# Complete Croquet

## A Guide to Skills, Tactics and Strategy

# Complete Croquet

## A Guide to Skills, Tactics and Strategy

James Hawkins

THE CROWOOD PRESS

First published in 2010 by
The Crowood Press Ltd
Ramsbury, Marlborough
Wiltshire SN8 2HR

**www.crowood.com**

**British Library Cataloguing-in-Publication Data**
A catalogue record for this book is available from the British Library.

ISBN 978 1 84797 168 5

**Disclaimer**
The author and the publisher do not accept any responsibility in any manner whatsoever for any error or omission, or any loss, damage, injury, adverse outcome, or liability of any kind incurred as a result of the use of any of the information contained in this book, or reliance upon it. If in doubt about any aspect of croquet, readers are advised to seek professional advice.

Throughout this book 'he', 'him' and 'his' have been used as neutral pronouns and as such refer to both males and females.

Photograph previous page: former British Women's Champion, Debbie Cornelius.

Typeset by D & N Publishing, Baydon, Wiltshire.

Printed and bound in Malaysia by Times Offset (M) Sdn Bhd.

# CONTENTS

# CHAPTER I

# THE GAME OF CROQUET

Everyone knows – or thinks they know – something about croquet, whether they have played themselves, seen it or read about it. Croquet is one of the most recognizable and distinctive of games, yet it is also one of the most misunderstood. Devotees have ranged from Leo Tolstoy to the Marx Brothers, from Winston Churchill to Bart Simpson. After 150 years of evolution and adaptation, croquet has become the dominant garden game in England, played at home by innumerable families, many of whom make up their own rules to suit their surroundings.

*Two-times World Champion Chris Clarke in play.*

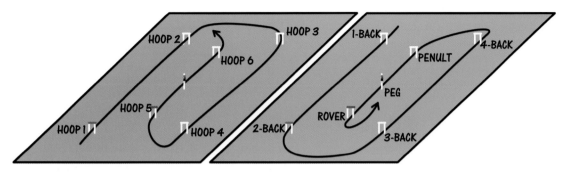

*The circuit of twelve hoops.*

The official game of croquet – or Association Croquet – is a game of tactics, with long sequences of strokes strung together, as in snooker, pool or billiards. It is played at international level, and in regular tournaments at clubs in many countries. Because it is a game of strategy and accuracy, there is no restriction based on age, and no bias between genders. The handicapping system allows novices and champions to meet on equal terms.

This book aims to pick apart the complexities of the tactics of croquet. It takes the reader from the basics of break play to the esoteric realm of the world-class supershot. Before delving into all that, however, you will need a brief outline of the game.

## The Basics of Croquet

Croquet is a contest between two sides – Red and Yellow versus Blue and Black. It can be played as a game of doubles, but competitive croquet normally involves just two players, one of whom has the Red and Yellow balls, the other the Blue and the Black.

Each ball has to complete a course of twelve hoops in a certain order. The first side to complete the course with both balls wins. When a ball scores its hoop – or *runs the hoop* – it earns another shot, and when a ball hits – or *roquets* – one of the other balls, it earns another two shots.

The first of those two shots is the *croquet stroke*, in which you must place your ball in contact with the ball you have just hit, and play a shot so that both balls move. The second extra shot – the *continuation stroke* – is a normal one, in which an astute player will try to make another roquet or run a hoop.

Once you have made three roquets, one on each of the other balls, your turn ends. However, if you score your hoop, you earn the right for another three roquets and croquets. If you place the balls correctly, you can score several hoops in a turn, and engineer some elaborate strategies.

## Equipment

It is possible to buy a children's plastic croquet set from a supermarket for the same price as a cappuccino. Tournament-quality equipment, needless to say, has a much higher specification. Modern hoops are constructed from chunky cast iron or steel, rather than thin bent wire, as supplied in many garden sets. The clearance between hoop and ball is at most an eighth of an inch. At championship level, that clearance may be as tiny as a thirty-second of an inch. High-level tournaments have even been held where the hoops have zero clearance, with the ball having to graze both uprights in order to pass through. In such a situation, precision and pre-planning are the keys to victory.

*The clearance between hoop and ball.*

As the game has developed, so has the technology of equipment manufacture. Balls are made from plastic resin, with increased durability and consistency of bounce. Many top players now favour carbon-fibre mallets, whose extreme weight distribution provides some advantages over the traditional wooden design.

## A Brief History of Croquet

The early days of croquet are shrouded in mystery. There is evidence dating back centuries, and possibly as far back as 800 years, of games played with balls, hoops and sticks. The oldest surviving trace is possibly the Dutch game of *beugelen*, which goes back at least to the mid-seventeenth century, and which lives on, played in a handful of clubs in the province of Limburg, in the southern tip of the Netherlands. Beugelen requires an indoor clay court, one large metal ring, and wooden balls, about the size of a football. There is a superficial similarity with croquet in terms of equipment, but the game has no concept of bonus shots – roquets, croquets and continuation strokes – and shares few of the playing characteristics.

Circumstantial evidence links beugelen to a slightly later game, originating in the same part of northern Europe. Documents show this game, *pall mall* (or *paille maille*, *pell mell*, *palle-malle*, or *jeu de mail*), being played in the French royal court, now with smaller balls and recognizable mallets. The game had spread to London by 1661, when Samuel Pepys noted that he had been 'to St James's Park, where I saw the

> ### EXTREME CROQUET
>
> Cheap croquet sets have their place, and some individuals favour the cheapest and most disposable equipment available. Awkward childhood memories of backyard croquet games have given rise to a new phenomenon – that of 'Extreme Croquet' – which provides an opportunity for grown-ups to relive their youth, but usually with more alcohol.
>
> The first documented game was in Sweden in the 1970s, where a group of friends bought a cheap croquet set and laid out the hoops in the middle of a forest. The craze seems to have spread and become more popular recently, particularly among university students in the USA. 'Lawns' – such as they are – may be laid out with hoops on rock outcrops, up trees, or across drainage channels. The game combines many of the finer characteristics of golf, orienteering and picnicking, but has little in common with organized croquet.

Duke of York playing at Pelemele, the first time that I ever saw the sport'. The playing area was a strip of land 1,000 yards long, called 'The Mall'. Shopkeepers lined the route, and thus was created the world's first shopping mall.

Many historians attempt to trace croquet's ancestry back to these early games, but the evidence is scant. Enthusiasm for pall mall seems to have waned, and croquet emerged suddenly around a century later. Here was a radically different game in every aspect. It retained none of

*Oak carving of a mallet game (seventeenth century).*

*Cheltenham Croquet Club.*

pall mall's rules, except for the use of a mallet to hit a ball through a hoop. What is more, its origins seem to have lain, not in London or Paris, but in Ireland.

### Jaques and Whitmore

The credit for introducing croquet to England seems to be attributable largely to John Jaques II. The Jaques family had trained as ivory-turners, and had successfully cornered the market in supplying sporting goods to Victorian England. They had introduced the Staunton chess set, and were later responsible for the invention of – among other games – Snakes and Ladders and Table Tennis. John Jaques visited Ireland in 1852, and saw a new game called Crookey being played. He brought it home and marketed it to the growing Victorian middle classes. Croquet was soon established as the latest craze.

Jaques's early rules were rudimentary, and croquet might have fizzled out were it not for the efforts of Walter Jones Whitmore. Whitmore was not a practical man – he was a failed poet, failed novelist and failed inventor – but he did see the potential for developing the strategy of the new game. He tweaked the rules, and formulated the first guide to tactics, published in *The Field* magazine in 1866. In 1867, the game's first open tournament was held in Evesham, Worcestershire, and Whitmore became croquet's first official champion.

### The All England Lawn Tennis and Croquet Club

As the game grew in popularity, clubs started to spring up. Worthing (the earliest club) in West Sussex was founded in 1860. The game spread along England's south coast, and around the south-west (Whitmore's area of influence). Whitmore and others saw a need for a national centre in London, and formed a club that would become world-famous – the All England Croquet Club at Wimbledon.

The formation of the All England Croquet Club was rancorous. Whitmore's appointment to the committee was quickly seen as a mistake, but he did not step down with much grace. Instead, he formed a rival splinter organization, the National Croquet Club. It continued for a short period, but was soon absorbed into the AECC. Whitmore continued to dissent, and went on to form a third body, the Grand National Croquet Club. With Whitmore's early death in 1872, the GNCC folded.

Croquet had more to worry about than such internal bickering. Soon a new game had emerged to challenge croquet's place – a game called 'Lawn Tennis'. Tennis had several advantages – the playing area was half the size, games were shorter, and all participants were kept simultaneously active. Croquet started to fade from the public's gaze. Wimbledon allocated some space to the upstart game, and soon rebranded itself as the 'All England Croquet and Lawn

Tennis Club'. By 1882, croquet had vanished almost to nothing, and was dropped from the name of the club. Although it was reinstated in the title, largely for sentimental reasons, in 1899, today only one croquet lawn remains at the game's first headquarters.

# Development

Enthusiasts saw the need to coordinate the disparate clubs that were starting around the country. The Croquet Association (CA) was established, and eventually found a permanent base at the Hurlingham Club in south-west London. The CA relocated in 2002 to Cheltenham Croquet Club, home to many of the UK's top events.

---

### CROQUET AT THE OLYMPICS

Croquet's popularity had spread globally by 1900, so much so that it featured at the Paris Olympics that year. This was the first Olympic sport to include women (and one of the few, even now, to feature women competing alongside men in the same event). In many other respects, however, it was less than successful.

There were just ten competitors, nine of whom were from Paris. The sole outsider had made the journey from Belgium, but he failed to complete the first round of play. This was perhaps understandable, as the event was inconveniently held over three successive weeks, which may have explained the absence of any other visiting nations. France won all the medals, although it is not certain whether more than one pair entered the doubles event.

Publicity was poor. At least one participant went to his grave years later, still unaware that he had competed in the Olympic Games. And, over the whole event, there was just one single spectator – an elderly Englishman who travelled from Nice to watch.

Four years later, croquet, of sorts, returned to the Olympics in St Louis, USA. There was some anti-English resistance to the recognized game, so it was renamed 'roque', and underwent some rule changes, to make it more 'American'.

Roque is played on an octagonal court with a hard surface. The boundaries are marked with a low concrete wall, allowing players to bounce the (rubber) balls round corners. Once again, the host nation took every single medal at the Games. By 1908, the IOC had tightened up the regulations for inclusion in the Olympics. Neither croquet nor roque has featured since.

Sadly, roque is now all but obsolete. Infighting and a dwindling interest led to the bulldozing of many roque courts in the 1950s and, as car ownership grew, many were concreted over to become parking lots. The game does live on in American literature, with mentions in both John Steinbeck's *Sweet Thursday* and Stephen King's *The Shining*.

*Reg Bamford winning the 2005 World Championship.*

British – and particularly English – croquet has blossomed over the last thirty years. Through the seven-month playing season, hundreds of tournaments across the country cater for the thousands of dedicated participants who play each week at the many clubs affiliated to the CA. This current stability comes as a welcome relief after years of hardship.

## The Fall and Rise

Lawn tennis almost killed the game of croquet, but not quite. The end of the nineteenth century was a difficult period for the game, but popularity comes in waves, and croquet had bounced back by the first decade of the next century. The onset of the Great War inevitably halted the game's expansion once again but, by the early 1920s, croquet had again resurfaced. This decade was, perhaps, the game's heyday – these were happy post-war days when England's burgeoning middle classes had the time and opportunity to enjoy their leisure time to the full.

It was the Second World War that represented the greatest threat to croquet, and the game barely survived. Many clubs closed, and the wartime gloom threatened to drive it to extinction. And yet croquet clung on, unloved and out of fashion.

## Modern International Scene

The resurgence in croquet's appeal can be traced back to the early 1960s. By the 1980s, croquet was attracting a generation of youngsters, among them Chris Clarke, Robert Fulford and David Maugham in the UK, and Reg Bamford in South Africa.

Croquet had been strong in Australia and New Zealand since its earliest days, and interest was growing in North America. The World Croquet Federation was created in 1986, with plans to develop the game throughout the rest of the world. The WCF now has twenty-six member countries, and the game's reach has spread to much of mainland Europe.

## Competition

### World Singles Championship

The staging of the WCF World Croquet Championship has done a great deal to raise the profile of the game. Croquet remains untouched by the professional status of many sports. Players have their travel expenses financed by national associations, but there is no expectation that anyone will grow rich as a croquet player. There are no cash prizes – winners receive the handsome Wimbledon Cup, and the simple glory of victory.

### The MacRobertson Shield

The MacRobertson Shield is the main international team event. The shield was donated by Sir MacPherson Robertson in 1925, and the test series is now contested by the game's four dominant nations. The 'Mac' now carries a great deal of prestige, and competition for selection is fierce. Presumably, in 1925 selection was based only partially on playing ability – matches in that first year were played over the course of ten weeks, and visiting teams had to provide their own finance for the three-month campaign.

Demand for a world team championship grows. The 2010 Mac will see an English, rather than a British, team. Ireland, Scotland and Wales are developing their own standings in the world; and alongside them are strong performers from Canada, Sweden, Italy, Spain and Egypt. The future is unknowable, but it looks strong for worldwide croquet.

---

**WORLD CHAMPIONS**

| Year | Winner | Runner-up | Host venue |
|---|---|---|---|
| 2009 | Reg Bamford (RSA) | Ben Rothman (USA) | Palm Beach, Florida, USA |
| 2008 | Chris Clarke (ENG) | Stephen Mulliner (ENG) | Christchurch, New Zealand |
| 2005 | Reg Bamford (RSA) | Robert Fulford (ENG) | Cheltenham, England |
| 2002 | Robert Fulford (ENG) | Toby Garrison (NZ) | Wellington, New Zealand |
| 2001 | Reg Bamford (RSA) | Robert Fulford (ENG) | Hurlingham, England |
| 1997 | Robert Fulford (ENG) | Stephen Mulliner (ENG) | Bunbury, Australia |
| 1995 | Chris Clarke (ENG) | Robert Fulford (ENG) | Fontenay le Comte, France |
| 1994 | Robert Fulford (ENG) | Chris Clarke (ENG) | Carden Park, England |
| 1992 | Robert Fulford (ENG) | John Walters (ENG) | Newport, Rhode Island, USA |
| 1991 | John Walters (ENG) | David Openshaw (ENG) | Hurlingham, England |
| 1990 | Robert Fulford (ENG) | Mark Saurin (ENG) | Hurlingham, England |
| 1989 | Joe Hogan (NZ) | Mark Avery (ENG) | Hurlingham, England |

## THE MACROBERTSON SHIELD

| Year | First | Second | Third | Fourth | Host venue |
|---|---|---|---|---|---|
| 2006 | Great Britain | Australia | USA | New Zealand | Australia |
| 2003 | Great Britain | Australia | USA | New Zealand | USA |
| 2000 | Great Britain | New Zealand | USA | Australia | New Zealand |
| 1996 | Great Britain | New Zealand | Australia | USA | Great Britain |
| 1993 | Great Britain | New Zealand | Australia | USA | Australia |
| 1990 | Great Britain | New Zealand | Australia | | New Zealand |
| 1986 | New Zealand | Great Britain | Australia | | Great Britain |
| 1982 | Great Britain | Australia | New Zealand | | Australia |
| 1979 | New Zealand | Great Britain | Australia | | New Zealand |
| 1974 | Great Britain | New Zealand | Australia | | England |
| 1969 | England | New Zealand | Australia | | Australia |
| 1963 | England | Australia | New Zealand | | New Zealand |
| 1956 | England | New Zealand | | | England |
| 1950–1 | New Zealand | England | | | New Zealand |
| 1937 | England | Australia | | | England |
| 1935 | Australia | England | New Zealand | | Australia |
| 1930 | Australia | New Zealand | | | Australia |
| 1927–8 | Australia | England | | | Australia |
| 1925 | England | Australia | | | England |

*The MacRobertson Shield.*

# CHAPTER 2

# THE SINGLE BALL SHOT

Most people pick up a croquet mallet, decide what swing feels comfortable, and stick with that for the rest of their playing career. Unfortunately, what may be a natural swing is often not a very successful one. None of the game's top players earned their status without practising and refining their swing from its raw and natural state to an unnatural, but seemingly effortless, one.

The muscles of the elbow and shoulder are designed for heavy-duty work, while delicate movements are performed by the wrist and finger muscles. A good swing is controlled

*Former British Men's Champion, Pete Trimmer.*

by the large muscles in the upper arm. A competent cro-quet player will make shoulder movements that are smooth, unified and consistent. At the same time, wrist and finger movement needs to be minimized; the tiniest involuntary twitch of a finger can represent the difference between hitting and missing, and, therefore, between winning and losing.

# Grip

The key to problems with fingers is to form your hands into a consistent and comfortable grip. There are essentially only three ways of holding a croquet mallet.

## The Standard Grip

This is how most players naturally pick up a mallet. The lower hand (the dominant one) holds the shaft with the palm facing forward, and the upper hand holds the top of the shaft with knuckles facing forward. Beginners often start with their hands well apart. Ideally, the two hands should be just touching, so it is advisable as you are learning to move the lower hand gradually up the shaft each time you play. Having the hands together should reduce stretching of the lower arm, which tenses one shoulder more than the other.

As you swing, both forearms should be at right-angles to the mallet. This should help straighten your backswing, and allow you to hit hard shots more effectively.

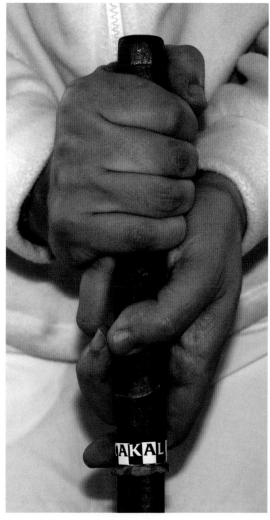

*The standard grip (left-hander shown).*

## The Irish Grip

This was popularized in the early twentieth century by three Irish players, Cyril Corbally, Duff Matthews and Leslie O'Callaghan. Both hands grip the shaft with the palms facing forward. Again, the hands should be held close together, and many players have their hands slightly overlapping, as with a golf grip. The hands are held slightly lower, and many devotees favour a mallet shaft that is slightly (just a couple of inches) shorter.

As you bend your wrists back, there is a tendency for the wrists to twist inwards (to pronate), which results in a crooked backswing for many Irish-grip players. This can be resolved in several ways. Many players forego a large backswing, playing many shots as a gentle poke. When you need to play a hard shot, stand half a step further away from the ball as you hit it. That provides you with more room on the backswing before the wrists pronate.

Alternatively, you can just learn to live with the crookedness. Robert Fulford, five times World Champion and arguably the greatest ever player of the game, has a swing that turns markedly to the left on the backswing. Timing your follow-through may require a greater degree of natural coordination, so his natural style may be a difficult one to mimic.

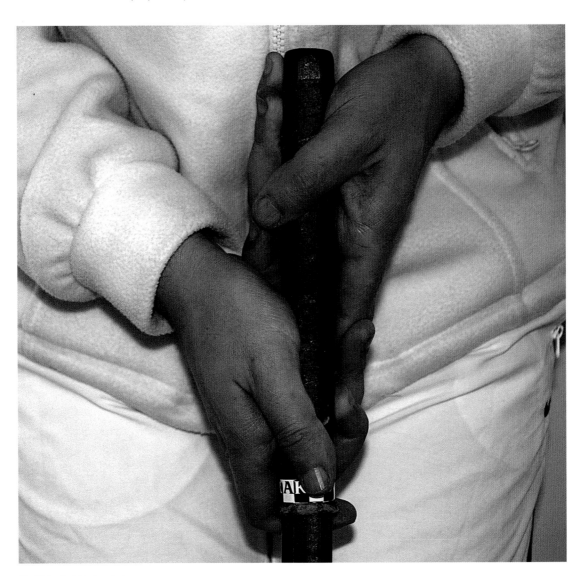

The Irish grip (right-handed).

*Stephen Mulliner's Irish grip has a small backswing.*

## The Solomon Grip

The Solomon grip was conceived in the 1950s by John Solomon, who dominated the British game until the 1970s. Both hands grip the shaft with the knuckles pointing forwards. This may be more successful with a slightly longer mallet – it is often the swing adopted by children who find either of the other two grips uncomfortable on a mallet that is too tall for them.

I am no great fan of the Solomon grip. For me, there is not enough support for the back of the mallet shaft, which wobbles in my hands at the point of impact with the ball. Maybe my fingers are too short or too weak to grip adequately. It may be possible to resolve this worry by having one or both thumbs raised. Try placing a thumb on the top of the mallet, rather than wrapping it round the side of the shaft. With the length of the thumb-bone resting against the back of the shaft, you may be able to brace your shots.

In spite of my doubts, the Solomon grip has a number of fans in the top flight of the game.

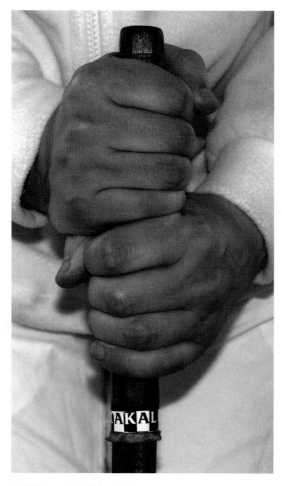

*The Solomon grip (left-handed).*

## Training Your Grip

It is crucially important that your grip is consistent whenever you play. There is no other way but to program the position of your hands into your memory. Every time you pick up your mallet, your hands should adopt a comfortable position. But, it is possible to train yourself to do this, even when you do not have a mallet near by.

Take a couple of sheets of A4 paper, or one sheet of newspaper folded in two, and roll them into a long tube. You want the tube to be about the same thickness as your mallet shaft – do not be tempted to use a cardboard tube, as its diameter will be too thick. Hold the tube as if it is your mallet. Experiment until you find a grip that is comfortable.

Stand up and look down. You should be able to see the floor through the tube. Swing the tube backwards and forwards, as if you were playing a shot. Throughout the swing, you should still be able to look through the tube and see the floor. Practise this routine for a couple of minutes a day, and you should become more and more confident of your grip and your swing.

The advantage of this practice technique is that it does not require any equipment. It is ideal as a winter routine, as you need not even step outside. Try it standing astride a line on the floor – the edge of the carpet, or a gap between tiles in the kitchen. Do your swing, and make sure that line remains visible through the tube.

In reality, this exercise is not replicating your swing 100 per cent faithfully – your elbows and wrists will extend slightly at the back of the swing and tense as you follow through. However, it will help you to affirm your grip, as well as coordinating your shoulder movements. It forces you to keep your fingers and wrists still, basing your swing around your elbows and shoulders.

*John Solomon in play at Southwick.*

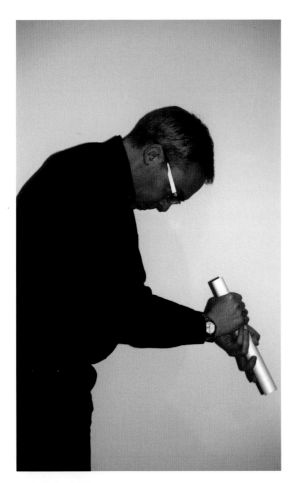

*A paper tube makes a useful grip trainer.*

## Shoulders and Legs

### Style

In croquet's early days, most players played side-style, with the shoulders facing square on to the direction of the shot, and the mallet swung to one side of the body (the right side for a right-hander). The style is problematic in a number of ways. The right arm is held straight, while the left is stretched across the chest. That makes it difficult to coordinate the motion of the two arms – one side of the body is tensed, and there is a tendency to swing crookedly, right to left, on each shot. The left arm provides little in the way of power, making long, firm shots inaccurate, if not impossible. What is more, the player's eyes are one foot to the left of the line of travel. The cure for this would be for the player to lean all their weight on the right side, which, in turn, creates major problems with balance. Unless you have

a compelling reason to play side-style, it is not advisable to do so.

### Stance

Beginners often stand with their legs straight and their feet very wide apart, presumably because they feel that this stance lessens the risk of the mallet hitting the ankles.

A wide stance forces you to straighten your legs and therefore tenses the calf muscles. That in turn tenses the back, and creates unnecessary tension in the shoulders. If your body is not relaxed, your swing will not be. In the normal course of the day you would find such a stance uncomfortable, so it is not recommended when you are playing croquet.

The important thing is to stand so that you are relaxed. Whether you play croquet to win, or whether you play for the simple enjoyment of the game, no swing should make you feel uncomfortable.

*Side style.*

*A wide style increases tension in the muscles.*

*Centre style (left-handed).*

NB: The illustrations of stance here and in Chapter 3 show the author, who is left-handed. Copying my stance exactly may be uncomfortable, so readers are invited to experiment with their own style.

Some players advocate standing with one foot slightly ahead of the other. I think it hardly matters. The important aspect of stance is that your shoulders should be square to the direction of the shot. Placing one foot far forward might spoil that alignment. Modern fashions favour keeping the feet together and almost level, but Chapter 3 explains how that stance should be varied for other shots.

Problems often arise when players stand too close or too far from the ball. For most standard-grip players, the mallet will hit the ball full on when your toes are level with the bottom of the mallet shaft. If you stand closer, you will hit down on to the ball; if you are further away, you will hit up. Irish-grip players may prefer to stand so that their toes are level with the back edge, or *heel*, of the mallet.

## Casting

*Casting*, or practice-swinging, is the subject of much debate. There seems to be a generational divide among players. Much as it offends the aesthetic sensibilities of established players, casting has become widespread among the new crop.

Previously, most players would take aim, adopt their stance and *ground the mallet*; placing the mallet on the floor before taking the shot helps to steady the swing. After grounding, they would then start the backswing, and hit the ball.

Nowadays, many (but by no means all) players hold the mallet above the ball, repeatedly swinging the mallet up to the horizontal. It is said that this helps to check the alignment with the target, as well as ensuring that the swing is consistent. Some multi-swingers claim to cast precisely four times, and some will swing at least twenty times before their actual stroke. Once they are satisfied with the line, they drop their shoulders and elbows, and play the shot.

*Jenny Clarke casting the mallet before hitting.*

## REG BAMFORD AND THE SWING TRAINER

In the late 1980s, the English player Eric Solomon advocated the use of a swing trainer, to teach muscles a repetitive routine for a perfect swing. Few people adopted the suggestion until 2001, when South African Reg Bamford chose to employ the technique – to devastating effect.

Bamford commissioned John Hobbs, a British mallet-maker, to construct a trainer from two plywood sheets fixed in parallel, so that the mallet could swing between them. Each evening, Bamford would practise swinging along the groove, narrowing the gap until there was less than a millimetre's clearance between the mallet and each sheet.

*Reg Bamford practising with a swing trainer.*

After two weeks of this routine, spectators watched Bamford shoot balls at the centre peg on one of the lawns at Surbiton Croquet Club. Of sixty-four balls shot at the peg from 42ft (over 12m) away, Bamford scored sixty-three hits. Moreover, each hit rebounded by the same amount, and in the same direction.

Bamford, already a world-class shot, had perfected a way of training his swing to be absolutely consistent. Using this training method, he became World Champion in 2001, and top-class croquet entered the era of the supershot.

That gives a smooth transition between practice swing and the genuine swing.

Players argue that it helps with relaxing their swing and gauging the pace of a shot. I am a caster, and I think it makes me hit straighter. But there seems to be no real consensus either way. The only advice I can offer is to do what feels right.

## Curing a Twitchy Swing

Most players go through phases during which all their shots seem to miss. Often they feel themselves missing consistently by the same amount on the same side. Something feels wrong, but it is hard to diagnose the problem precisely.

The cause is often muscle tension. If you are not relaxed, one shoulder – or one foot, or one wrist – may be stiffer than the other. You may not notice it yourself, but you could be leaning a tiny bit to one side, and not swinging evenly at the ball. Tension in your upper body often arises from tension in your legs. If you are tense and uncomfortable before you have started swinging the mallet, you will probably miss. Many players have certain rituals that they follow

before taking a shot – do not be afraid to loosen yourself up by performing some quick neck exercises, or flexing your fingers, or jumping up and down on the spot. Once you have taken your stance for the stroke, try rebalancing yourself by quickly doing one of the following exercises:

- wiggle your toes;
- tense and relax each foot in turn;
- 'pedal on the spot' – alternately lift each heel off the ground, slightly bending and straightening your knees.

You can do each of these without altering your position. As soon as you lift your feet off the ground, you have disturbed the aiming line you have chosen, so it is worth taking aim again.

If none of that works, and you are still missing, you may have a problem with your grip. The tiniest of twitches in a finger can cause your mallet to twist imperceptibly. It is not enough for you to notice, but it can make you miss a crucial shot. With most croquet grips, the most likely cause is a tiny squeeze of the thumb, or tension in the tendon that joins your third and fourth fingers. The following rebalancing exercise may help with this:

- Hold your mallet above the ball, and slightly loosen your grip.
- Spin your mallet in your hands, so that the opposite end-face is pointing forwards.
- Feel the swing of the mallet, and tighten your grip back to normal.
- Loosen your grip, and rotate the mallet again.
- Keep ungripping the mallet and re-applying your grip, until your fingers adopt a comfortable and familiar position.

If that does you no good, then the problem probably lies elsewhere. Concentrate on the shot itself – as long as you have aimed correctly, and as long as your swing is straight, then all you have to worry about is making a clean contact between the mallet and the ball. Keep your head down, focus on the ball, relax and hit.

## Aiming

### Stalking the Ball

Once you have acquired a straight swing, you need to determine where to point your body. If you stand close to your ball, you often cannot see whether you are facing in the right direction. The habit that all players need to adopt is to *stalk the ball* before each shot. Stand several yards back from your ball, and walk towards it, along the line of the shot. By standing back, you can see whether your ball is in line with its target. Walk along that line, and your body will continue to face forwards. If your shoulders face in the right direction, your swing should be directly towards the target.

This is one technique that is almost impossible to teach – some people are better natural judges than others. However, there are a few tips that might improve your aiming.

### Crouching

It is hard to see whether the balls are aligned, particularly with long shots. Suppose you are playing Red, and you want to roquet Black. Your mallet is close up, Red is in the middle distance, and Black is in the far distance. The angles are such that you cannot see everything at the same time. Crouch down, holding your mallet in its correct grip, but with its head resting on the ground in front of you. This lets you look along the length of the mallet to the Red to the Black, and have all three in your field of vision at once.

*Robert Fulford crouches to get a better view.*

---

### ILLEGAL ASSISTANCE

Some years before I started playing croquet, there was a player in the north of England who employed an ingenious – but illegal – means of aiming his long shots.

Apparently, he played with a mallet to which he had fixed the polished brass gun-sight of an antique rifle. Before each shot, he would bend down, line up the target through the telescopic sight, and then take his stance and play the shot. By all accounts, it did him no good. He had a terrible swing, and missed everything. And, with each shot he played, he would stab himself in the thigh with the gun-sight.

---

### The Parallax View

From a distance, you might think that your body, the Red ball and the Black ball are aligned. If so, then moving slightly left or right will cause everything to move out of alignment. Look along the line of Red and Black, and very gently rock towards your right foot, back to your left foot, and then back into equilibrium. Alternatively, if you prefer, slightly tilt your head right and then left. You should see the following:

- balls aligned;
- Red missing on the left;
- Red missing on the right;
- balls aligned again.

If that is what you see, then your body is aligned correctly.

### Draw a Dotted Line

Look at the mallet, your ball, and the target. Mallet – ball – target – mallet – ball – target. With a long shot, your eyes are jumping from one point of focus to the next. Try moving your eyes gradually from one to the next. Focus on your mallet, and follow an imaginary dotted line to your ball. Continue the line, and focus on each dot in turn, right up to the target ball.

These principles might help you orient yourself correctly before the shot. But remember – if you are not pointing the right way, do not settle for shuffling your feet until you find the right line. Stop, stalk the shot again, and check your alignment.

There is no shot in croquet that is so short that it does not need careful aim. However, once you have learned to swing straight and aim straight, you then only need to concentrate on hitting your ball cleanly.

## Hoop-Running

Going through a hoop – *running* or *making* the hoop – is, pretty obviously, a fundamental skill of the game. Most coaches draw a distinction between straight hoops and angled hoops, and adopt a different aiming technique. With tournament hoops set firmly in the ground, the clearance between ball and hoop is very small. However you play the shot, your attempt at a hoop will almost certainly reach one upright, or *wire*, of the hoop before the other. If your ball hits the near wire, it will not go through.

### Aiming a Hoop Shot

Imagine a length of drainpipe the exact diameter of a croquet ball. Aim your hoop shots so that this imaginary drainpipe runs from your ball towards the hoop, just missing the near wire. Many players stalk their hoop shots, lining the edge of their ball with the inner edge of the upright. Instead, stalk the shot along the line of the imaginary channel. No matter how straight or acutely angled your position, this principle will still apply.

When this method is put into practice, it is remarkable what angles of hoop can be run. In theory, any hoop is runnable if your ball can hit the far wire and bounce inwards into the hoop, rather than outwards away from it. Look at the hoop from the far side – if you can see more than half the ball between the uprights, then you *might* have a chance. With a bit of clever technique, experts can score when the angle is as sharp as 60 degrees. You will have to wait, as that is a topic for a later chapter.

*Visualize a channel between the ball and the hoop.*

*Acutely angled hoops are theoretically possible if most of the ball is visible from the other side.*

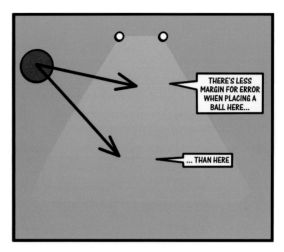

*The 'fan of success'.*

## The Stroke

The first rule of hoop-running is not to jab at the hoop. Imagine you are threading a needle, or that the mallet is a giant paintbrush. Ideally, you want a smooth stroke with some follow-through.

Jabbing has two negative effects: first, it stops the ball from spinning forwards, and second, it amplifies any crookedness in your swing. Following through, on the other hand, evens out that crookedness. It is hard to swing badly if you keep your mallet travelling along the line of aim.

As the angle of a hoop tightens, your ball will hit the far upright more fully. This will absorb much of the energy of the ball, so angled hoops need to be hit much more firmly.

## The Fan of Success

Straight, close hoops are much easier to run than long, angled ones. The more you practise, the more you will feel comfortable with difficult hoops. One practice routine involves the 'fan of success'.

To follow this routine, you visualize a fan on the ground in front of the hoop. This represents the area from which you are comfortable scoring. Initially, you will be happy with short and straight shots, and will be less confident of long or angled hoops. As you get more experienced, your fan of success should become bigger and wider. In the context of a game, you should make yourself aware of what your optimum position is, so you can position your ball to guarantee scoring. When you are very close to the hoop, scoring should be easy, provided that your shot is dead straight; long and straight is generally much easier than close and angled. For comfort, you should try and place your ball as close to the middle of your fan as possible.

## Hitting Another Ball

Roqueting each of the other balls extends your turn from one stroke to seven. Running a hoop resets your allocation of roquets, and, in theory, grants you up to ninety-one successive shots. The ability to roquet is, therefore, crucial. As always, a long follow-through will straighten your swing. Play each shot smoothly and, as with hoops, avoid jabbing.

---

### GOLF CROQUET

Golf Croquet was originally conceived as a simplified game for those unprepared for the subtleties of Association Croquet. Each turn comprises one shot, and there are no roquets, croquets or continuation shots.

Golf Croquet had a dedicated following among British servicemen in officers' clubs in Cairo during the war. By the 1990s, the Egyptians had adopted Golf Croquet as their national game, improving the rules to suit a more adventurous playing style.

Egyptian golfers have an awesome hoop-running ability, regularly crashing through hoops from twenty yards. Some players favour deliberately leaving themselves severely angled and at an eight-yard distance; they claim (with some justification) that the angle helps them bounce through, and have a better chance of scoring two hoops in one stroke.

This spectacular game attracts a loyal following in Egypt. It is played at night on floodlit lawns, and often has extensive television coverage. So far, Egyptians have yet to make a serious mark on the Association game, where the range of stroke play is wider. Only the top handful of Association players – including Reg Bamford and Robert Fulford – have come close to overcoming their astonishing firepower.

*David Maugham plays a rush.*

## Rushing

You will often want to do more than just roquet another ball. You will often want to roquet it to an exact position. This is called a *rush*.

In a normal roquet, you just have to concentrate on getting your ball (Red) to hit the other ball (Yellow). In a rush, you also need to think about strength and direction.

**Dolly Rush** The *dolly rush* is an easy, straight rush. Red and Yellow are no more than a foot or two apart, and pointing in a direct line towards where you want to go. The angle of the mallet is vital, so you need to be aware of the

### CLIPS

As the game progresses, it is often hard to keep up with which hoops have been scored by which balls. Coloured clips are placed on the hoops to indicate the next hoop. Clips on the crown indicate the outward journey (Hoops 1 to 6), and clips on the side the return journey (1-back to Rover).

The clip positions, or clippage, will often lead you into attacking or defensive strategies.

*Clips on a hoop.*

positioning of your feet. Your feet should be positioned as for any normal shot, so that the mallet is flat at the moment of impact. If you stand too close, the mallet will be hitting downwards on to your ball, which will cause Red to spin more; you will lose energy as the balls impact, and there is a danger that Red will bounce in the air and skim the top of Yellow, or even jump clean over it.

Standing too far away from Red is a less serious error. You will hit Red at the start of the follow-through. It will make

Red stop shorter, and send Yellow further. That saves on effort, but it builds inaccuracy into the shot. For many, there is a danger of twisting the mallet at the point of impact. There is a great benefit to playing this stroke – a *stop rush* or *stun shot* – if you are a Golf Croquet player, but in Association Croquet its advantages are few. For consistency, you should keep your normal stance, and vary the extent of your follow-through to regulate the pace of the shot.

**Cut-Rush** Usually, you will not want to hit Yellow in a dead-straight line, preferring instead to clip it on one side or the other. This is a *cut-rush*.

If Red hits the left half of Yellow, Yellow will go to the right; if Red hits Yellow on the right, it will go left. The difficulty relates to the amount of angle you can put into the Yellow, and how hard to hit. Cut-rushing is technically one of the hardest of skills to master in croquet, requiring judgement of both pace and direction. There are four stages:

1 *Select the direction you want Yellow to go.* Look along the line in which you want Yellow to travel. Draw an imaginary line from the destination towards Yellow – some players even draw this line in mid-air with a finger. Trace that line back to Yellow. This is Yellow's *rushline*.
2 *Visualize where Red will be at the moment of impact.* Red must hit Yellow exactly on this rushline. Imagine that another ball is in contact with Yellow, sitting on the rushline nearer Red. Red must pass straight through this imaginary ball.
3 *Aim at the phantom ball.* This is the hard part, and it only comes with experience. You have to stalk a shot where Red is going to hit an invisible ball. You are not allowed to place an actual physical ball in front of Yellow, so you will have to use your imagination.

Focus on the spot on the ground where that ball would sit, stalk the shot, and take your stance.
4 *Hit Red.* Strike Red, and follow through. Cut-rushes need you to hit much harder than straight rushes, so do not play this half-heartedly. Do not be tempted to stand too far forward, or you are likely to jump over Yellow. Neither should you stand back and attempt a stop rush – it will not work, and you will endanger a miss.

As a measure of difficulty, look from Red towards the destination for Yellow. If you need to turn your head to do this, the shot is a very difficult one. Do not be discouraged if you are a novice, but play within your limitations. Confine yourself to narrower angles and shorter distances.

## Greed

Much of this book will make little sense unless you learn how to rush a ball. I spent my childhood playing garden croquet, in long grass with wooden balls that bounced very little. We played no rushes, and lost much of the game's strategic subtlety. Rushes are not the end-product of a successful turn, but they are one of its most valuable components.

Readers should not be too greedy with rushing. One of the commonest mistakes is the over-ambitious cut-rush. You play hard at a ball, intending to clip it on one side and bring it a foot closer to your hoop. Cut-rushes are difficult shots, and this is the sort of shot that is often missed.

The most certain cure is to make sure that all your rushes are dolly rushes. At least, make sure that they are comfortably hittable, and lead on to other, easier shots. For that, you must master the shot immediately before, and immediately after, each roquet – the croquet stroke.

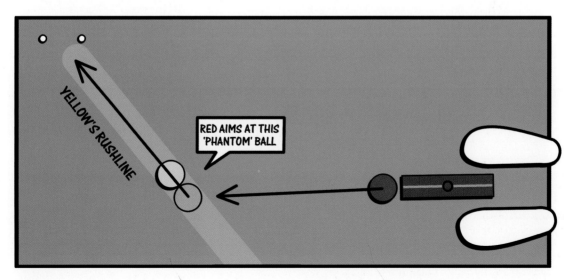

YELLOW'S RUSHLINE

RED AIMS AT THIS 'PHANTOM' BALL

*Cut-rushing.*

# CHAPTER 3

# THE CROQUET STROKE

In any croquet stroke, you need to make both your ball and the other ball move. If you play the shot right, you can control the position of both balls. Your ball (Red) will land in position to make your next shot easy, and the other ball (Yellow) will land somewhere advantageous.

## Placement

You have roqueted Yellow, and must now place Red in contact. However you hit Red, Yellow will always move in the same direction – along the line of the two balls. It is always

*A croquet stroke.*

*The balls are placed in contact.*

worth checking that this line is correct. It takes a couple of seconds, but it can make such a difference that Yellow will finish off-line by several yards.

There is not much else to add, except that you should always make sure that Red and Yellow are actually in contact. A gap between them will affect the shot, and may produce the wrong outcome. If Red insists on rolling away when you try to place it, press the grass with a thumb under the spot where Red will lie. Alternatively, many players use their foot to put a gentle weight on their ball.

Now, position yourself on the direct line through Red and Yellow. Take a normal stance, and hit Red.

## The Drive

A normal hit on Red should produce a consistent result. If the mallet is flat at the point of impact, and there is no angle between the two balls, then Red should move about a quarter of the distance of Yellow. This is a *drive* shot.

There is nothing complicated about this, the most basic of all croquet strokes. Each time you play it, whatever the strength of the shot, you should get roughly the same ratio between the balls. For some, Yellow to Red is 3:1, for others the distances are nearer 5:1. The proportions vary depending on your technique, your mallet and the type of balls you are playing with. A lightweight garden set might give a ratio of 2:1; modern championship balls have a more receptive bounce, and might give as much as 5:1 for some players.

Make a note of this ratio, as your playing strategy will be dictated by how you play this shot.

*The stance for a drive shot.*

## The Stop Shot

If you change the way you hit Red, you can make Yellow travel twice as far. Red will stop, as Yellow continues to travel. This is a *stop shot* and it may take a while to master.

Instead of hitting Red with the flat of the mallet's end-face, you will hit it with the mallet pointing upwards, and with almost no follow-through. Hold the mallet at the top of the shaft and place the mallet behind the ball as for a drive, then take half a step backwards. The mallet should now be tilting towards you. At the exact moment when you hit Red, the back edge, or heel, of the mallet should hit the ground sharply, in a downward motion. Yellow should travel at least seven times, and maybe as much as ten times, further than Red.

## The Half-Roll

Standing back and playing with less follow-through causes Red to hold back in the croquet stroke. Doing the opposite causes Red to roll on. In the *half-roll*, Red will travel about half the distance of Yellow – a Yellow/Red ratio of 2:1.

Because you are moving both Red and Yellow, roll shots require more force than other croquet strokes. If your technique is wrong, you will struggle to play the shot. You will also risk damage to your wrists. To avoid this, you want your upper arms to do all the work.

In a roll, your forearms should be at right-angles to the shaft of the mallet. That will let you keep your wrists rigid, and swing the mallet from your elbows and shoulders. The procedure is as follows:

- Hold the mallet with a standard or Solomon grip. Irish-grip players should reverse their top hand so the knuckles face forward; few people have wrists flexible enough to retain their normal grip and absorb the shock of impact.
- Place your lower hand (right, if you are right-handed) halfway down the shaft. With a standard grip, you will have the palm forward, and you will brace the shaft with the base of your hand.
- Place your upper hand slightly down from the top of the mallet. Your knuckles are forward, so you can rest the back of the shaft on the ball of your thumb. I like to stabilize my grip by extending my thumb upwards.

*The stance for a stop shot.*

*The half-roll, side view. Note the angle at which the mallet hits the ball.*

*The half-roll, front view.*

- Place one foot forward, toes level with the Red ball. (If you are right-handed, this will be your left foot.) If you lean a bit more weight on this foot, your body, and the mallet, will tilt forwards.
- Do not play the shot yet, or you will hit yourself in the face with the mallet shaft. Straighten your forearms, so that they are nearly parallel. That will angle the mallet across your body, away from your face, and towards your shoulder. Your elbows should now be able to swing forwards and backwards at the side of your body.
- Hit Red with some follow-through. All the movement should be from your elbows and shoulders.

## The Full-Roll

The transition from drive to half-roll is gradual. Depending on the exact ratio required, you will bring your hands a little bit lower, and stand a little bit further forward.

Continue the movement of hands down the mallet, and you can play a roll where Red and Yellow travel the same distance. This is a *full-roll* and the procedure is the same:

- Place the lower hand a few inches from the mallet head. Maintaining a (standard) grip at right-angles may be uncomfortable here. I change my fingering slightly, and hold the shaft with just my thumb and first two fingers. I do not need to bend my wrist so far, and it gives me enough firmness in the grip.
- Place the upper hand halfway down the shaft. As before, brace the shaft with the ball of the thumb.
- Red should be level with the instep of your forward foot. Place your backward foot well back – you will need your feet well apart for balance.
- Bend your knees, and lean your weight on to the forward foot.
- Angle the mallet across your body.
- Punch Red with follow-through.

*The full-roll, side view. The mallet hits down even further on the ball.*

*The full-roll, front view.*

*The pass-roll. Because of the steep angle of the mallet, the striker must avoid follow-through.*

## The Pass-Roll

The *pass-roll* is quite a sophisticated shot, which many players shy away from. Instead of getting a Yellow/Red ratio of 10:1 (stop shot), 4:1 (drive), 2:1 (half-roll) or 1:1 (full-roll), experts can achieve ratios of 1:2 or 1:3. Red accelerates, and overtakes the Yellow. It goes as follows:

- Take the same stance as for a full-roll, although you may want to experiment with tilting the mallet even more.
- Turn both hands knuckles forward in a Solomon grip. Place both thumbs upwards, to brace the shaft of the mallet.
- Rather than swinging in an arc, as for every other croquet stroke, punch Red sharply, moving both shoulders equally. That will move the mallet in a straight line, and the mallet head will not flatten its trajectory during the stroke.
- Do NOT play this with any follow-through. Pull the mallet back as soon as you have punched Red. Following through will probably produce an illegal push shot, as well as causing damage to the lawn.

Do not play the shot if you want Red and Yellow to travel dead straight; Red will bump into Yellow as it tries to overtake.

The only person I have seen who could play that successfully was the late Andrew Bennet, who coached me as a beginner. He could perform a straight pass-roll where Red jumped clean over the top of Yellow, re-touched it on the far side, stole some of its momentum, and rocketed off into the distance. Startled referees would be so surprised to see a 1:5 pass-roll that they would sometimes declare it illegal in disbelief. I have seen it with my own eyes, and it is legitimate, although I cannot say whether it is reproducible.

## Alternative Roll Technique

The transition between croquet strokes is not clear, and you will often have to play 'a drive with a little bit of stop', or 'a sort of a slight roll', or 'a three-quarters roll'. I strongly advise playing all croquet strokes with the same grip and the same style, achieving the transition by adjusting the feet and moving the hands down the mallet.

For some players, that is uncomfortable, and they prefer to play roll strokes side-style – swinging the mallet on one side of the body, with the upper hand reaching across the chest. It does not work very well – you will not be able to hit hard, and you will hurt your wrists – because two things are going wrong. The lower arm is virtually parallel to the shaft, so the shot relies on wrist muscles rather than elbows, and the upper forearm is moving across the body, causing the shoulder muscles to turn rather than push forwards.

If you really must play rolls side-style, try holding the lower hand near the head, and the upper hand at the very top of the shaft. That should make you less hunched, stopping you from reaching across, and allowing you to bend from your elbows.

## Split Shots

Much of the time, your croquet strokes will not be perfectly straight, and you will want Red and Yellow to travel in different directions. This is a *split shot*.

Once Red and Yellow are in contact, Yellow's line is determined. However you hit Red, Yellow will travel straight. If you swing the mallet along a different line, Red will be squirted out sideways. That is going to depend on your choice of shot. The procedure is as follows:

- Decide where Yellow will finish.
- Line Red and Yellow up, pointing to this spot.
- Decide where you want Red to finish.
- Your aiming position is halfway between Yellow's finishing spot and Red's finishing spot. Swing the mallet towards this point.
- To put it another way: draw a triangle from you to each of the two targets, and aim halfway along the opposite side.

---

### GATEBALL

Croquet's early spread meant that equipment manufacturers were publishing their own rules faster than the authorities could standardize the game. To this date, some garden games still permit croquet strokes that send either ball hurtling off the lawn, or are played with a foot on the striker's ball. Under official laws, either results in an immediate end of the turn, and the latter has long been illegal.

Both of these elements play an integral part in the Japanese game of Gateball. The game was invented in 1946 as an inexpensive diversion for children. It is played on a hard surface, much smaller than a croquet lawn. There are just three (very wide) hoops, or gates, and a central peg, or goal-pole. Ten players form two teams, and the strategy is largely concerned with touching (roqueting) the opponents' balls, and sparking (croqueting, with a foot on the striker's ball) them out of play.

Gateball has seen impressive growth, both in Japan and across the Far East. Rather than being just a children's game, it has become a popular pursuit for the elderly. Time will tell how Gateball spreads westwards across China but, in Japan alone, it is estimated to have two million followers.

*An alternative roll technique. Keep the lower elbow bent.*

*Lining up a split shot.*

*BELOW: Australia's Martin Clarke plays a split-roll with Blue.*

There are other methods of aiming split shots, but this technique is more accurate, and also gives you some indication of the strength of the shot. Psychologically, aiming at a specific spot, which may be several yards away, should help you to gauge the pace of your croquet stroke.

Widening the angle of split has a significant effect on the ratios of the shot. The wider the split, the further Red will travel. Even with a stop shot, Red will keep moving, and you will often find your 10:1 ratio becomes impossible. On the plus side, these wide shots have much less need for big, awkward full-rolls. As an example, you will sometimes need to send Red and Yellow the same distance, at right-angles to each other. This is the most extreme angle of split – aim straight down the middle, and play a stop shot, a drive or a roll. You may be surprised to see that you will consistently achieve a 1:1 ratio.

Do not be afraid of split shots. By controlling the accurate position of both balls, you open the door to all sorts of clever procedures.

## The Take-Off

The take-off is one of the basic building blocks for many of the tactical manoeuvres of the game. It is a very extreme split shot, where Red moves a long way, and Yellow barely travels. This will be close to a 90-degree split shot, and you will swing close to the direction you want for Red. Legally, you cannot play exactly at a right-angle to Yellow. You must hit into the angle to make Yellow move, even if it is just enough to cause it to shake.

A take-off is played as follows:

- Place Red touching Yellow. Where the balls touch, their curvature forms a 'V' shape.
- Align Red so that the 'V' is pointing very slightly to one side of the target position for Red (the side further from the Yellow).
- Aim at a point the same distance away from the target position, on the side nearer Yellow.
- Play the stroke as if you were just hitting a single ball. Yellow will take virtually no energy from the pace of the shot.

*The 'V' between the balls. Red must hit the take-off slightly in towards the Yellow.*

*USA's John Taves plays a take-off.*

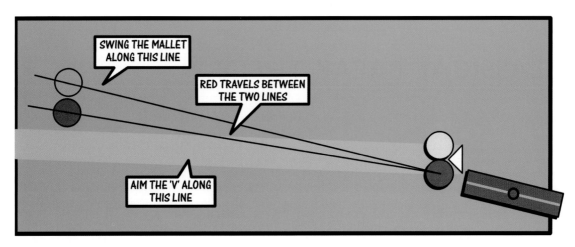

*Lining up the take-off.*

If you wanted to send Red to its hoop, you could place Red to the right of Yellow, align the 'V' one foot to the right of the hoop, and swing the mallet one foot to the left.

Some beginners develop a phobia of playing take-offs from one side of the ball, and will play constantly from Yellow's right. It is important that this does not happen to you. There are points where you will need to leave Yellow precisely on one spot, or move it just one inch in one direction or another. Take-offs where Yellow barely moves are called *thin take-offs*. When you want to move Yellow some distance, you will play a *thick take-off*. It is possible to send Red some distance and cause Yellow to move several yards.

There is nothing complicated in a thin take-off. Direction is easy to work out, and you only need to worry about pacing Red correctly. For this reason, this is often the shot of choice for beginners.

## Choosing the Shot

Choosing between a stop shot and a roll requires a conscious physical thought. You can measure the ratios you need, and select your shot based on that. There is a point during the playing of a croquet stroke when subconscious thought takes over. Judging the exact strength or the exact ratio of a shot is something that moves from your brain to your central nervous system.

Once you have got the balls where you want them in a game, you can govern which shots you play. Most players will steer clear of complicated split-rolls, and try to leave themselves drives and stop shots. The advantage of the stop shot is that most of the energy goes into the Yellow ball. If you misjudge the strength, Red will be barely affected – if Yellow goes a yard too short, Red will be short by a tenth of a yard (a ball's width). For this reason, stop shots are the best shots to play when you want to place your ball (Red) accurately, and drives are a better choice when you are placing the other ball (Yellow).

Practise all the shots, and determine where your strengths and weaknesses lie. Once you are prepared with a full range of strokes, croquet is primarily a game of tactics.

*David Goacher places Red for a take-off.*

# CHAPTER 4

# CLASSICAL BREAK THEORY

It is an obvious thing to say, but the way to win games is to score all your hoops before your opponent does. That statement can be dressed up in many more complicated ways, but the essence is the same – you need to score at a faster rate than your opponent. To do that, the key is giving yourself the opportunity of a *break*, in which you run several hoops in sequence during one turn.

The concept of the break has been around for a very long time, and it involves a conventional pattern, comprising four distinct but fundamental elements.

*A break in progress.*

## The Hoop Approach

The first rule of break play is that it is impossible to make much progress without taking croquet, and earning continuation shots, from the other balls. To get to a scoring position, the sequence goes like this:

- Red roquets Yellow.
- Red plays a croquet stroke, landing in front of Red's hoop.

- Red runs the hoop.
- Red makes a roquet (usually Yellow again).

This cycle repeats at each hoop during the break. Most of the time there are some intervening shots where Red hits Blue and Black, but that detail will be added later. The key ingredients are the following:

- a croquet stroke that places Red in a scoring position; and
- having a ball on the far side of the hoop, near enough for Red to hit it.

The croquet stroke immediately before the hoop is called the *hoop approach*, and is one of the most important elements of the game. It is vital to place Red in scoring position, but, at the same time, Yellow should be sent to a spot beyond the hoop where Red can roquet it again.

## The Pioneer

An accomplished player could, as a last resort, play a break round all twelve hoops using just Red and Yellow, ignoring Blue and Black; this is a *two-ball break*, in which every croquet stroke is a hoop approach. With just two strokes between each hoop, Red has to get into a runnable position with very little margin for error. Two-balling is very much the technique of the adventurer; when a two-ball break goes wrong, it goes wrong catastrophically, and with no chance of recovery.

Adding a third ball to the set-up gives you the opportunity of more croquet strokes, and another two shots between hoops. The second fundamental principle of break play is to have this third ball ready at the next hoop, while still concentrating on Red's current hoop. A ball placed like this at the next hoop is called a *pioneer*.

The sequence of shots, then, is as follows:

- Red roquets Yellow;
- Red approaches Hoop 1, sending Yellow beyond the hoop;
- Red runs the hoop;
- Red hits Yellow.

This time, the Blue ball happens to be near Hoop 2, so Red can use it as a pioneer, to approach the next hoop. The sequence proceeds as follows:

- Red plays a croquet stroke, sending Yellow towards Hoop 3, and landing near Blue.

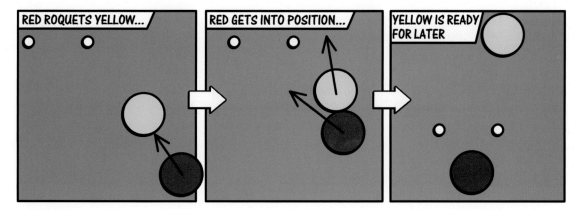

Approaching a hoop.

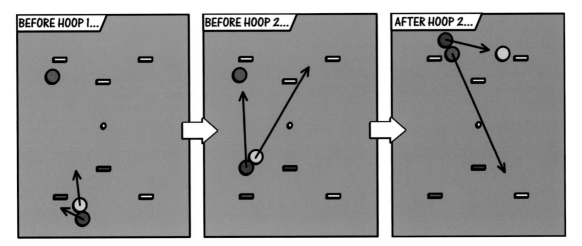

*Use of a pioneer – the three-ball break.*

- Red roquets Blue.
- Red approaches Hoop 2.
- Red runs the hoop and hits Blue again.

As Yellow is at Red's next hoop, Red can use it as a pioneer for Hoop 3. Blue can be croqueted to Hoop 4, where it becomes the next pioneer. The sequence repeats itself for the rest of Red's break.

## The Pivot

Introducing Blue as a third ball has certainly improved Red's chances of progress. This – the *three-ball break* – is a big improvement. Red can roquet, and take croquet from, both Yellow and Blue between hoops, allowing another two

strokes. Unfortunately, all those extra strokes are likely to be very difficult ones. In theory, Red *could* play the croquet strokes described above, with Yellow going to Hoop 3 and Red landing near Blue. In practice, that particular shot is a huge, wrist-breaking, thirty-yard split-roll, with no guaranteed success for any except the most expert of players.

Let us introduce the Black ball. Its function is to simplify Red's task. To ease that big difficult split shot, Black is put in the middle of the lawn, near the peg, affecting the shot sequence as follows:

- Red roquets Yellow, approaches Hoop 1 and scores the hoop.
- Red now roquets Yellow again, with the intention of sending it to Hoop 3.
- Red no longer needs to attempt the difficult split shot,

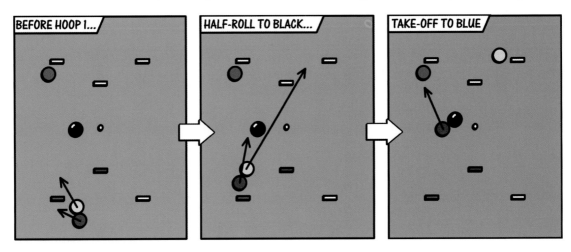

*Use of a pivot – the four-ball break.*

so plays a straight half-roll, sending Yellow to the desired spot, and landing close to the Black.
• Red hits Black, and takes off towards Blue.

After Hoop 2, Red roquets Blue and sends it to Hoop 4. Without Black at the peg, this would be another expert shot. With Black in the middle of the lawn, it is another straight stroke. Blue goes to Hoop 4, Red stops near Black, and can use it to get towards Yellow.

This is the essence of the *four-ball break*. Yellow and Blue are used throughout to make Red's attempt at each hoop easier. Black's function is to help with the positioning of the other balls. As Red sends balls ahead to distant hoops, the play rotates around the Black. For this reason, Black is called the *pivot ball*.

## The Forward Rush

You now have most of the basics in place. Using all three of the other balls, you are earning an extra six shots between hoops. Your objectives should be as follows:

• have a pioneer ready at each hoop before you get there;
• use the pivot to get your ball close enough to that pioneer; and
• hit the pioneer, approach the hoop, and score.

The pivot ball makes a big difference, by giving a series of straight shots. What it does not provide is a series of straight, *short* shots. To help achieve that, we need to back-track, and add some more detail.

Red has just roqueted Yellow, and needs to get in front of Hoop 1. As well as placing Red in a good scoring position, you need to put Yellow beyond the hoop, so that it can be roqueted again after scoring. The point at which Yellow is

placed governs whether the next shot is an easy one or not.

Red's plan is this: Yellow will be sent towards Hoop 3, and Red will stop near the peg, so it can roquet the pivot ball (Black). As Red runs Hoop 1, Yellow should be in a spot where it can be rushed in a useful direction. A rush after a hoop, towards the centre of the lawn, is called a *forward rush*. This rush allows Red to take croquet from Yellow at the exact spot where the next stroke is easiest.

The principles can be summarized as follows:

• RULE 1: Use another ball, and croquet it to get position in front of each hoop.
• RULE 2: Use the third ball to make sure there is a ball ready at the next-but-one hoop.
• RULE 3: Use the fourth ball, placed in the middle of the lawn, to make shots straighter, easier and more accurate.
• RULE 4: Get rushes after hoops, to make shots shorter, and improve accuracy.

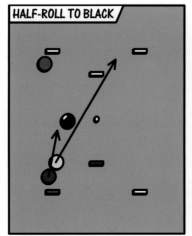

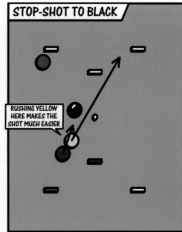

*Making the shots easier with a forward rush.*

---

THE ONE-BALL BREAK

In theory, a player can string together ninety-one successive shots during the course of a turn, allowing all twelve hoops to be scored in one visit to the lawn.

Apocryphal stories abound about more outlandish scoring attempts. Croquet myth describes a group of young players at Cheltenham Croquet Club in the 1970s and early 80s, who perfected the one-ball break – extended turns without the striker making a single roquet. Scoring Hoops 1 and 2 in the same shot is not unheard of, although it is never anything more than a fluke. It is said that the Cheltenham Set practised, and regularly achieved, the break nicknamed 'The Simple Six' – the six hoops from Hoop 3 to 2-back, scored with just six shots. It seems an appealing prospect, although some of the shots involved are challenging, to say the least.

## Technique

### The Hoop Approach

Understanding the pattern of a four-ball break is one thing, but putting it into practice is quite another. There are a few aspects of technique with which players need to be familiar before everything fits into place.

Some players argue that the hoop approach is the most important shot in the whole game. If your approaches land you six inches dead in front of each hoop, you have every chance of scoring. A good approach gives you the opportunity of an easy hoop, which, in turn, is likely to make your subsequent shot easier.

It is important that you get the hang of the approach shot, and there are a few questions to ask yourself before playing it. (As before, this example has you playing Red, and taking croquet from Yellow.)

- Where do I want Red to finish, to give the best chance of scoring?
- Where do I want Yellow to finish, to give the best chance of continuing after the hoop?
- What shot do I need to play to get both balls into the right positions?

The easiest way to look at approaches is to work through a series of examples.

**A Simple Approach**   Once your break is under way, the commonest approach is where Red is taking croquet from Yellow somewhere close to the hoop, and straight in front.

Red is already in a runnable position, but just needs to be closer. Yellow needs to be on the far side, and well clear of the hoop. The balls are lined up for a croquet stroke with a slight split, which should be played as either a stop shot or a drive. Red should drop into position, with Yellow about three

to six feet beyond, to give a good chance of a forward rush.

**Long and Straight**   Option Two has a similar set-up, but the situation is less well controlled. Red is approaching the hoop with Yellow, but from much further away. The position is more speculative, as Red has no guarantee of success. Red may prefer to *roll up* – to approach the hoop with a half-roll or full-roll. Top players often frown at the roll-up, as an inelegant and often inaccurate shot. Because it keeps the two balls close together, it is less likely to give Red the chance of a forward rush after the hoop, but that often has a defensive advantage for the less confident player. For more on this, see Chapter 8.

**Short and Angled**   Approaching from an angle presents a different challenge. Red may be very close to the hoop, but travelling from an unrunnable position, to try to find a spot where the hoop may be scored. Here we return to the concept of the 'fan of success' (see page 25). Red must land somewhere in the fan in order to score. If you go too close to the hoop where the fan is narrow, there is a risk of losing position; if you go too far back, there is more likelihood of finding a straight position, but a much longer hoop. The approach from the side is a trade-off, where Red must find the most comfortable spot within the fan's area. At the same time, Yellow needs to be on the far side to wait for Red after the hoop. It is a stroke that requires a split shot, and you may find yourself playing it as a stop shot, a roll or a take-off.

**Long and Angled**   The long approach from the side is a speculative shot. Again, Red is aiming to land within the fan. This time, the shot is played from a considerable distance, risking either going too close to the hoop and getting no useful position, or landing in a very deep position within the fan, leading to a very long hoop attempt. Even the best players will struggle to control a shot such as this, inevitably played as a half-roll or full-roll with plenty of split. Even so, speculation sometimes pays off, and the pay-off of scoring often outweighs the difficulty of the shot.

*Brian Wislang plays a simple hoop approach.*

*Stephen Mulliner rolls up from further away.*

*Jonathan Kirby approaches from the side.*

**Approach from Behind** Many croquet players (including me) dread this position – Yellow lands immediately behind the hoop, but only a couple of feet away. All Red has to do is to play a take-off, just missing the hoop, and landing in position on the far side. This shot, the *reverse take-off*, requires only one thing, and that is judging the delicate pace of placing Red in position. Provided you have lined up the balls correctly for the croquet stroke, it should be straightforward to tap Red into a perfect position.

Often, though, this shot is a psychological torment – players frequently misjudge the strength, and Red either fails to move more than a couple of inches, or it scoots way past the hoop, leaving a perfectly straight, but very long, shot. The take-off approach occurs very frequently, so players should have it on their regular practice routine.

As with any take-off stroke, Yellow barely moves in this shot.

Because of this, Yellow is often not far enough clear of the hoop to allow Red the prospect of a forward rush after scoring.

## The Backward Rush

Sometimes, Red does not want the rush after the hoop to point forwards at all. Occasionally, the preferred direction is back in the opposite direction. After Hoop 1, Red wants to move forward towards Hoops 2 and 3; but after Hoop 2, Red ideally wants a rush back to somewhere behind him, near the peg.

The principle is exactly the same as for the other types of approach, except that Yellow's finishing position should be somewhere behind the hoop, and to the right. Most players favour putting Yellow much closer, playing the approach with a half-roll.

*A long and speculative approach to Hoop 5.*

*A reverse take-off to the hoop.*

*Red requires a backward rush after scoring.*

## PRACTISING HOOP APPROACHES

Approaching hoops is a critical element in success at croquet. To practise the technique, try to get Red directly in front of a hoop, starting from croqueting position in contact with Yellow. Place Yellow two feet from the hoop, and move its starting point as if on a clock face. At six o'clock, Red would be right in front of the hoop for a simple approach; at three and nine o'clock, Red would be split from the side; and at twelve o'clock, Red would need to take off from two feet directly behind the hoop.

You should be prepared to approach the hoop from any angle. Once you have gained some confidence, try approaching from further away. Soon you will become more aware of where to place Red in order to score, and will understand the positions where you can exploit a forward rush on Yellow.

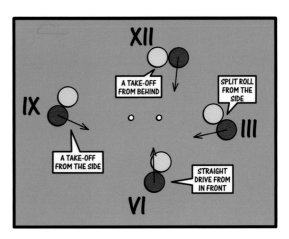

*Practise approaching from different positions.*

## The Take-Off

The classical model for break play relies extensively on taking off from the pivot ball at the peg to the pioneer at each hoop in turn. Typically, the length of that take-off will be about thirteen yards (roughly the distance from the peg to each of the four outer hoops). It is important that you are comfortable with judging the pace of the shot, so it is something you will need to practise regularly.

If Red lands well short in the take-off, you might be faced with a three-yard shot at your pioneer. Shoot at Yellow hard, and you risk knocking it a long way out of position. If you shoot gently, you risk missing completely, as the undulations of the lawn cause Red to waver and miss. It may be simple advice, but you must focus on where you want your Red ball to land, concentrate on the pace of your take-off, and practise, practise, practise.

With all shots, there is a way of making your next shot harder, and a way of making it easier. Red is taking off from Black, and landing near Blue, from which you are going to approach your hoop. If Red stops between Blue and the hoop, your roquet will knock Blue further away from where you want to be. Aim for Red to come to rest so that Blue is between it and the hoop. It is an important point – if you are slightly out of position with Blue, a take-off to the far side will let Red rush back towards an ideal approach position.

## Rushlines

You are about to play your take-off from Black towards Yellow, which is sitting three feet away from your hoop. You want to rush Yellow a bit closer to the hoop. Pace your

take-off right, and you can play that rush from on Yellow's rushline (see page 27). If you place Red close to the rushline, your next shot will be easier. If you place Red wide of the line, you are faced with a tricky cut-rush.

The take-off from Black should aim to land on, or very close to, that line. Taking off towards the rushline from an angle gives you a much better chance of hitting your target. Playing the shot from square on gives you much less margin for error.

### BUMPY LAWNS

It is disappointing for the perfectionist player, but even the flattest of croquet lawns have hidden bumps and undulations to deflect the most accurate of shots. As often as not, this happens just at the crucial moment in front of a hoop. The reason (usually) is a bad shot, but it is always at such crucial moments that hills and valleys suddenly appear on the lawn's surface.

The process of setting hoops firmly in the ground, coupled with the constant compaction of feet, followed by repair to the surface, often leaves a small mound around the hoop. Most clubs reset their hoops periodically and move them a foot or two in either direction, to overcome the worst of the effect. And most players will, for their entire croquet career, be oblivious to the hazard.

Some players develop a high level of skill at excusing their own mistakes, whether these result from surface imperfections or from a lack of roundness in the balls. Some claim the scientific justification of side spin resulting from the direction of mowing, or the gravitational pull of the Coriolis Effect.

Good shots sometimes curl off line, and bad shots sometimes curl on. Such things are essential elements of the game, with which players have to learn to live.

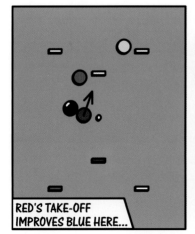
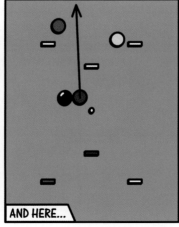
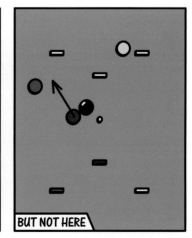

*Think about where to play your take-off. You can make your next shot needlessly difficult.*

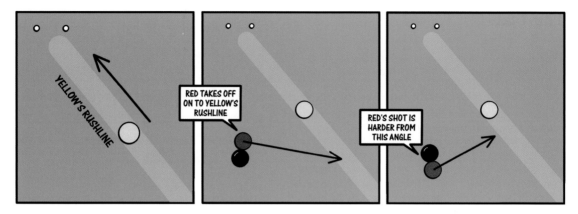

*Landing on Yellow's rushline is easier if played from an angle.*

Rushlines become more and more important the deeper you look into the tactics of the game. They make difficult shots much easier, and turn risky strategies into safely achievable ones.

## The Rush on Yellow

You will find, with practice, that it is perfectly possible to play a break without getting a forward rush after every hoop. Some of the time, you will not even get the opportunity. Red will often whizz through a hoop much further than you expected, or just squeeze through by a tiny amount. In either case, you are likely to find that your carefully placed Yellow is not going to rush to anywhere useful.

All is not lost. The point of the four-ball break is that it is adaptable, and can accommodate any such misfortunes. Your next croquet stroke is likely to be more difficult, but you still have every chance of getting back on course. Be cautious, though, because problems can be made worse with the wrong choice of shot.

So, Red has come through Hoop 1, and managed to hit Yellow. The diagram (right) shows what might happen, depending on where Yellow lands.

*Point A* results from coming through beyond Yellow, and having no option but to roquet it into a much worse position. You might feel that the croquet stroke to place Yellow at Hoop 3, whilst stopping Red near Black, is beyond your ability. There is an alternative play; for more on this, see Chapter 6.

*Point B* results when Red has hit Yellow, but has not been able to rush it anywhere useful. Red simply has to play a long, straight half-roll, sending Yellow to Hoop 3 and stopping near Black.

*Point C* is Yellow's ideal position. Red just needs a straight drive to send Yellow to the next-but-one hoop.

*Point D* is far from ideal. It is physically impossible to send Yellow closer to the hoop at the same time as sending Red closer to the Black. Red's only hope of getting Yellow into position would seriously endanger the next shot. Yellow will have to be left where it is, in order to guarantee that Red will be able to hit Black.

The moral is this: the forward rush after the hoop should allow you to play your next shot so that you land near Black. Rush Yellow where you like, but, whatever you do, do not attempt to rush Yellow to the far side of Black.

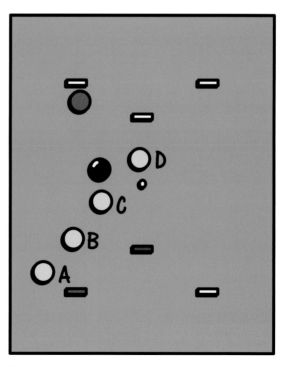

*The outcome of the roquet on Yellow after Hoop 1.*

## The Rushed Pioneer

Ambitious players may consider the option of running Hoop 1, landing so that Red is just short of Yellow, and rushing Yellow directly to Hoop 3. It sounds like a great idea – you do not need to worry about which croquet stroke to choose, and you do not need the Black ball to simplify the shot.

Never, ever, think about rushing a pioneer into position like this. The beauty of a croquet stroke is that you can line it up, and dictate the direction in which Yellow will travel. The scope for error in a rush, even one that looks perfectly straight, is huge. If you hit off-centre by a tiny amount, over a distance of twenty yards that will become magnified to a horrendous degree. Stop shots and drives are controllable and predictable, even over long distances. Whatever your standard of play, rushing over great distances is a risky business.

The Classical Break provides the fundamental framework on which all tactical thinking in croquet rests. The principle of preparing for the next hoop before scoring the current one is the key to a winning strategy. Chapter 5 deals with the ways in which it has adapted and evolved over the last forty years, allowing ever more elaborate tactical manoeuvres to be carried out.

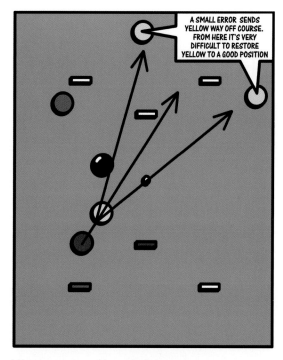

*What can go wrong with a rushed pioneer.*

# THE MODERN BREAK

## A Critique of Classical Break Theory

The classical model remains the most popular among beginners and intermediate players, but its use has fallen significantly from fashion among the top players in the game.

For previous generations, and those not having the luxury of top-class lawns and equipment, the Classical Theory has proved ideal. The key elements of this traditional technique are the take-off from the pivot to each hoop, and the occasional straight roll, required whenever there is no forward rush available after a hoop. Each of these has its place, and they suit the personal style of many players.

*Reg Bamford in play.*

On the other hand, critics of the take-off avoid its over-use, particularly on a fast lawn, where balls can go scooting well past their target; or on a lawn with an uneven pace, where accurate judgement of the correct strength is something of a lottery.

The first few hoops of a break often see the striker trying to get control of the balls, and frequently involve a string of difficult shots before things settle into shape. The Classical Break requires a rigid structure, which is often not in place at the start of the turn when it is most needed. Now is the moment when that long, twenty-five-yard half-roll is needed – Yellow has to land exactly at Hoop 3, with Red stopping a foot away from the Black ball at the peg.

Many players see the classical structure as being good enough to allow them to score hoops, but lacking sufficient flexibility for dealing with testing conditions.

## The Intuitive Leap

The difference in thinking between the traditional break and its modern counterpart seems a small one, but it has a huge effect.

In the classical technique, the pivot ball (Black, in each example here) remains near the peg, and the striker's ball (Red) covers the thirteen-yard distance from the middle of the lawn to each hoop. In the modern game, the pivot ball moves, so that Red does not have to.

What this creates in theory is a very fluid arrangement of the balls. Black moves around the lawn, and is positioned in almost any place *except* near the peg. Rather than relying on take-offs and half-rolls, Red's game now focuses on stop shots and rushes.

## The Moving Pivot in Practice

Let us return to a standard break, and walk through the shots in sequence. In this example, though, Black is not at the peg – it is a bit closer to Hoop 1. Watch what happens:

- Red runs Hoop 1 and hits Yellow.
- Because Black is closer, Yellow can be sent to Hoop 3 with a drive rather than a half-roll. It is a softer shot, and more reliable. Red lands short of, and to the right of, Black.
- Red *rushes* Black somewhere just beyond Blue at Hoop 2.
- Red stop-shots Black to a position well short of the peg, and lands very close to Blue.
- Red runs Hoop 2, and stop-shots Blue towards Hoop 4, landing to the right of Black.
- Black is rushed beyond Yellow at Hoop 3.
- Red stops Black back into the lawn, landing near Yellow.

And so it goes on. Black does all the work, travelling out to the edges of the lawn, and being sent back inwards; Red moves only small distances, so lands close to the pioneer at each hoop.

Under the classical convention, your break is bound by rigid rules, but here you have a great deal of artistic freedom, allowing you to improvise and correct any positions. The break is governed by choices – where Red aims the rushes on Black, and where Black is placed to optimize the next few shots.

## Pivot Placement

There is some leeway in where you place the pivot. It depends on how the ratios on a croquet stroke work for you. If you are good at stop shots, keep the pivot closer than recommended here. If they are not your forte, place it further towards the centre of the lawn.

My rule for placement is to put the pivot ball between a third and halfway between your current hoop and the middle of the opposite boundary. So, if you are going from Hoop 1 to Hoop 2, place the pivot a third of the way between Hoop 1 and the centre of the North boundary. Going from Hoop 2 to Hoop 3, place it a third of the way between Hoop 2 and the centre of the East boundary.

This may sound complicated, as it is very precise advice about the optimum positions. There is a great deal of tolerance, so there is plenty of scope to experiment with the placing. However, these specific positions should achieve the following:

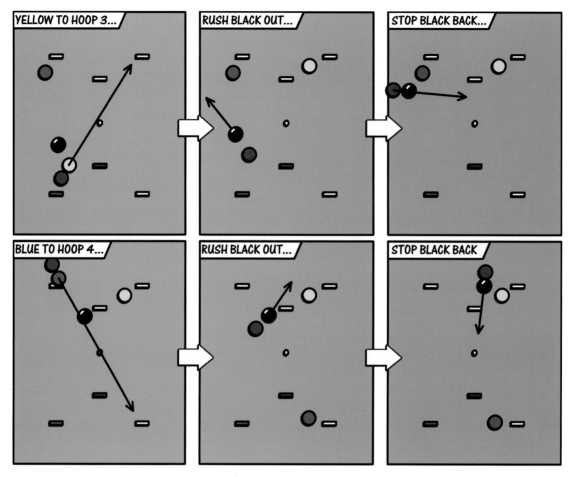

The modern break. The pivot continually moves around the lawn.

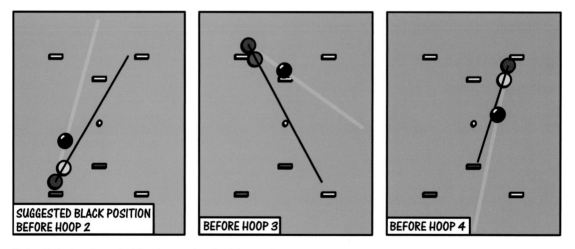

Placing Black along the marked line gives a series of straight stop shots.

- they should give you a straight drive to the next-but-one hoop, with Red dropping near the pivot;
- they should leave Red so it is always on the correct side of Black, ready for the rush to the next hoop; and
- Yellow should be allowed a clear path up to the next-but-one hoop, without fear of accidentally colliding with a hoop or peg.

In practice, very few players theorize to any obsessive extent about placement of the pivot. An alternative plan would be to keep Black (a) somewhere on your side of the lawn, and (b) in a general area that is between five and seven yards away from the peg.

## Rushing the Pivot

Rushing is a fundamental feature of the modern break. You can play a turn with lots of long, angled cut-rushes, or you can play it with short, straight rushes. To make this easy, you need to be constantly aware of each ball's rushline — the imaginary line between where a ball is now, and where you want it to be when you croquet it.

If a player wants to rush a pioneer into a better position, Red needs to land close to the line for that shot. In this example, Red wants to rush Yellow closer to the hoop. In the Classical Break, this would require a long take-off

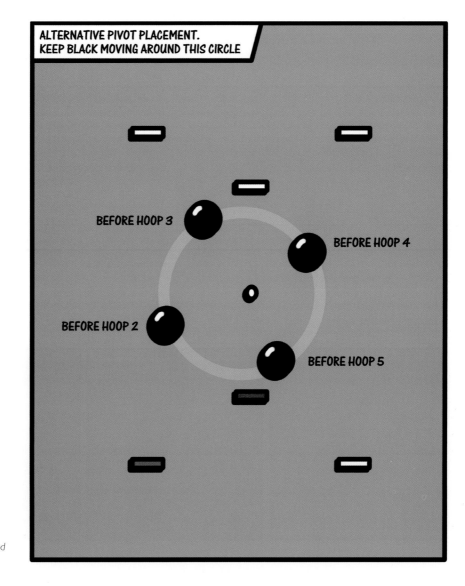

ALTERNATIVE PIVOT PLACEMENT.
KEEP BLACK MOVING AROUND THIS CIRCLE

BEFORE HOOP 3

BEFORE HOOP 4

BEFORE HOOP 2

BEFORE HOOP 5

*Black can occupy any convenient position around the circle.*

## AVOIDING THE FURNITURE

Croquet would be a much easier game if you did not need hoops. The hoops and the peg – the furniture – are never in the right place where you want them to be, and they are often in the wrong place, where you do not want them. One of the shortcomings of the Classical Theory is that there is a ball, the pivot, permanently stationed very close to the peg. It is very easy for Red to come through Hoop 1, and play the half-roll to send Yellow to Hoop 3, only to see Yellow curl off course and smash into the peg. Yellow either stops there, thirteen yards short of its target, or is deflected off, travelling several yards in a completely different direction.

Many other problems can arise when the peg gets in the way. Maybe you have a good enough line to send Yellow direct to Hoop 3, but Red comes to rest very close to Black, and completely obscured by the peg. Red has no ball to hit, so the break comes to a premature and abrupt end.

The moral is this: however the position of the balls changes during the game, the six hoops and the peg will always remain in the same place. You have only yourself to blame if you become entangled with them; you must place balls far enough away to avoid any unnecessary problems.

The modern technique is very good at allowing the player to steer clear of any of the furniture. Black is no longer shackled so closely to the peg. It is a two-second check to make sure that no furniture is in the way of the next shot. Often, Red just needs to tap Yellow an extra foot forward, or a foot to the right. Little things make the difference between having a shot that is totally obscured by hoops, and having one where there is nothing in the way.

from Black, in the hope of getting a good angle on Yellow for the next shot. The Modern Break requires the player to rush Black closer to the rushline – the distance is shorter, the angle is better, and the results are more accurate.

There is a huge amount of leeway in Red's choice of where to rush Black to get position for the next stroke. Here are the options:

*Position A* – the ideal spot. Red will take croquet from Black in a position that is already on the rushline. Red can play pretty well any type of shot, sending Black back in towards the middle. As Red has already found its position on the right line, it just needs to edge closer to the Yellow.

*Position B* – you have overhit the Black, but there is nothing much to worry about. Red can stop close to Yellow, sending Black back towards a mid-lawn position. It is a straight croquet stroke, and Red just needs to

concentrate on stopping short of the Yellow.

*Position C* – you have accidentally cut Black in the wrong direction. This needs a bit of care, but should be OK. Red needs a small split shot to send Black back into its position, stopping near the Yellow.

*Position D* – Black has gone short, but the result is good. Play a take-off, leaving Black where it is. It is a reasonable pivot position for Black, and Red gets the rush you wanted. Be satisfied with this outcome, which many players prefer as their ideal spot for taking croquet. For those playing on heavy lawns, or without a powerful swing, it is ideal.

*Position E* – your rush has failed, and you have only just skimmed the Black, which has barely moved. Not a disaster by any means – it is the position you would be in if you had opted for a standard Classical Break. There is no reason why you cannot carry on as normal from this position.

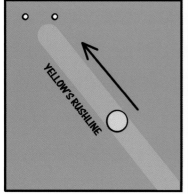
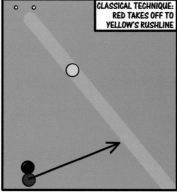
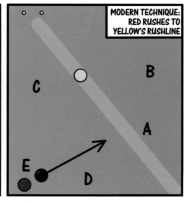

*Rushing towards Yellow's rushline.*

Practice will tell you which of these options is best for your own technique and ability.

## Adding More Detail

That is about all there is to say about the basic concept of the Modern Break. Classicists and Modernists agree on most details of the turn, except for the most reliable way to get Red from one hoop to the next. The old style uses take-offs; the new one uses rushes and stop shots.

The tactics you read about in a book do not necessarily match the tactics you would employ in a competitive game, so you should experiment with both systems, take something from each, and opt for whichever is best for you.

Either way, there is more subtlety and detail to add to the basic pattern, and you need to learn also how to strengthen your break-making ability.

*Chris Clarke – a leading exponent of the precision break.*

## CHAPTER 6

# ENHANCING THE BREAK

So far, the descriptions of break play have been quite rigid. Whether you are a follower of tradition or favour the modern method, there are several ways to depart from the strict pattern. If you are playing well, there are some clever manoeuvres to try, which will keep things tidy. And, if you are playing badly, there are some additional tricks that will help repair difficult situations. First, let us look where problems might occur.

*Tony Le Moignan rolls away from the boundary.*

# The Geometry of the Croquet Lawn

A healthy break, however you choose to play it, allows you some discretion about where to place the four balls. Balls can stray into some areas of the lawn without concern, while balls accidentally placed in other areas will require remedial attention. Before getting into the detail of how to improve your break position, here is a brief analysis of how the areas of the lawn fit together.

## The Inner Rectangle

The area having the first four hoops at its corners is often called the *inner rectangle*, or just the *rectangle*. All six hoops lie within this area, and you will play most of the shots of your break from within the rectangle. In terms of area, the inner rectangle comprises only about a third of the whole playing surface. If you can keep all four balls within this area throughout your turn, the lawn will seem a whole lot smaller. Roquets, rushes and croquet strokes are all much more manageable if you try not to stray from the middle.

## The Quarters

At any one time, you will probably be using only half of the inner rectangle. If you divide the rectangle into *quarters*, the four balls will probably be in the quarter nearest your current hoop, and the quarter nearest your next hoop. In fact, you will probably have three of the balls in your current quarter, and the fourth one in the next quarter. So, at Hoop 1, Red (your ball), Yellow (the Hoop 1 pioneer), and Black (the pivot) are ideally placed in the First Quarter, and Blue (the Hoop 2 pioneer) should be in the Second Quarter.

If in doubt, keep the four balls inside the inner rectangle, and ideally keep them in the quarter nearest you. Balls that lie in the quarters that you are scheduled to visit next are described as being *in front of the break*. Balls that are not on your scheduled path are *behind the break*.

## The Hoop Circuit – Problem Hoops

If you study enough games, you will notice that players *break down* (in other words, fail in their break attempts) at the same hoops. The first three hoops are often thought of as the most difficult, when you have not yet got the balls organized into the layout you want. Of these, Hoop 3 is the one that frightens many players the most.

You have placed the Hoop 3 pioneer right at the start of your break, just after scoring Hoop 1. Your pivot was not ideal – you had to play a long split-roll over a twenty-yard distance, and you have not yet gauged the pace of the lawn. Hoop 3 is hard because the pioneer is often the most badly placed.

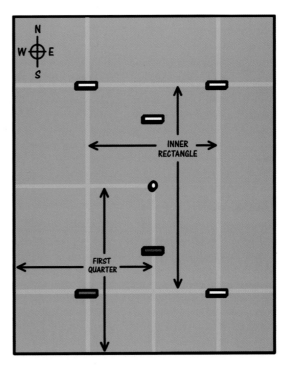

*Areas of the lawn.*

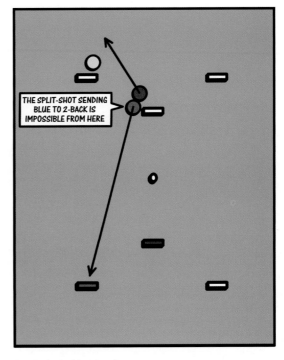

*2-back: the problem hoop.*

If you manage to get past the third hoop, everything looks good. Hoops 4, 5, 6 and 1-back – *the middle four* – are very close to each other. This is the opportunity to tidy up your break, and organize yourself for the later hoops.

The second major obstacle in the break is 2-back, which often takes inexperienced players unawares (diagram previous page). Hoop 6 is the point at which the clockwise circuit around the hoops switches to an anticlockwise circuit. That means that your next hoop (1-back) is in the opposite direction from the subsequent hoop (2-back). If your break is well organized, there is a special trick for dealing with this.

## The Boundary

When the four balls sit inside the inner rectangle, you should always feel more confident about your prospects of scoring. By area, the inner rectangle represents only a third of the playing surface, so any balls lying here remain close to the action. There is plenty of room to get to the far side of a ball and rush it somewhere useful. Margins of error are bigger, distances are shorter, and you have the space to play elaborate and daring croquet strokes without fear of sending a ball off the lawn.

If Yellow is on the *yardline* – one yard in from the boundary – the picture is very different. Red wants to take

---

### INTERNATIONAL BOUNDARIES

Under the rules of Association Croquet, balls that go out of play, or that stray too close to the boundary, are replaced one yard in. In practice, that is measured with the player's mallet. Typically, a mallet shaft is around thirty-six inches, so provides an accurate and straightforward means of doing this. Some players have mallets custom-made to a length of thirty-four and three-sixteenths of an inch (half a ball's width less than a yard), or thirty-seven and eleven-sixteenths of an inch (half a ball more), to make measurement easier.

However, the USCA Rules of the North American game stipulate a 'yardline' that is only 9in, measured with the mallet head. Balls placed near the boundary become difficult to bring back into play, leading to very defensive situations.

Balls sent off the lawn in Egypt are, under the rules of Golf Croquet, replaced exactly on the boundary line. This has proved a popular rule change, and has now been internationally adopted.

Japanese Gateball treats the boundary differently, and much skill is focused on sending as many balls over the boundary as possible. Balls sent out of the playing area are not replaced, and remain out of play for a full turn. Gateball is a team game for ten players, but it is possible to reach a situation where there is not a single ball on the lawn.

---

### THE PROBLEM WITH BOUNDARIES

Attempting to land your Red ball inch-perfect behind a yardline ball is often very dangerous indeed. Local knowledge can useful in this situation, as the boundary area is often the most inconsistent part of any croquet lawn.

I have played on one lawn that has a four-foot drop from one end to the other, and another where it was not even possible to see the far boundary. In both cases, any ball that landed within the yardline area would come to rest, wobble, and then hurtle under the force of gravity over the boundary, ending my turn and my prospects of winning.

I have also played on saucer-shaped lawns where there is a gradient in the other direction. Before a tournament a few years ago, I caught one player practising trying to send a ball out of play. No matter how hard he hit the ball, he was unable to make the ball stay within the yardline area, and watched it curl round each time in towards the lawn.

Boundary problems are often a side-effect of long-term maintenance of a croquet lawn. To avoid excessive wear around hoops, clubs often move entire lawns by a few feet from time to time over the course of a season. Sometimes, the redrawing of boundaries moves the strip of grass that was a foot outside the lawn to one foot just inside. The earth could be more, or less, compacted, the levels could be different, and the surface could run faster, or slower, than the rest of the lawn. Players must rely on local knowledge to take advantage of such features of the lawn.

---

advantage of Yellow, but now the opportunity is greatly reduced. There is often no realistic prospect of rushing Yellow into play, unless Red can get in the narrow strip between Yellow and the boundary.

During your turn, only Red is allowed to stray into the yardline area. As soon as any of the other three balls stop within three feet of the boundary, they must be replaced on the yard. Rescuing such awkward balls calls for some special techniques.

## The Corners

A ball in a corner is even harder to exploit. This is the point where one awkward yardline meets another. Inexperienced players often hate the prospect of drawing out corner balls, because of the hazards of getting into the narrow space behind. There is very little room to set up a rush, so the alternative is to croquet the ball into play with an ineffective take-off or an ugly roll. At the same time, many experts love corner balls.

The subject of defensive boundary positions, and the advanced technique of bringing corner balls into play, will be covered later.

# Problems and Solutions

### A Short Pioneer – the Pivot Swap

You have planned everything right: you have come through Hoop 1 with Red, you have hit Yellow, and played a croquet stroke to send it to Hoop 3. Red has landed next to Black, the pivot ball. The one thing that has gone wrong is that Yellow has landed seven yards short of Hoop 3. Do not worry. Misjudging distance early in the break happens all the time, and there is a simple solution.

Yellow just is not good enough as a pioneer to guarantee success at Hoop 3. So, hit Black, and croquet it to Hoop 3, with Red finishing close to Blue at Hoop 2. Yellow (your intended Hoop 3 pioneer) has become the pivot, and Black (your intended pivot) has become the pioneer.

There are times when you might want to swap pivots, even when you are not in trouble. Pivot swaps become a useful trick for more complicated manoeuvres.

### Rescuing a Lost Pioneer – Doubling the Pioneer

Here is the same scenario. You have come through Hoop 1 and sent Yellow to Hoop 3. This time, instead of sending it too short, you have sent it way beyond the hoop. This is a much nastier position. To draw Yellow back into play, you would have to go to the far side of it, into the narrow area between the ball and the corner. As before, Yellow is a bad pioneer, so you should use the Black ball as a replacement. This time, it is not such an instant fix, so here is a walkthrough of the sequence of shots needed to repair the damage. The first step is to send Black down to Hoop 3. Where it lands will dictate what happens next. If you can place Black in a comfortable pioneer position, then all is well. You can get back on track immediately with the following sequence:

- Make Hoop 2 with Blue. After the hoop, Blue will become the pivot. Ideally, you want Blue somewhere near Hoop 6 or the peg. If you can rush it a couple of yards towards that area, so much the better.
- Now take off towards Yellow. Blue will naturally get nudged in towards the centre of the lawn where you want it.
- Yellow will become your Hoop 4 pioneer. If stop shots are not your forte, you might want to rush it a bit further out towards the corner. That will give you more room to play the next shot.
- Yellow is sent to Hoop 4, with a long stop shot. Red stops near Black, and Blue is now the pivot.

By reshuffling the roles of each ball, you have got back on track. Black (pivot) has become the Hoop 3 pioneer; Blue (your intended Hoop 4 pioneer) has become the pivot; and Yellow (your Hoop 3 pioneer) has instead been sent to Hoop 4.

You will need a bit more patience if you sent Yellow too far, but have not been able to send Black to a spot about which you are confident. You could try exactly the same play as above, but Yellow's final stop shot could be a cumbersome roll.

There are so many ways of rectifying this position, and it all depends on your specific predicament. Here is one example:

- Make Hoop 2 with Blue. Stick with your original plan to send it to Hoop 4.
- Try the shot to send Blue down the lawn, but focus on leaving Red close to Black.
- Rush Black off the lawn towards Yellow. This may be very close to Yellow, or a few yards away.
- Croquet Black to bring it a bit further in to the lawn, but make sure you get a rush on Yellow towards Hoop 3.

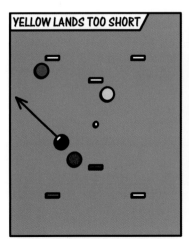 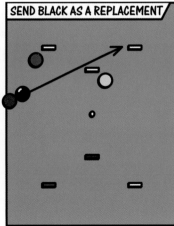 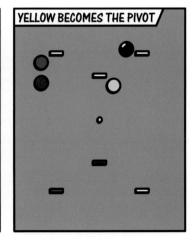

*Replacing a short pioneer with a pivot swap.*

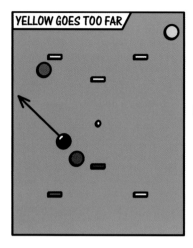 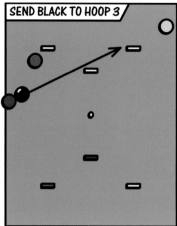 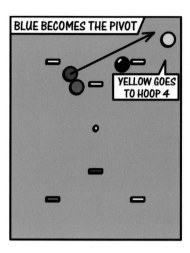

*Replacing an overlong pioneer.*

- Score the hoop, and try to rush Yellow off the lawn again, somewhere near Black.
- If you have brought Black in at all, you should now have the space to stop-shot Yellow into the rectangle, holding on Black for a rush.

In this second example, you have changed your plan about which shots to play, but each ball has retained its role – Black is the pivot, Blue is the pioneer to Hoops 2 and 4, and Yellow is the pioneer for Hoop 3. It is not possible to orchestrate an instant fix, so you have had to coax Black and Yellow in gradually, until you have enough room to play a decent stop shot. After Hoop 3, and only once you have cured your short-term problem, you have then swapped pivots – Yellow will be left near Hoop 3, while Black becomes the pioneer to Hoop 5.

There is a need, especially when you are playing badly, to make things up as you go along. It is right to have a plan about how to play your break, but it is wrong to stick too rigidly to it when the balls do not land where you want them. Be prepared to improvise.

## The Hoop 6 Turn and the Early Pioneer

There is a useful trick for dealing with the difficult 2-back pioneer. 2-back is the point at which you come out of the easy stretch of four hoops close together. Because Hoops 4 and 5 are so close together, it is often the time when you can turn a ragged break into a nice tidy one. And that is the key for dealing with 2-back.

This is an optional extra, for those with the luxury of a break that is starting to fit together. Instead of sending the

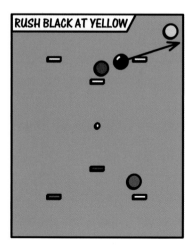  

*Gradually easing Black and Yellow back into play.*

### A MATTER OF PRIORITIES

At every stage of the break, there is one ball that is more important than the others, and that is the ball with which you are playing your turn.

This is especially true when things are not going well. Players often look for a quick fix for their problems, at the expense of scoring. If you have failed to send a decent pioneer to the next hoop, you certainly want to repair the damage, but you do not want to do so at the expense of keeping the turn going.

Some players will coax a break back into life over the course of three or four hoops. They will play to guarantee their next hoop, gradually drawing the balls in from the boundaries with a series of rushes and take-offs. I am much more of a rolling-all-the-balls-into-the-middle kind of player. Patience and caution are virtues in a croquet player, and I have neither. This is an instance where you should follow what I say, but ignore what I do.

2-back pioneer to its hoop after Hoop 6, try sending it after Hoop 5. Black, your pivot, is sent as your pioneer to 1-back, so you will play the next three hoops with a pioneer at each, and no pivot ball.

Here is some detail. After Hoop 4, put Black somewhere beyond Hoop 5, and somewhere to the left (on the side nearer 2-back). Approach Hoop 5 off Yellow, run the hoop and hit Yellow again. Yellow now goes directly to 2-back with a stop shot. Red stops short of Black, which is then sent up towards 1-back.

The early pioneer to 2-back is something I will do as a matter of course in almost every break. There are players who perform a similar manoeuvre to send an early ball to Hoop 6 after Hoop 3, or a ball to Rover after 3-back. In the first case, I never normally play that well so early in the

break; and in the latter, my concentration has usually lapsed by that late stage. You are welcome to experiment and see if this technique suits your style of play.

### Rescuing a Lost Pivot – Back-Rushing

If you watch someone else playing, you can often see, better than they can, the point where a problem occurs. If this problem is left uncorrected, things can go from bad to worse, without the striker being aware of how the mess came into being.

Much of the time, the only thing that holds your break back from being difficult is a well-placed pivot ball. You will sometimes have to leave it behind while you deal with a tricky situation, but you still need to bring it back under your control, and keep it in a useful position.

The key shot here is the hoop approach. Here is an example. You are at Hoop 5, and everything is laid out fine – Yellow is a good Hoop 5 pioneer, and Blue is looking good at Hoop 6. However, in order to get this perfect layout, you have had to leave Black behind, somewhere near Hoop 4.

Whenever this happens, stop and think about your hoop approach. Normally, you would plan to play a little drive, to send Yellow a few feet beyond Hoop 5. Red would run the hoop, landing just short of Yellow. Red would then rush Yellow up the lawn, ready for you to croquet it over towards 1-back.

Instead, you want to bring the Black back into play, so approach the hoop with a roll. Red finishes in position in front of the hoop, with Yellow just a bit alongside, and to the right. However hard Red comes through, you will have the chance of a rush, either down to the South boundary past Black, or over to the East boundary. Depending on where the rush goes, you should now be able to do one of the following:

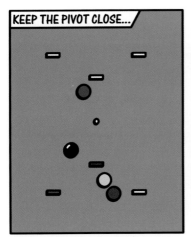

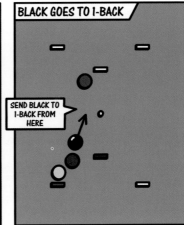

*Placing an early 2-back pioneer.*

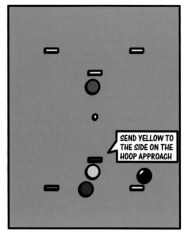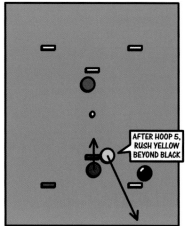

*Back-rushing: Red returns to collect Black.*

- place Yellow at 1-back, putting Black towards the peg;
- place Yellow at 2-back, bringing Black up the lawn, to send to 1-back; or
- place Yellow as the new pivot, bringing Black up to become the new 1-back pioneer.

In this example, this is a very low-risk strategy, because you have control of Yellow at Hoop 5 and a good pioneer at Hoop 6. When things are going well, your chances to improve positions are great.

## Digging Out a Corner Ball

Most errors in a break occur in the first couple of hoops. You have managed to place two of the other balls in approximately the right place, as you valiantly attempt difficult approaches and long hoops. Things will improve once you have coaxed the fourth ball into play, but right now it is stuck tight in a distant corner.

---

**THE HOGAN ROLL**

Theoretically, there is a way of bringing a corner ball into the lawn immediately, but it does not bear thinking about. Joe Hogan, croquet's first World Champion, played the astonishing Hogan roll during the course of the Championship Final in 1989.

Red has just started a three-ball break, and Black is in the fourth corner. Red roquets Black after the first hoop, and plays a forty-yard pass-roll. Red stops near Blue at Hoop 2, and Black goes to Hoop 3. The description does no justice to the shot itself, which is inconceivably difficult.

---

The easiest way of bringing a ball into play is to wait until you are in that neighbourhood. Imagine Red is for Hoop 1, and you have a tidy three-ball break waiting for you. Alas, Black is buried deep in Corner 4, and you can see no easy way of fetching it.

For a ball in Corner 4, the best advice for fetching it is to wait until Hoop 4. Instinct would tell you to play your turn like this:

- Make Hoop 2 off Blue.
- Send Blue in front of Hoop 4, going to Yellow at Hoop 3.
- Make Hoop 3 off Yellow.
- Rush Yellow down the lawn a bit, and send it to Hoop 4, going to Blue.
- Run Hoop 4, hoping to come near to Black.
- Hit Black, and you have all four balls.

A much better way is to use a pivot swap, as follows:

- Make Hoop 2 off Blue.
- Send Blue to Hoop 4, ideally hitting it a bit harder than usual. The best place is a couple of feet to the left of Hoop 4, and a foot or two beyond the hoop.
- Make Hoop 3 off Yellow.
- Do not pay much attention to what happens to Yellow, which will now become your pivot ball. Take off to Black.
- Hit Black, and play a straight drive. Black goes direct to Hoop 5 as your new pioneer, and Red stops short of Blue. You have a perfect set-up.

The important point is that, when you are retrieving a ball from the boundary, the easiest method is to offset your pioneer, so it is further from its hoop, and nearer to the ball you want to fetch.

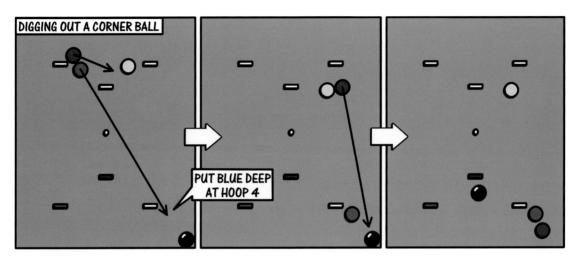

*Digging Black out of Corner 4.*

Here is a similar example, where Red is for Hoop 2, and you want to dig Black out of Corner 1. You have very little prospect of doing that for some time, but your nearest point is when Red reaches Hoop 5. Send your Hoop 5 pioneer a couple of yards towards Hoop 1. After Hoop 4, it is now possible to roquet Black, and play a half-roll out of the corner. Black goes to Hoop 6, and Red lands near Yellow. Bringing Yellow just a couple of yards towards the corner turns this from a very difficult full-roll, needing a lot of precision, into a manageable half-roll. As so often in croquet, planning is everything.

## The Complete Break

That is more or less all you need to know about breaks. If the game relied solely on starting an established break at Hoop 1, continuing to the peg, and then stopping, you would not need to read any further. But what happens when you have no break?

*Jenny Clarke approaches 2-back, to give a rush back up the lawn.*

# CHAPTER 7

# OUTPLAYER TACTICS

Knowing how to play the perfect break is not much use to you when you are losing. An hour into the game, you are on your third coffee of the morning, you are slumped in a chair, and you have yet to make your first roquet. You know you are a better player than the other guy, but he just has not given you a chance to get going. This chapter is all about how to seize control, how to stop your opponent and how to make sure that you are on the lawn, and not just watching.

## The Outplayer

The advantage is with your opponent. His Blue and Black are together, and your Red and Yellow are split. He has the *innings* – unless you do something, each of his turns will start with a short hit on his partner ball. Until the situation alters, he is going to do all the scoring.

Three things will bring about a change:

1 you make a long roquet – or *hit in* – to regain control;
2 you force him to make a mistake; or
3 you stop him making any progress.

## Choice of Ball

It is possible to over-analyse the tactics of the game. If there is a ball that is close enough for you to be guaranteed of hitting, you probably do not want to think more deeply. Control passes to you if you make a roquet, so hit first, and only then think about what to do with your croquet stroke. Ask yourself, 'Have I a guaranteed hit?' If the answer is 'Yes', just play the shot.

Things get more complex when you are not 100 per cent sure of hitting. At the front of your mind should be the question, 'Which ball would my opponent prefer me to leave where it is?'

If your Red ball is near Black's hoop, you should certainly think about playing Red. The most dangerous positions for Red are the following:

- Red is at Black's hoop.
- Black has a rush on Blue directly towards Red.
- Red is at Black's subsequent hoop.
- Red is somewhere in the middle of the lawn.

Whichever of Red and Yellow features higher on this list is the more vulnerable. The safest option would be for you to play that ball.

There is some pressure off you if there is no clear-cut safe option. Maybe Red is near Black's hoop, but not quite near enough, and you are prepared to risk leaving it. Perhaps Red and Yellow are equally safe – or equally dangerous.

ABOVE: *Players wait for their opponents to finish their turns.*

LEFT: *Outplayers at Southwick.*

*Reg Bamford watches Ed Duckworth in play.*

You now have the luxury of playing the ball you want to, rather than the ball you think you ought to.

Here is your third question: 'Which ball do I want to play?'

In general, the ball you would like to play is the one that gives you a better scoring opportunity. If Red has a ball near its hoop, or the chance of an easy couple of shots to dig out a playable break position, then you will be tempted to opt for a shot with Red.

Even better, you might be spoilt for choice, with a promising start for either Red or Yellow. In this case, it is normally better to play your *backward ball* – the ball with more hoops still to score. So, if Red and Yellow are for Hoops 1 and 4-back, Red has the promise of a twelve-hoop break, while Yellow can only hope for three hoops. Red is the clear candidate for the ball you would rather play next.

# Selecting the Target

Now you have chosen which ball to play, you need to decide what to do with it. Your options are limited.

### Option 1: Blue and Black Together, Yellow Near the Boundary

Red shoots at Yellow. There is the chance of a roquet, which gives control back to you. If you miss, Red is joined up with Yellow, and Blue is joined up with Black, some distance away from you. Sometimes this is a good idea. Your opponent will almost certainly try to split you up. That is bad news if he is an expert, as he will stand a good chance of getting a rush on one of your balls. It is a chance for him to score.

*Free shots.*

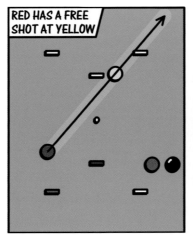

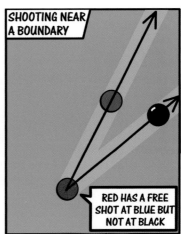

If your opponent is weaker, joining up can be fruitful. It forces him to concentrate on safety play – split Red and Yellow apart before thinking about approaching a hoop. In some games it is the best tactic for coaxing a mistake from your opponent.

## Option 2: Blue and Black Together, Yellow Towards the Middle of the Lawn

There is hardly ever a scenario when it is a good idea to shoot at Yellow gently. Leaving Red and Yellow together in a mid-lawn position is asking for trouble. If you plan to shoot at Yellow, you should aim to reach the boundary if you miss. Shooting hard makes Red less vulnerable to all the bounces and swerves of an imperfect lawn, but it also leaves you much safer.

This is often the best choice of shot for Red. There is the option of a roquet on Yellow, but a miss leaves Red safely on a distant boundary. This is a *free shot*, and gives Red an attacking option, which lands defensively after a miss. Hit or miss, there is no real penalty to you. Keep an eye out for free shots – if one presents itself, you hardly need to search further for which shot to take.

## Option 3: Shooting at Blue and Black

I was taught that it is a bad idea to shoot at the opponent. If Blue and Black are joined up on the boundary, a missed shot at them just donates a third ball to play with.

Constantly shooting at the opponent is the trademark of a player who is either a fearless straight-hitter, or someone who never learns from their mistakes. However, there are times – and very specific ones – when you can get away with it. If you do hit, the pay-off is usually great. You earn a croquet on Black, with Blue close by. Bearing in mind that it is the start of your turn, and you have not yet taken

croquet from Yellow, the prospects look good.

When to shoot:

- Red can land well past Blue and Black if you miss. If Blue and Black are mid-lawn, you have a possible free shot. If they are on the boundary, but you are shooting from an angle, it is possible to shoot, miss, and land well out of reach.
- Red has a *double target* at Blue and Black. The gap between the two balls is so small that you can aim for the middle, and expect to hit one or other of the balls.
- Black has a very short rush on Blue, very close to the boundary. If you shoot Red at this, Black will turn down the rush on Blue, and hit Red first; Black will then play a tiny stop shot, hoping to get back to his original position; Black will then rush Blue. There is a chance that Black could sacrifice his position to mess about with Red, and then not regain the rush. Even if he does, Black and Blue are now mid-lawn, and Red is safely on the boundary. Black's rush, left so close to the boundary that he cannot exploit the nearby Red, is called an *unguarded rush*.

When not to shoot:

- Blue and Black are joined up with a rush, but now the two balls are a few feet in from the boundary. This time, shooting at Black leaves you very vulnerable. This will be Black's response: Red is a few feet away, so Black turns round and hits it; Black has room to play a decent stop shot – at the very least, he should be able to send Red to the edge of the inner rectangle; Black lands back in position for the rush on Blue. Black has defended the boundary with a *guarded rush*. By moving a few feet further in, he has enough space to bring Red back into play. Shooting Red at a guarded rush is a sign of desperation or recklessness. A miss will often concede an immediate break for Black.

- Blue and Black are joined up on the boundary, but with no useful rush. Shooting and missing presents Black with a third ball to play with. From here, it is possible to convert a poor position, with no rush to Black's hoop, into a profitable one.

In summary, you should avoid shooting at the opponent when his two balls are a couple of yards off the boundary. On the boundary is a different matter – when Black has a poor rush, shooting at him can only make his position better; shooting at a good rush can only make his position worse.

### Option 4: Blue and Black Joined; Yellow Already Safely on the Boundary

There are times when you can rule out all the above as options. Red at Blue/Black gives an immediate break; Red at Yellow gives too much away; you are not hitting straight,

and your opponent is unlikely to make an error when you present him with an easy prospect. If you think your chances of hitting are outweighed by what you surrender if you miss, then it is time to play defensively.

You have thought about the alternatives – Red's shot at Blue and Black gives away an instant break; Red's shot at Yellow is not much better. Your next best bet is a *wide join*.

Instead of shooting at Yellow with the intention of hitting, you place Red a few yards away. You are close enough to worry Black, who thinks you might hit on the next turn, but you are far enough apart to give little away. Black has to split Red and Yellow up, but you have placed the balls in an awkward position where there is no easy rush opportunity for him.

There are a number of points to remember:

- Attempt a wide join only when Yellow is on, or very close to, the boundary. If Yellow is well in, you are just presenting your opponent with a chance of bringing Yellow further into play.

*James Le Moignan shoots Red at a double target.*

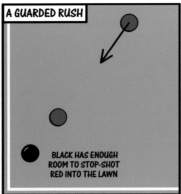

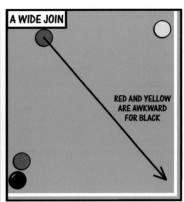

*Defensive positioning.*

## DOUBLE TARGETS

Placing two balls close to each other provides a much wider target for the opponent. Some players have a policy of always shooting at a double target, and you should be wary about how you line up the balls, in order to avoid giving such a generous gift. Before you make the declaration that you will always shoot at doubles, it is important to understand a bit about the geometry.

A target ball, so it is said, is really two balls wide. You can hit it dead centre, or go half a ball's width on either side, and you will still earn a roquet. Trace a path along which the centre of your ball would need to travel – the width of the target is 7¼in, or twice the width of the ball you are aiming at.

You can use the same principle to work out the real size of a double target. The perfect double has two target balls, with a gap between just wide enough for your ball. If you go through the gap, you will scrape both balls; 7¼in to the left, and you will still hit the left ball, and the same distance to the right will allow you to hit the right ball. This perfect double target is, in effect, twice as wide as a single ball. Mathematically, that equates to a shot which is (more or less) twice as close, and twice as easy to hit.

Occasionally, you might be presented with a target where all three of the other balls are close: you can see Blue, then a gap, then Black and another gap, and then Yellow. In croquet jargon, this is known variously as a triple target, a Baillieu double, or a pawnbroker. Often you will see it where Yellow is close by, but Blue and Black are in the far distance. Many players find these shots irresistible – the effective width is three times that of a single ball, making the shot appear a third of the distance away.

As the gap between the target balls decreases, so too does the attractiveness of the shot. Two balls in contact are just one and a half times wider than just one ball. As the width drops further, the benefit of shooting drops further still.

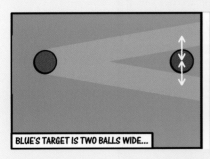

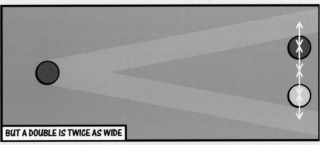

*Measuring a double target.*

- Do not be tempted to place Red and Yellow too close, or too far apart. The distance between them should be such that your opponent thinks you *might* hit. But, at the same time, the balls should not be so close together that there is an easy pick-up for him. Conventional wisdom dictates that Red and Yellow should be at the distance where your hitting chances are about 50 per cent. The defensive advantage is lost by going closer than a couple of yards, so the novice should stay somewhere in the region of four or five yards. Even an expert will very rarely set a wide join longer than eight yards. At that point your wide join ceases to be a join at all.

- Try to keep Red and Yellow on the same boundary. If Black decides not to split your balls, you are faced with a shot of Red at Yellow or Yellow at Red. Hitting lets you back in, but missing often leaves you with another wide join further along the boundary. A good ploy is to set your wide join by placing Red midway between Yellow and the nearest corner. That way, Yellow can shoot back and forth without fear of going too far past Red.
- If you do put Red and Yellow on different boundaries, it is a very defensive position. If Yellow is five yards from a corner on one boundary, try placing Red five yards from the corner on the other boundary. There is no positional advantage to you, but it leaves your opponent with virtually no prospect of a rush on either Red or Yellow. A very negative tactic, admittedly, but it is something to consider when you want to bide your time against a weaker opponent.

- Avoid setting a wide join anywhere that is useful to your opponent. If Black has a rush on Blue pointing straight at Yellow, you should not even consider the join. You are courting danger if you join up near Black's hoop. And, for the ultra-cautious, do not join on the boundary nearest Black's next two hoops (in other words, the West boundary, when Black is for Hoop 1), where there is a faint chance he will manage an attempt at an approach.

## Option 5: Cornering

There are times when even the wide join is not going to save you. You cannot shoot, you cannot join up. Playing any shot with either ball concedes a break. You still have one option, and that is to run away and hide. There is no immediate chance of getting the innings back, so you need to stop Black's progress, and be ready to pounce when there is an error.

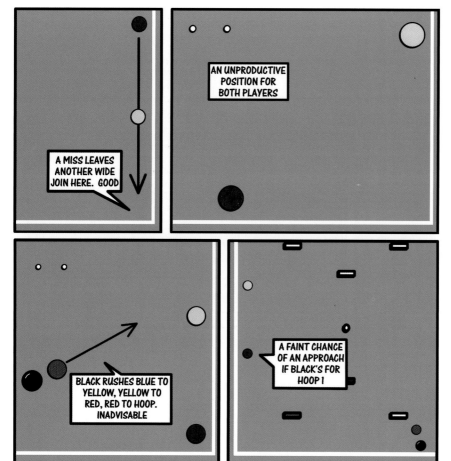

*Good and bad positions for Red to lay a wide join.*

The key defensive points are the four corners of the lawn. Burying Red deep in a corner is often your best bet for impeding Black. Your only question is which corner to choose. Let us suppose that Black is for Hoop 1. Here are your choices:

1 *Red into Corner 1*. Generally, this is the least satisfactory shot against all but the weakest of players. You put Red into the corner; Black will just move you out again. There is a chance that he will manage that with a speculative attempt at a long hoop approach, and, if that works, you risk giving away a break.

2 *Red into Corner 2*. This is the passive-aggressive shot to take. You assume that Black will limp through the first hoop, but without a reasonable rush up the lawn. He cannot afford a tentative roll approach, because you have taken control of the territory around Hoop 2. He could abandon Blue (hopefully mid-lawn), hit Red, and try to approach the hoop from the corner. That is a much harder shot than the approach to Hoop 1 from Corner 1 – the angles and distances are wrong when approaching from behind. Red, placed in this position to ward off trouble, is called a *policeman*. If Black does come closer, there is a good chance that Red will get an early hit after Black's failed hoop.

3 *Red into Corner 3*. Hoop 3 is always difficult, especially at the early stage of a break where Black has no pivot ball. If Black gets this far using just Blue and Yellow, it is straightforward to pick up Red. What you are counting on is that Black will struggle to get here. The more hoops you force him to play without being able to incorporate Red into his break, the more chance you have of the collapse of his turn.

4 *Red into Corner 4*. This is the ideal shot for defensive play. Black will have had a hard slog through the first three hoops. If he has managed to organize himself, Hoop 4 is his first chance to bring Red into play. If things are still scrappy, he will struggle with even that.

Whichever hoop Black plans to score, Red can make progress difficult by cornering. The corners closest to where Black will go next are in front of the break. Safe defensive policy is to hide your balls anywhere behind Black's break, in the last corner on his itinerary.

Often, you can regard a cornered ball as a precursor to a wide join. When Red and Yellow have both been in vulnerable positions, you can hide Red, wait for another turn, and then bring Yellow to the boundary, ready for Black to make an error.

## Option 6: Run Your Hoop

There is one other choice that is often disregarded, and always frowned upon by purists. Blue and Black are joined, and have inadvertently left Red near Black's hoop. As it happens, this is also Red's hoop, and there is a chance of scoring. This is your last resort.

There is one good reason why you should not do this – a miss is disastrous. But there is also one good reason why you should. If all your shots at other balls are unpromising, but your shot at the hoop is guaranteed, have a good think. Running the hoop and landing four feet beyond might make your dangerous shot at Yellow suddenly seem much safer. Or your difficult shot at Blue and Black might suddenly become a perfect double target. At the very least, it is another point on the scoreboard. Bear it in mind – people will call you reckless, but it might be your golden chance to steal back the innings.

Whatever you choose to do, you will find it impossible to win a game unless you gain the innings at least once. That does not necessarily mean that you need to hit lots of long shots. Many matches are won by forcing your opponent to miss short roquets, and fail easy hoops. By lying in wait, there are times when you can take victory without ever having to attempt a long shot.

Your next consideration is how to keep control once you have it, and how to convert your initial hit-in into break perfection.

## CHAPTER 8

# KEEPING THE INNINGS

We have seen how there are a number of ways of regaining the innings when your opponent has control of the balls. Now, you need to consider things from the point of view of the other player. How do you retain control, while at the same time strengthening your position? And how do you build that position from nothing into a perfect break?

Ambition gets the better of many players, who instinctively want every visit to the lawn to deliver a perfect scoring turn. While experts are adept at digging out breaks from unpromising starts, you will often have to settle for rearranging the balls, and readying yourself for a better prospect on the next turn. If there is no break available this turn, you might have to settle for a *leave*, in which you set up the balls for your next turn.

*Planning the next move.*

This is a balancing act between four objectives:

1 leaving yourself a hittable shot;
2 leaving your opponent with a missable shot;
3 creating a good chance for you if the opponent misses; and
4 creating a bad chance for the opponent if he hits.

Not all players manage this balancing act very well. There are a number of ways in which it can all go wrong.

## Aunt Emma

### A Guide to Bad Croquet

You have just hit. You pick up Red, place it in contact with the other ball, and now you do not know what to do. You want to score some hoops, but your first priority is to keep Blue and Black out of play. So you shuffle the balls around, put some distance between Blue and Black, put Red and Yellow together, and park yourself as far away from the opponent as possible.

Everything looks fine – you have got the innings, oppo has a long shot, and you can think about how to improve things in a couple of minutes when Black misses. You are not playing confidently, and you have got to work hard to put together a break. The natural tendency is to try to keep the initiative at all costs, in the hope that a scoring opportunity might suddenly appear.

Just as you figured, Black shoots at Blue, and misses. You are joined up, but he is too close together for comfort. So you roquet Yellow gently, take off to Black, shove it back into the same position, and join up again.

The identical set-up, and Black plays the same shot. It worked last time, so you play the same sequence of shots. You are together, Blue and Black are split. Maybe you will get a chance to score your hoop next turn, but the priority is to keep the innings, and to keep the opponent apart.

Half an hour later, you are still in the same position. As long as Black fails to hit, this can go on all day until one of you gives up and goes home.

This is the classic 'Aunt Emma' strategy. The player with the innings (that is you) wastes the advantage, and both players' time, by aimlessly moving the balls around. It is boring for both players, and it is not helping either of you to progress.

### The Problems with Aunt Emma

What has happened when you have embarked on the Aunt Emma routine is that you have lost sight of two of the objectives of a leave. Yes, it is perfectly effective in retaining control – you have a short shot, and the

---

**AUNT EMMA**

Nobody knows who the original Aunt Emma was, or, indeed, whether there was ever such a person. This technique of unadventurous and destructive play has certainly been around for more than a century, however.

Arthur Lillie referred to Aunt Emma in his book *Croquet up to Date*, published in 1900, under the chapter title 'Cowardly Tactics'. Since then, every writer who has had something to say on the matter has been overwhelmingly negative about the strategy. Indeed, nothing produces a more splenetic response among the game's commentators; their descriptions include phrases such as 'silly', 'excruciatingly dull', and 'selfish, and generally boring'.

So who was the original Aunt Emma? One theory suggests that it refers to Emma Clutton-Brock, the ageing aunt of Walter Jones Whitmore. Her dreadful croquet and addiction to port certainly made her unpopular with the Jones Whitmore clan, although there is little evidence to prove that 'Aunt Emma' was more than a generic Victorian archetype of lacklustre, unenthusiastic players everywhere.

---

opponent has a long one – but, in terms of a profitable position, it is virtually useless. It is hard for Red to score, and Black is always just one hit-in away from stealing everything back from you.

Players are sometimes overcome with the stress of playing Aunt Emma tactics. Once you take the focus away from scoring, you are left with just the anxiety of hoping your opponent will continue to miss. Think about the percentages – even if you manage to score an occasional hoop during your Aunt Emma routine, you are giving your opponent a chance of a long shot as many as twenty or thirty times during the game. You will be very lucky if every one of those misses, no matter what the distance. What is more, the burden is all on you throughout the game. Blue/Black has the opportunity of gaining control if any one of his shots hits, or if any one of yours misses.

Croquet has two types of tactics – those that win games, and those that lose them. It may be boring, and it may be against the spirit of the game, but, in the long run, the real problem with Aunt Emmaing is that it will cause you to lose games, and your croquet experience will be less fulfilling.

## Setting up Your Chance

It is only a small difference between a bad leave and a good one. The formula for Aunt Emma play is simple: split opponents and join up. The same thing applies for more sophisticated play, but the crucial difference is the way in which each of those tasks is achieved.

ABOVE: *Stephen Mulliner in confident form.*

BELOW: *Splitting the opponent – the right way and the wrong way.*

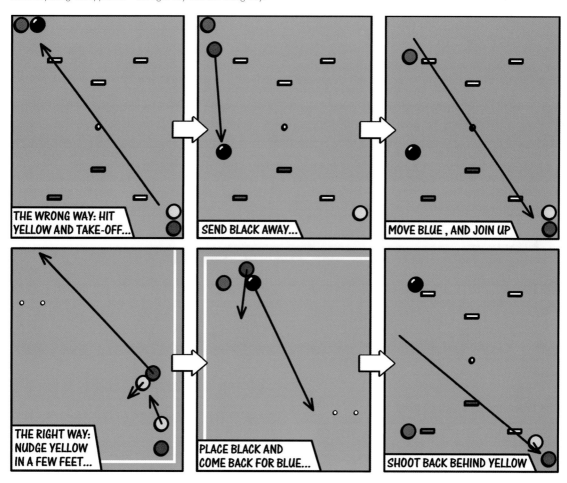

### Splitting the Opponent – The Wrong Way

Blue and Black are together, and you want to arrange the balls in a better position. Red's for Hoop 1, so it would be useful to send one of them towards Hoop 1 and one towards Hoop 2. Then you can join up, and everything will be fine.

You roquet Yellow, and take off to Blue and Black, leaving Yellow on the boundary. You hit Black, and stop-shot it towards Hoop 1. Black goes most of the way there, and Red travels just a couple of yards. Blue is close enough for you to hit, so you turn round and make the roquet. Now you play another stop shot, sending Blue towards Hoop 2. That works fine, so you play your last shot back down towards Yellow.

The opponent plays, and moves Black away from Hoop 1. Red's pioneer has gone, and the scoring chance looks much less promising. Your clever leave has vanished straight away.

### Splitting the Opponent – A Better Solution

Imagine playing that again, but with two small refinements. You roquet Yellow, but this time you cut Yellow a couple of feet in from the boundary. The take-off to Blue and Black nudges it a couple more feet in towards the lawn.

Now, you hit Black. Instead of sending it towards Hoop 1, you decide to send Blue there. Generally, when splitting the opponents, it is easier to place the closer ball and then the further one, in that order. So, you send Black towards Hoop 2; it is a much gentler shot, and you are closer to Blue for the subsequent roquet. You hit Blue and play a big drive/roll shot. Blue goes to Hoop 1, and Red stops somewhere in the middle of the lawn.

Because Yellow is a bit further in, you can play Red off the boundary, and you have a laid rush for the next turn. And, because of the way you have played the shot on Blue, you have a better angle for playing this last stroke of your turn. You shoot Red to a point wide of Yellow, and your turn ends. When Red is placed back on the yardline, you have a rush on Yellow, and a much more powerful position.

## The Squeeze Leave

By taking a bit more care, you have created something more subtle than the Aunt Emma position. This new leave is often referred to as a *squeeze*. Neither Black nor Blue has an easy shot, and you are handed a strong position no matter which of the two plays the next turn.

*James Death takes on a long shot.*

## Example

In this example, Blue is at Red's hoop; Black is at Red's next hoop; Red has a rush on Yellow towards Black.
Blue/Black has the following choice of shots:

1 *Shoot Black at Blue.* Red has an immediate four-ball break if the shot misses.
2 *Shoot Blue at Black.* Red can rush Yellow to Hoop 1, or else bring Black in towards Hoop 2, getting a rush on Blue to Hoop 1.
3 *Shoot Black at Yellow/Red.* A miss from Black will land in range of Red, granting an instant four-ball break.
4 *Shoot Blue at Yellow/Red.* Red can bring Blue into play, improving the rush on Yellow. Red has the break.

Only the second option requires Red to do much work to get going, and Blue may well choose to retreat to a corner, rather than risking a shot. Even then, Red has the option to continue with a three-ball break.

The key elements are the following:

- Black and Blue are left close enough to the respective hoops to leave your opponent in no doubt that he is in a vulnerable position. You have an excellent chance of progress whichever ball is left.
- Red has a useful rush on Yellow. By coming a yard or two in from the boundary, this rush is *guarded*. If the opponent shoots and misses, there is enough space behind Yellow for Red to roquet the ball, stop-shot it into the lawn, and retain the rush on Yellow.
- Assuming all the balls are still for Hoop 1, Red and Yellow have laid up in a *safe corner*. They are away from Blue/Black's hoop, and a hit-in will leave the opponent still with a great deal of work to assemble a break.

## Some Variations on the Squeeze

There are all sorts of variations on the same basic leave, which you can construct depending on which hoop each ball is for.

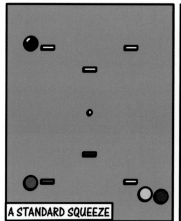

A STANDARD SQUEEZE

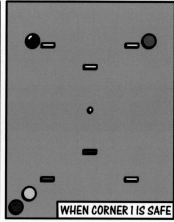

WHEN CORNER 1 IS SAFE

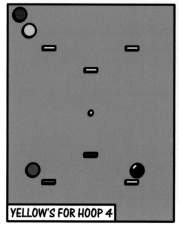

YELLOW'S FOR HOOP 4

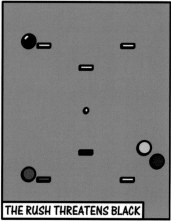

THE RUSH THREATENS BLACK

*The squeeze and its variants.*

**Take Control of the Safe Corners**  If Red still requires Hoop 1, but Blue and Black are for a different hoop, Corner 1 becomes safe, so it is safe to lay up here, with the opponents at Hoops 2 and 3.

**The Double Squeeze**  If Red is still on Hoop 1, but Yellow is for Hoop 4, you might consider this. Blue is at Red's hoop; Black is at Yellow's hoop; Red has a rush on Yellow from Corner 2. Blue decides to stop Red's break attempt, by shooting away from Hoop 1. You have trapped Blue and Black into joining up near Hoop 4, so you may opt to play Yellow instead. Whatever happens, you threaten a four-ball break with either ball.

**The Defensive Squeeze**  When Blue and Black are for different hoops, you have the option to introduce a defensive element. Imagine the standard squeeze, where Red and Blue are for Hoop 1, and Yellow and Black are for Hoop 2. So, you leave Blue at Blue's hoop, and Black at Black's hoop. For the opponent to make any progress, he must move a ball away from its hoop, hit a long shot, and then travel all the way back. Whatever shot he attempts, there will be no ball near his destination.

**Threatening the Fourth Ball**  With Blue at Hoop 1 and Black at Hoop 2, Red has a choice about where to point the rush on Yellow. You can aim the rush towards Blue at Hoop 1 – Blue moves, Red plays the rush, approaches the hoop, and the break is set; or you can aim the rush towards Black at Hoop 2 – Blue moves, Red rushes Yellow to Black, and Black to Hoop 1.

There is a school of thought that you should always leave your rush pointing directly at the less useful of the opponent's balls. Whichever shot he takes, you have a commanding position. With your rush pointing towards Black, it is now reckless for him to shoot Blue towards Black. The likely outcome is that Blue plays defensively into a corner.

Where you point the rush is a matter for personal preference. I prefer my opponent not to corner, thus leaving me with easy access to all four balls. Pointing the rush at Hoop 1 gives me fewer shots that can go wrong. The choice is left to you, depending on your own ambition and confidence.

# After the Miss – Picking up the Break

You have managed to construct an adequate leave. The opponent has taken a shot and missed. You now have two choices: you can improve what you already had – make that poor rush on Yellow into a perfect one, draw the other balls into play, and prepare for a perfect break next turn; or you can attempt the break now. Either way, the balls are probably not perfectly placed yet, so there are a few tricks you might need, in order to get everything exactly as you want it.

*James Le Moignan shoots.*

## The Stop-Shot Approach

Here is an unpromising position. You had a nice leave – Black at Hoop 1 (ready for Red), Blue at Hoop 3, Red with an easy rush on Yellow – but Black has retreated to a corner, and your chance has gone.

There is a neat solution to this. Take the rush to Hoop 1 as planned. Leave Yellow where it lies, and take off to Black in Corner 1. A hard stop shot sends Black safely towards Hoop 2, with Red landing somewhere near the hoop. This speculative shot is the *stop-shot approach*. If you play it right, Red finishes in position, scores the hoop, hits Yellow, and the break is established. If your shot is imperfect, you remain joined up at your hoop, with a good leave. Either way, you have a sound outcome.

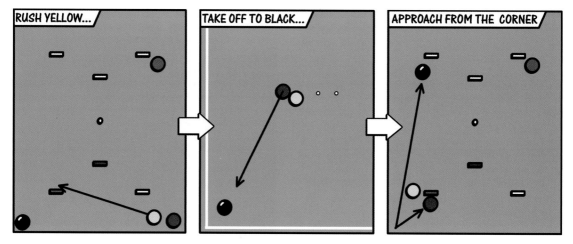

*The stop-shot approach to Hoop 1 from Corner 1.*

## Commitment

As you take the first quavering steps towards your break, the question in the mind of many players is, 'What happens if I fail this hoop?' Caution tells you not to commit Yellow to the middle of the lawn until you are sure of progress with Red. But then, taking Black over towards Hoop 1 leaves Red within the opponent's close firing range if you fail the hoop. The worry for some players goes deeper – I have heard the argument that it is best not to send Black towards the peg until the break is established, because it will land nearer to Blue at Hoop 2.

The upshot, of course, is that the break never becomes established. You either commit fully to playing a break, or you do not. Even so, there are a couple of safety principles you can adopt that will take away some of the risk.

More often than not, your break will start with an approach to the first hoop with your partner ball. If Red is approaching a hoop with Yellow, the situation is obviously safer than with Blue or Black. Even the worst failure leaves you joined up, and at your hoop.

If you have not yet established your momentum, then your confidence is likely to be low. So, if you are bothered by what you give away, you can add some defence to the hoop approach. If you are using Yellow, play more of a drive/roll, to keep your partner ball close by; if you are using Blue or Black, play the approach as a stop shot, to send the enemy ball a couple of yards further from you in the event of a failed hoop.

Breaks seldom start with all four balls in play. A two-ball break often evolves to a three-ball break, and only then do you get the chance of graduating to the perfect four-baller. For caution's sake, your safest option for a two-ball break is to play it with Red and Yellow, while Blue and Black remain split. Sooner or later, you will have the chance of bringing one or other of the opponent colours into play. And a short while after that, you should have all four balls.

There is an interim period in the process where you have three balls mid-lawn, and the fourth still tucked away near the boundary. If you have to engage in a prolonged three-ball break, try to make sure that you are using Blue and Black only, with Yellow safely out of the way. Whatever happens – a bad rush or a failed hoop approach – you have the option of retreating. Your break may have failed, but your fall-back is a leave on the boundary, with two pioneers still in place.

## Avoiding a Crash Landing

Scoring all your hoops is only half the battle. A player who scores well, but immediately concedes the initiative to the opponent, is going to make little progress towards winning consistently. Running hoops is important, but so too is the need to stop the other player from gaining the advantage as soon as his turn starts.

In an ideal world, you would play all your breaks right through to their natural end, leaving the lawn gracefully and handing your opponent no chance of snatching the innings. In real life, however, things go wrong. From time to time, you will overhit a shot, miss a roquet or fail a hoop.

Even when your break does collapse in a heap, do not lose sight of the possibility of salvaging some sort of advantage.

It is not always the end of the world when things go wrong. If you totally misjudge the pace of a croquet stroke, you still have one last continuation shot in which to place Red as best as you can.

*An unscheduled early finish from Tom Anderson.*

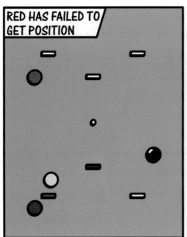
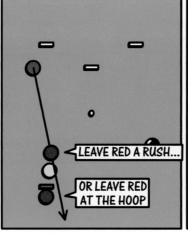
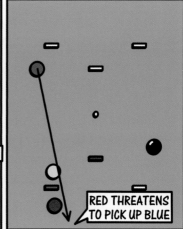

*Options for Red after a hoop approach goes short.*

## A Failed Hoop Approach

Red has just played a roll approach to Hoop 1 with Yellow, but has landed in a position where the hoop is impossible. Blue and Black are split, so staying near the hoop feels safe.

The novice's response is to use Red's last shot to take position a foot in front of the hoop. Next turn, you can tap Red through, hit Yellow, and carry on. Two things can go wrong with this. First, your positional shot comes out wrong, and you are no better off. Second, Yellow is not ideally placed.

A better option is to position Red behind Yellow. You will start your next turn with a rush on Yellow, promising an easy approach, an easy hoop, and an easy forward rush on Yellow.

There is an alternative choice here, which stops Blue taking control. You decide that, whether you take position or leave a rush, Blue is likely to shoot at you. So you take a long position, maybe a yard from the hoop. Now, Blue has a problem. If he shoots at Yellow and misses, the following will happen:

- Red roquets Blue.
- Red stops Blue back to Hoop 2.
- Red roquets Yellow and proceeds with the break.

If Blue turns down the shot on Yellow, Red just hits Yellow, and continues.

This third way is not for everyone. It is only sensible in the following circumstances:

- if you think Blue will shoot at Yellow, and want to stop him;
- if you can threaten to continue when Blue declines the shot; and

- if you can plausibly threaten to turn round and hit Blue after he misses.

## Exposing Your Partner

It is generally a bad idea to end a turn with both your balls in the middle of the lawn. If Blue or Black hits anything, you are presenting him with a very good chance of a short rush to somewhere useful. Often, that will lead to a break.

There are times when you can get away with it, but there are times when a mid-lawn lay-up will be the very last shot you take before losing the game. A defensive option is usually better.

Here is an example. Something terrible has just happened. Maybe you have accidentally roqueted your ankle, and Red has moved just a few inches. Or maybe you have just hit a hoop and ricocheted to somewhere a long way from your target. However you got there, you now have a situation where Red needs to get to Black but is too far away from where you want to be.

You have a few options. The obvious one is to try for a hit-in, on whichever ball you have not already roqueted. Less obviously, you may be able to block Black's shot at Yellow, with a *deep guard*.

You decide that Black will probably shoot at Yellow, but there is a chance that he will miss. So, you put Red on the boundary beyond the Yellow. If Black does miss Yellow, he lets you straight back in. And if Black hits, Red is safely hidden on the boundary. Do not get carried away with this – it will not work if you leave a double target with Red and Yellow, or if Black is guaranteed to hit Yellow anyway.

Very rarely, there is the chance for another interesting option. Instead of defending Yellow from Black, you decide to attack Blue. You place Red in a wide join with the

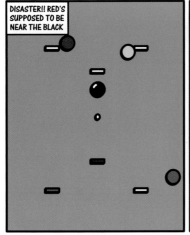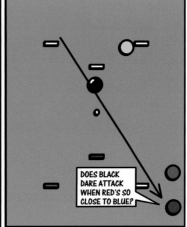

*Protecting Yellow – some creative options to consider.*

opponent on the boundary. Black still wants to take on the shot at Yellow, but now you threaten his partner ball. Does he play Blue at Red, with the danger of handing you a four-ball break? Does he hit Yellow with Black, and then have to sort out the wide join? Does he risk missing Yellow, and conceding the initiative?

Psychologically, it is a response designed to weaken a nervous opponent. If he would rather play Blue anyway, it is a pretty terrible choice of tactic. Only try it if you want to stop Black, and you are ready for a long defensive exchange between the two of you.

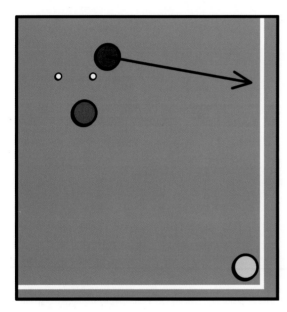

*Constructing a triangle.*

## Triangles

Nothing affects an opponent more effectively than a sense of doubt. If you have presented him with a moderately short shot, it is often no bad thing to present a second shot of the same length. Above is an example, where Red has misapproached Hoop 4 with Blue. Yellow is in the corner, about eight yards from Blue. You play Red to the boundary, so that Yellow-Red, Red-Blue and Blue-Yellow are all approximately the same length. Under normal circumstances, Blue might have fancied the shot at Yellow, but now there is a threat that he will be punished for a miss.

The formation of a triangle on the boundary has many of the positive benefits of a wide join and a deep guard. In this example, Blue can barely afford to shoot at either Red or Yellow. His best response may be to abandon all thoughts about taking back the innings this turn.

### If All Else Fails...

The break is going nicely. You have got all four balls in the middle of the lawn. You have played an approach, and skidded a foot past the hoop. You have just one shot left, but everything is so close that you are in serious trouble. Your only option is to wreck the position, and hope to get yourself safe. It is time for a *scatter shot*. You plan to hit another ball with Red, but, because you have used up your entitlement of roquets, it will not earn you a croquet stroke, and your turn will end immediately.

Tactically, there is nothing much to say about scatters. For most players, it is a case of pointing Red at one of the other balls, hitting hard, and seeing where everything ends up. Hopefully, you will get Red safely out as far as the boundary, and maybe get one of the other balls out of harm's way. There are a number of points to bear in mind:

- A scatter shot is played as if it is a rush on another ball, but it is not a roquet. Legally, there is much more chance of a fault, so be careful.
- If you plan to clear Red and the other ball as far as possible, you probably want to play the shot as hard as you can. That carries the risk of missing everything completely, so temper the urge and do only what feels comfortable. Do not force the shot.
- Hitting the other ball dead centre will send it a long way, but will cause Red to stop where it is. If you want Red out as far as the boundary, play for a wide cut-rush. If you want Red to hold position, play the shot hard and straight.

> **THE LEGALITY OF SCATTER SHOTS**
>
> Scatter shots can end very badly, and it is often a good idea to consult a referee if you are playing a serious game and you are in doubt.
>
> When Red and Yellow are very close, it is possible for Red to hit Yellow and bounce back on the mallet. The laws of croquet turn a blind eye when this happens in a roquet, but this is not the case in a scatter shot.
>
> If Red and Yellow are within a foot or less, there is a chance that a scatter shot might cause Red to ricochet on to the mallet. You should play the shot either with no follow-through, or with a bit of cut. Otherwise, you risk a fault, and the premature end to your turn.

## Making a Graceful Exit

Enough talk about disaster. What you really want is to complete your turn exactly as you planned, and for your opponent to miss, allowing you to win the game immediately after.

Much of the earlier discussion about leaves still applies. The key elements to a good leave are the same:

- Leave Blue and Black with difficult shots.
- Leave Yellow an easy shot.
- Make a break hard for the opponent in case he hits.
- Make the break easy for Yellow if the opponent misses.

Laying a leave at the end of a break is a luxury. You have had time to think about what you want to do, and you have had more chance to manoeuvre the balls into the right positions. The leave you produce now should be more polished and refined than the quickly improvised leave you put together in your previous turn, before the break started. There is one important trick you need to learn to make this easy:

Never score your last hoop with your partner ball.

As long as you remember this, the rest is straightforward. You want to end your turn by rushing Yellow to a safe boundary, and then fine-tuning Red's position. The best way to guarantee the rush is to make the last hoop with one of the other balls, but to have Yellow close by.

The way in which you engineer the last few shots of your break is up to you. To illustrate, here is the same leave played in various ways. Red is for Penult, and you want to set up a standard squeeze – Blue and Black at Hoops 1 and 2, with Yellow and Red down in the fourth corner.

## Yellow as Pivot

Red is approaching Penult with Black. There is just one more hoop to go, so Black has no further part to play in the break. There is a short and easy shot to send it to Hoop 2 immediately.

- Red scores Penult, and sends Black towards Hoop 2.
- Red rushes Yellow, and brings it closer to Rover.
- Red roquets Blue, and scores Rover.
- Red plays a little split shot, sending Blue towards Hoop 1.
- Red rushes Yellow to the far boundary.
- Red rolls both balls together towards their final resting place.
- Red's last shot gives Yellow a perfect dolly rush in towards the lawn.

OPPOSITE: *Red and Yellow are together, as Bruce Fleming hands the play to Chris Clarke.*

## Yellow as Penult Pioneer

This time, Black is the pivot, and Red is approaching Penult with Yellow. Now, it is easier to place Blue and Black after your last hoop.

- Red scores Penult, and stops Yellow down towards Rover.
- Red roquets Black, and brings that down towards Rover.
- Red roquets Blue, and scores the hoop.
- Red plays a stop shot, sending Blue to Hoop 2.
- Red hits Black, and sends it to Hoop 1.
- Red rushes Yellow, and sets up for the rush.

## Yellow as Rover Pioneer

This course of play is not advisable, but you can still salvage a decent leave out of the situation.

- Red scores Penult with Black, and sends it towards Hoop 2.
- Red rushes Blue towards Rover.
- Red stop-shots Blue into its final position at Hoop 1.
- Red roquets Yellow and approaches Rover.

Now, Blue and Black are already placed well, so you need not worry about them. Your best hope is to have the chance of a rush on Yellow into a neutral position. If that has happened, you are fine. If not, it is time for desperate measures. Roquet Yellow, and roll both balls towards a safe boundary. Leave the rush with your last shot.

It is a clumsy end. You might not get Yellow far enough to guard against a shot from the opponent. You might not get the chance of a tight rush. Console yourself in the fact that you have scored as many hoops as you had planned, and hope that your opponent misses.

# The Wisdom of Defence

There was a time in my youth when I would set out to shoot at every long shot that was presented to me. Without regard for wisdom or my own hitting standard, I would occasionally hit a dangerous shot – and win – but I would often miss, too, and have to face the consequences.

Each generation produces players who learn how to shoot straight before they learn when it is not appropriate. Tactics evolve, and many top-flight players now attach much less importance to the skill of guarded boundaries, wide joins and defensive traps.

Even so, the tactics of defence remain a core skill of the game. Not everyone has the superlative hitting ability of a champion. It is a unique element of croquet that a beginner can rely on tactical wits above technical expertise, and defeat the strongest of opponents.

# CHAPTER 9

# HANDICAP PLAY

All this talk about the perfect break is very depressing. Most players will need several years' practice to master the break consistently. Help is at hand, however, in the form of croquet's handicapping system. It is vital to learn how to incorporate the skills of break-building and prudent defence into the rules of handicap play.

*Tournament play at Wrest Park.*

## How Handicaps Work

If you play at club level, you will receive a handicap. Beginners start with a handicap of 24 and more experienced players have a lower one. The higher-handicapped player receives a number of extra turns, or *bisques*, calculated as the difference between the two players' handicaps. So, a 20-handicap playing a 5-handicap would receive fifteen bisques. A tally of these is usually kept by placing white sticks in the ground beside the lawn.

*As a novice, Pete Trimmer played his first season of handicap-level croquet without losing a single game.*

There are a number of important things to note:

- A bisque is an extra *turn*, not just an extra *stroke*. The striker can use a bisque to roquet and croquet each of the other balls, and to score hoops as in a normal turn.
- Bisques can only ever be taken at the end of the striker's turn. For example, I might opt to play my normal turn so that Red lands close to a faraway ball; my turn would normally end, but I can then use a bisque to make the roquet, and gain the subsequent bonus shots.
- Bisques may be taken in succession. For example, a player might play their normal turn, then take a bisque to use the other three balls, then take a second and third bisque to use the other three balls again.
- Sometimes *half-bisques* are used. A half-bisque is one where the other three balls may be hit, but no points may be scored for any ball. The half-bisque is most useful for tidying up an awkward position, or using in conjunction with a whole bisque.

## Using Bisques

It is difficult to reduce the essence of bisque-taking down to a simple formula. There are times in a game when it is a good idea to use bisques, and times when it is not productive. As a general principle, the more bisques you receive, the stronger your opponent is. Clearly, if that is the case, you need to start scoring early in the game, with a plan for a quick win.

Bisques are at their most powerful if used together, one after the other. Try to use your standard turn to get control of the game, a first bisque to set up a break, and a second bisque to start scoring.

### Using a Bisque Mid-Break

Maybe your opponent has made an error, and handed you a perfect set-up. Maybe you have expended a few bisques to get here. Either way, you are on the lawn, and you have got all the balls in their perfect positions – Red and Yellow are together at Hoop 1, Black is in the middle, and Blue is at Hoop 2. The important thing is to keep the break going. Fortunately, you have a row of bisques to help you do that.

Sometimes, use of the mid-break bisque is obvious, and needs little explanation. Here is a key example. You are at Hoop 1, you hit Yellow and approach the hoop with Red. All is well. You then mishit Red, it rattles in the hoop, and sticks where it is without going through. Your turn ends, and all for the sake of a ball which has landed an inch short of where you wanted it. Take a bisque, tap Red through, and carry on with the break.

## THE HANDICAPPING SYSTEM

There is a danger of players in British croquet clubs taking handicap play for granted, but it is not universally adopted. In Australia and New Zealand, handicaps have often been used as a means of sorting players into classes, but without bisques featuring in the game. So, beginners would play each other, but not mix with intermediate or expert players.

This is a great shame. The joy of handicap play is the development of fresh tactics depending on the ability and playing style of a variety of opponents. Notionally, any player should have a 50-50 chance of winning a handicap game, whether it is against a raw beginner or the World Champion.

Perhaps British players are spoilt by the healthy state of the English tournament scene. Players frequently meet within their clubs, in league matches against neighbours, and in tournaments against visitors from other parts of the country.

In bygone days – as recently as the early 1990s – the prize-giving ceremony at the end of a tournament would include announcements from the Tournament Handicapper, listing those improvers whose handicap was deemed (at the handicapper's discretion) to have been reduced. Now, an automatic system operates; players gain or lose points depending on a game's outcome, with a series of five net wins earning a reduction in handicap level.

Originally, the system was conceived to have a fixed range, with beginners starting at 24, and improving to expert level at 0 (scratch). Systems evolve, and the minimum handicap no longer has a limit of zero. There are currently around a hundred 'minus players' in the UK, whose handicap has improved beyond that of the theoretical expert. The World Champion plays off a handicap of –3.

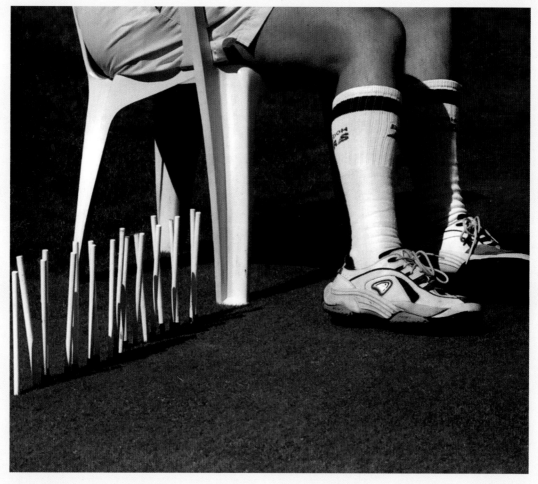

*A row of bisques.*

Continuing with this turn, you score Hoop 1, roquet Yellow, and send it to Hoop 3. Red lands six feet from Black, and you have a ball at each of your next hoops. You play your shot at Black, but you miss. Red finishes six feet on the far side of Black. For the use of one bisque, you can hit Black, and carry on as before. Do it. Everything is set up, and you still have an ideal scoring opportunity.

That can, of course, go wrong. If you have missed one six-footer, you could miss a second, and find yourself in the following unpleasant situation:

- Red misses Black from six feet.
- Red takes a bisque.
- Red misses Black again.
- Red takes another bisque.
- Red misses Black a third time.
- Red has to take a third bisque.

*Windscreen-wiping* – moving back and forth without making the vital roquet – happens to every player as he is learning the game, and it is something you will grow to recognize. You have chosen to take a bisque, and it was the right decision. One, two, or even three vital misses are disheartening, but the decision to carry on with the break was still the correct one. There are times when you will miss successive roquets, but your handicap should have been set at a level to give you plenty of bisques for dealing with this sort of error. Just take a deep breath, concentrate, and make sure of the roquet.

So, you have regained control. You have now roqueted Black (your pivot ball), and you have found yourself at Hoop 2 with Blue. You roquet Blue, approach the hoop, and overhit the shot. You have lost position, and are faced with an unrunnable hoop. Red is three inches away from where

you want it, but you have still got one last stroke before your turn ends, when you need to decide whether or not to use another bisque.

The obvious thing to do is to tap Red three inches back into position. Then you take the bisque, score the hoop, and everything is back to normal. Wait just a moment, though. There is a better option.

Instead of using a bisque just to carry on with what you already have, you can use it to improve the other balls. You have three options as in the diagram centre below:

A Use your last shot to tap Red into position at the hoop, and take the bisque to score.
B Play your last shot to the far side of Blue. Take the bisque, and have a second attempt at a hoop approach.
C Play your last shot to Black or Yellow. You can use the bisque to improve the position of one or both of these, before returning to Blue, scoring, and carrying on with a better break than before.

The first option is generally a bad idea. You need just one shot to continue. That might appeal to the lazy-minded player, as there are fewer things to go wrong. But if that one shot does go wrong, your turn is wasted. Tapping a ball a tiny distance is one of the hardest things to judge in croquet, even for the most experienced player. You are inviting trouble if you think you can rely on one difficult shot, rather than three easy ones.

The second option is much better. You are giving yourself the opportunity of another rush, another approach, and another hoop shot. This should give you a much better chance of success.

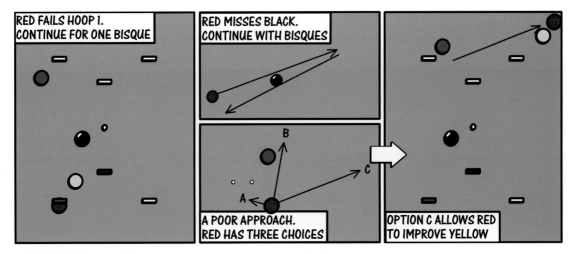

RED FAILS HOOP 1.
CONTINUE FOR ONE BISQUE

RED MISSES BLACK.
CONTINUE WITH BISQUES

A POOR APPROACH.
RED HAS THREE CHOICES

OPTION C ALLOWS RED
TO IMPROVE YELLOW

*Positions where a bisque is useful.*

You should never lose sight of the third option. Maybe your set-up is perfect already, in which case there is no need to worry. However, maybe Yellow is a long way past (see illustration previous page), or a long way short of, Hoop 3. Maybe Black has been left in a position which is not ideal.

Play your last shot just beyond Yellow, giving yourself a useful rush. Take the bisque, and improve the position. Now you have the option of tidying up Black before returning to Blue at Hoop 2. All the balls are tidied up for one bisque, and you can carry on with the break.

This sort of remedial attention could have been a simple matter of tapping Yellow a foot closer to Hoop 3 before taking off back to Blue, or it could have involved some drastic work. Here is a worked example of the sort of thing you could achieve.

Yellow has been sent to Hoop 3, but you have sent it too far to the right, and well beyond the hoop. What is more, Black is a bit out of position as the pivot ball. Now that you have lost position at Hoop 2, use your last shot to shoot Red to the left of Yellow. Red finishes on the yardline behind the Yellow ball, and your regular turn ends (see illustration below).

The key here is that Yellow had been hit so hard that it had stopped close to the edge of the lawn. So, Red starts the bisque turn within easy hitting distance. If you take your bisque, there is a rush on Yellow into the lawn. Play that, and then use your croquet stroke to land Red close to Black. You can improve your position greatly, just by a simple pivot swap. Yellow (wherever it now lies) can be used as the new pivot, and you just need to get Black to Hoop 3. Send Black to Hoop 3 in the way that is most comfortable for you – in this example, that is done with a rush followed by a straight drive. Black goes into position, with Red landing next to Blue; Red hits Blue, and you are back at Hoop 2. You have a fully repaired break for just one bisque.

Errors often come in flurries, where nothing goes right. So do successes. Many players become despondent, focusing on the awkward point of the break where several bisques fell in quick succession. There should be other periods during which you string together a sequence of winning shots, and motor through several hoops with little effort, and all because of a good set-up earlier.

## Using a Bisque to Get Control

It is not often that you will have the luxury of starting your turn with a laid four-ball break. Usually you will have to shuffle the balls into a better position, and often that means using bisques to get going.

Whatever problems your opponent sets you, and no matter how awkward the layout of the balls is at the start of your turn, you should expect to be able to set up a four-ball break using two bisques. Sometimes you will manage to get going for one bisque with little trouble, and sometimes you will trap yourself into some horrendously long and difficult shots before you get moving. There are a few basic techniques that should help to ease you on your way.

Your first problem occurs when you do not have the innings. Your opponent's balls, Blue and Black, are close together, and your balls, Red and Yellow, are split far apart. To gain control, you need to hit something, but that is not easy without using an extra turn.

Sometimes, you will prefer to bide your time and wait for a better opportunity to arise. A cushion of bisques is no substitute for the basic principles of defensive play, especially when your bisque supply is running low. However, there is at least one clear-cut situation, where you certainly should use a bisque right away (see illustration opposite top).

Yellow is already a good pioneer for you at Hoop 1. Blue and Black are together near Corner 2. Red should shoot at Blue and Black. If you hit, you have immediately got a scoring prospect for no loss of bisques. If you miss, you can start a bisque turn with a one-foot roquet. Blue can be sent directly to Hoop 2, Black can be nudged a bit further into play, and Yellow is a ready-made pioneer at Hoop 1. Red needs only take off from Black towards Yellow, and the break is under way. Admittedly, Black will need some tidying up to

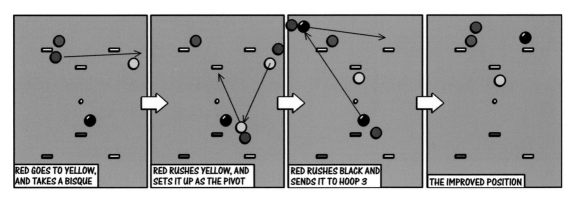

| RED GOES TO YELLOW, AND TAKES A BISQUE | RED RUSHES YELLOW, AND SETS IT UP AS THE PIVOT | RED RUSHES BLACK AND SENDS IT TO HOOP 3 | THE IMPROVED POSITION |

*A failed approach at Hoop 2 lets Red improve all the other balls.*

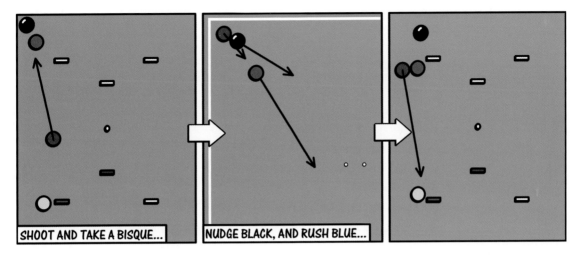

*An easy chance for an immediate break.*

get a standard layout, but this is well on the way to a healthy-looking break, all for the cost of just one bisque.

## Setting up for One Bisque

That is perfectly fine when your opponent hands you a position where the bisque is only used to grab control, turning a laid break for Blue into one for Red. Here is something that needs a bit more thought.

This time, you already have the initiative, but not much else. Red and Yellow are a foot apart, and Blue and Black are over on the other side of the lawn. So how do you get Red to Hoop 1?

### RULE 1: Count to Three

There is no need to panic when you are preparing for

bisque-taking. Often, people rush into a decision, and it proves expensive. When shots go wrong – as they often do – more and more bisques get wasted. Stop, think, and decide what you are going to do before you start.

### RULE 2: Make Sure of Your First Hoop

The first priority is to put Yellow into a perfect position. If there is no ball close to Hoop 1 (as in this example), put Yellow there now. So, here are your first few shots:

- Red roquets Yellow.
- Red croquets Yellow as close as possible towards Hoop 1 (probably with a stop shot or a drive). Concentrate on Yellow, as the placing of Red barely matters.
- Red has one shot remaining, so shoots at Blue in the far corner.
- Red takes a bisque.

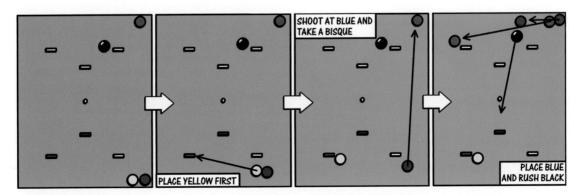

*Setting up for one bisque.*

*The model of a patient player, William Ormerod. His unusual playing style has evolved from playing cricket.*

Yellow is just where you want it. The bisque gives you a fresh turn, so Yellow is available once more for roqueting and croqueting. Your priority now is to send one of the other two balls to Hoop 2, the other towards pivot position, and to get Red back towards Hoop 1. Here is the rest of the sequence:

• Red roquets Blue.

• Red stop-shots Blue towards Hoop 2, with Red finishing near Black.
• Red rushes Black somewhere further towards mid-lawn.
• Red takes croquet from Black, taking off towards Yellow.
• Red roquets Yellow, and the break is fully laid out, and ready to play.

*Tony Le Moignan with the luxury of a ball already at Hoop 1.*

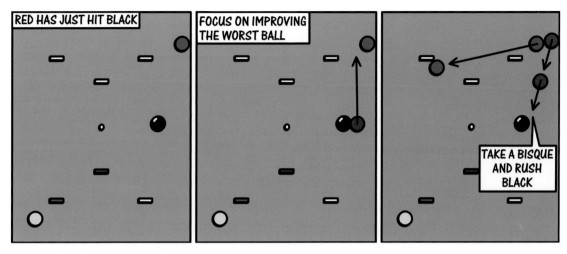

*Getting the other balls into play for one bisque.*

If you are setting up for a single bisque, your first priority must always be to get a ball to your first hoop. Once that is under control, think about how you can get a ball to the second hoop. Once those two elements are in place, you can think about placing the fourth ball as a pivot.

Here is another example, where some of the work has already been done for you. In the last turn, your opponent has let you in. You have managed to hit in on Black at the start of your turn, and find yourself about to take croquet. So what happens next?

Yellow looks OK as a Hoop 1 pioneer, but you are not confident of reaching it with a huge split shot on Black. However you choose to play the croquet stroke, you cannot get an angle to bring Red close enough to either Blue or Yellow. Blue is virtually useless to you anyway, so you will need some work if you want to get a break going. You might be tempted to soldier on without a bisque – leave Blue and Black where they are, take off to Yellow, hope to score Hoop 1, and then sort out all the balls later. In reality, the longer you leave an awkward position, the worse it will become.

## RULE 3: Do not Delay Taking a Bisque in the Hope of a Better Chance Later

It is straightforward to put this right now, and it will cost you only one bisque. You need to do the following:

- Red plays a take-off, to put Black into the lawn, stopping near Blue.
- Red roquets Blue, and sends it to Hoop 2 with a stop shot.
- Red has already hit Black this turn, so may not roquet/croquet it again. Instead, Red plays his last shot to finish close behind the Black.

That is the conclusion of Red's normal turn, so a bisque is taken.

This is much more comfortable. Red rushes Black towards the middle of the lawn, and the break is ready.

## RULE 4: Adapt your Pivot Position

These two examples show you how adaptable the pivot ball is. Your priorities are to put a ball to your first hoop, and a ball to your second hoop. The fourth ball (Black) is, in both cases, the pivot ball. During a break, you will shove it in the middle and mechanically follow the blueprint for a standard break. However, while you are improvising a break pick-up, you should put Black where *you* want it, to simplify your croquet on Blue.

The bad news is that your opponent will not always make things so easy for you. Often, you will have a position so hard that you will need two bisques to set up a four-ball break. Opponents will leave balls widely split, buried in corners, or on distant boundaries far from your hoop.

Such a situation calls for a different mindset. You are committing yourself to take two bisque turns before scoring. Your mission in the first of these turns is *not* to score – your intention is just to get as many of the balls into playable positions as possible. Scoring comes later, but, with your first bisque, you should do the following:

- Aim to get at least two of the other three balls into the inner rectangle.
- Aim to get at least one of Yellow and Blue (the two pioneers) into its final position.
- Get the fourth ball at least a foot off the boundary.

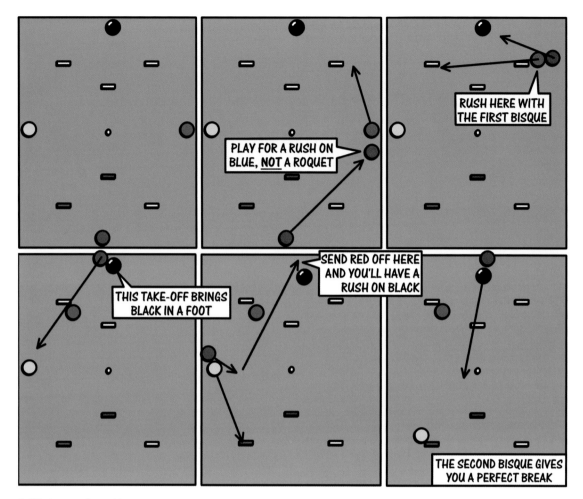

*A difficult set-up for two bisques.*

The third point probably makes little sense at the moment, so here is an example to explain why it is important.

Red and Yellow are for Hoop 1, and you have been handed this unpromising position. You have got a choice of several shots, and none of them appear inspiring. Below is a walk-through of the correct way to set everything up tidily, with just two bisques.

## RULE 5: Start with the Most Difficult Ball

The worst thing to do is to start by playing Red at Yellow, and trying to send it to Hoop 1 immediately. It is likely that you will find yourself four bisques lighter, with no hoop scored. Instead, focus on the Blue ball. It is as far from Hoops 1 and 2 as it can be. Go to the furthest ball first, and any later shot you play is going to be towards the action, rather than heading away from your hoops and the other two balls.

## RULE 6: Do Not be Greedy about Hitting

You have decided that your first shot is going to be Red at Blue, from where you will take your first bisque. There is a good chance that you can send Blue to Hoop 2, leaving Red near Black. That is going to be a tricky split-roll from where Blue lies, but you might want to blot that out of your mind for now. So, you play the long shot, Red at Blue.

Three things can happen in this shot:

1 Red misses Blue on the left;
2 Red hits Blue; or
3 Red misses Blue on the right.

Suppose you are having a good day, and you hit. You have saved yourself your first bisque, and you feel proud of yourself. Really, it is a false economy, as you are now faced with some horrible long shots. You roll Blue to Hoop 2; it goes too far; you land too far from Black; you miss Black, and have to take a bisque anyway. A better strategy would be to *miss deliberately*.

Face it – it is a long shot, and you would probably miss it anyway. Stick to your budget. You can get this break going for two bisques; you do not need the long roquet, so do not attempt it.

Missing on the left is going to make your situation worse. You will take a bisque, and you have a rush pointing even further away from Black and Hoop 2. If you miss on the right, there is an opportunity to rush Blue into a much nicer position.

## RULE 7: Play the Boundary

There is an important thing to bear in mind here. Red is aiming at Blue from an angle. Red is going to be replaced on the yardline opposite the point where it went off, not where it passed Blue. Red can miss Blue by four feet on the right, and still be replaced on its left. Your sole purpose in this shot is to set up a rush for Red – to get that, you should aim to miss Blue by at least five feet on the right.

When you use bisques for break construction, you will use the boundaries a lot. If Red crosses the boundary at the right point, you will start your bisque turn with it on the yardline exactly where you want it. Never play your shot at Blue, just hoping to land correctly; walk over there, take a good look, find the spot you want, come back, aim careful-ly and then, and only then, shoot Red off the boundary.

## RULE 8: Try to Straighten your Croquet Strokes

You should now have the prospect of a rush on Blue, point-ing somewhere towards Hoop 3. You are ready for your first bisque. The most important thing is not to miss Blue – you will land nowhere near another ball, and you will have wasted that extra turn.

Ideally, you want to rush Blue somewhere beyond Hoop 3, and somewhere just a bit in towards the lawn. The fur-ther you can hit it, the better your angle to send it to Hoop 2, landing near Black. Cutting the Blue a little bit inwards will shorten that shot.

Wherever Blue lies, play a croquet stroke to send it to Hoop 2, getting Red to stop within hitting distance of Black. Now hit the Black.

## RULE 9: Nudging a Ball into the Lawn

You still have two balls on boundaries, and nothing at your first hoop. Even if you are an expert, there is no way the Black ball is moving from where it is. But you have got bisques, so you have a trick to play here.

Play a take-off from Black to Yellow. Red lands close to Yellow, but – and this is important – Black moves a few

*Mark Avery coaxes a ball into play with a delicate roll.*

inches off the yardline. Now all Red needs to do is to hit Yellow, and roll it up close to Hoop 1. Red has one more shot before the end of the bisque turn. Red shoots at Black.

Now, at the end of the turn, Yellow and Blue are in place. Red has a short shot at Black. Red is on the yardline, but Black is a foot or two into the lawn. Red can take the sec-ond bisque, rush Black into the middle, and everything is set.

## RULE 10: Use Balls Just off the Yardline

Any ball that has been nudged a foot into play is useful for later bisque-taking. Red can play the boundary again: shoot off the lawn near Black, so that Red is replaced on the yard-line directly behind it. Use a first bisque to nudge a ball in a few inches; end the first bisque turn by joining up with the nudged ball; start the second bisque turn by rushing the ball into play.

## RULE 11: Tidy Up

Finally, you need to tidy up. In theory, you should be ready to go with a perfect break. In practice, there could be a bit of fine-tuning still to do. You still have the opportunity to improve the placing of each of the balls. You do not need to hit Blue and tap it closer to Hoop 2 if you do not want to; instead, you can go straight to Yellow, and start scoring points. But, even now, when you have dug out all the balls and put them into the shape of a break, you still have a few shots in hand to improve things. It is never too late, or too early, in a break to switch balls around, tweak positions, and make the best of your scoring opportunities.

*Outplayers at Cheltenham.*

## Ending the Break

It all seems like hard work – two bisques to move the balls around, even before you have got your own ball through a single hoop. Then, once you have finished your circuit with Red, you have got to do the same again with Yellow.

The good news is that it does not have to be like that. The example here looked at how to deal with your opponent leaving you in a very difficult position. As you near the end of your first break, you can put the balls in a position where it is difficult for Blue and Black to make any progress. There are times when you can use a bisque at the end of your turn, not for scoring, but for arranging the balls in a leave. For details of basic leaves – squeezing the opponent, keeping to the boundaries with a rush, and leaving the opponent exposed – see page 73.

## Half-Bisques

It is possible in croquet to have a handicap which is not a whole number. Rather than having 10 bisques in a game, the weaker player might receive 10½ extra turns.

A *half-bisque* is a turn that allows you to do all the normal things – roqueting and croqueting of the other balls – but does not allow you to score a hoop for any ball. You will only ever receive a single one in a game (so you may not split a whole bisque into two halves), but they are often useful when taken together with a whole bisque, or even used alone.

A half-bisque may be used in a number of ways:

- At the start of a break, when you would normally need two bisques to get going. Use a half-bisque for

---

**THE STOPPING BISQUE**

Croquet's early lawmakers experimented with all sorts of innovations, some of which have not survived. One such was the stopping bisque. Normally, you can use a bisque only at the very end of your turn, when you have run out of shots to play. This experimental rule allowed a player to trade in three normal bisques in return for a stopping bisque, which could be played at any time in the game, irrespective of whose rightful turn it was. A weaker player could wait for his opponent to do all the hard work of setting up a break, then immediately stop play, and take over from the given position.

It was soon realized that it was not actually a very good rule, giving free rein to time-wasting. A strong player could be punished, unless they deliberately played so scrappy a break that their opponent would have no desire to steal it. What is more, there are scenarios in which the playing of a stopping bisque could lead to immediate forfeiture of the game. The rule was soon abandoned.

*A busy day at Guildford. Three games are being played simultaneously on one lawn – Blue and Black are playing Red and Yellow; Green and Brown are playing Pink and White; and a striped set play a third game.*

setting up, followed by a whole bisque once you have got the break into a healthy state.

- At the end of the break, when you have no more hoops to score. Use the half-bisque to set up a leave for your opponent.
- In the middle of the break, when you have had a disaster that cannot be fixed easily.

An example of a mid-break disaster is the windscreen-wiper shot – Red misses Black from a short distance, and skates past to a distant boundary. Take a first bisque to hit Red gently enough to stop very close to Black. Then take a second bisque to hit the Black and carry on the turn.

Another, even more painful example occurs close to hoops. You are six inches in front of your hoop, you play the hoop shot, and miss. Red lands very close to the upright, in a spot where you cannot run the hoop, and cannot hit any other balls. Here, you have no choice but to give up, or to take two bisques – one to move Red two inches back in front of the hoop, and a second one to score.

In each of these examples, a half-bisque could easily have been used in place of the first bisque.

## Non-Break Bisques

Some players shy away from taking bisques early in a game, and will save them up for emergencies, in case they are needed later. They will wait until their opponent has an advantage, and then use a bisque just to destroy that position.

There is not much to be said in favour of this strategy. A strong opponent is not going to be held back for very long. They should be more accomplished at playing shots than you, and probably more experienced tactically. Defensive tactics have a place in croquet, but you should use bisques only for disrupting your opponent as a last resort, after all else has failed.

## Not Having Bisques

The novice's nightmare is the point at which the bisques come to an end, especially against a strong opponent. It is remarkable how many players claim they play better once all their bisques have been used. Psychologically, it may focus the mind, once you have accepted that your bisque safety net has been removed. But players really should not

*Wrest Park's six magnificent lawns in Bedfordshire.*

hold the loss of their bisques as something to look forward to.

The function of bisques is to build up an unassailable lead. Maybe that will get you past the finishing line. Maybe the supply will run out when you still have a few hoops to score. That is the time to switch to a defensive frame of mind – keep the innings, and put all your effort into finishing those last few hoops.

## The Last Bisque

There are players who burn their way through all but one of their allocation, and then cling desperately to the last bisque. Their plan is to save this final bisque for an emergency. It is not a great tactic.

The 'emergency' in question is a position where the opponent has crept round, has caught up, and is on the point of winning. Now you take your bisque to split him, and put together a leave in the hope of retaining the innings.

In essence, it is the use of a bisque in order to Aunt Emma the opponent. There are many reasons why it is a poor idea:

- Last-minute leaves like this are often scrappy. It would have been more profitable to use the bisque earlier

for a constructive leave, rather than now, for a destructive leave.
- You can use a last bisque only once, and you are very vulnerable immediately after.

---

### FULL BISQUE PLAY

A growing trend in UK croquet clubs is for full bisque play, in which both players receive a number of bisques. This allows each participant to set up and play breaks, making games quicker and more enjoyable.

The number of bisques awarded is related to a fixed base, often set to a value of 5, and players receive their own handicap, less that value. So a game between a 20 and a 10 would result in the receipt of 15 and 5 bisques for the two players. Where one player has a handicap less than the base, the calculation reverts to the standard method – so a 20-handicap playing a 2-handicap would be allocated 18 bisques as normal.

Full bisque has earned a loyal following in clubs, but has yet to become universal in external tournaments. There is a great deal of merit to the format, particularly in a game between two beginners with similar handicaps, as it allows the players the chance to experiment both with attacking and defensive tactics, while giving the satisfaction of extensive break play.

- Most of the time, it is not possible to spot when the emergency arises. The player who waits for the best time to spoil the opponent often misses the moment, and loses with the last bisque still in hand.
- Once your opponent realizes you have no intention of playing your last bisque, he no longer needs to play defensively, and can do what he likes without being punished.

Have courage. If you are playing with ten bisques, aim to use all ten. Using nine and then stockpiling the last one is a false economy.

## Giving Bisques

Of course, you have it easy. Your experienced opponent has no cushion of extra turns to make up for his mistakes, and he must rely on tactical experience to cause you to lose control of your bisques.

The objective of the bisque-receiver is to open up the play, in order to maximize the immediate scoring opportunity. The job of the bisque-giver is to shut down the action. Outplayer tactics become paramount, and you should expect to spend much of the first half of the game playing wide joins and cornering.

Sometimes, a free shot will give you the chance of an early break, but you need to be prepared to sit and wait for the inevitable mistakes from your weaker opponent. Sit back, relax and enjoy the sunshine. The time will come when you can snatch a narrow victory from your opponent's head start.

## In Praise of Handicap Play

Handicap croquet is the form of the game in which tactics are at their most varied. In a tournament, it is possible for a raw beginner or an experienced middle-ranker to compete against a world-class player. Tactics must be adjusted for each game, as the imperfections and idiosyncrasies of different opponents force you to improvise new ways of thinking. Depending on whether you receive 20 bisques, 5½ bisques or just a single one, your strategy must be different.

Whether it is because your opponent is a naturally good shot, or because he has access to a stack of bisques, you are often left with no hiding place. For this reason, you need to learn how to deal with cutting down his options for hitting, and to protect yourself from enemy onslaught.

*David Maugham is unusual among top players, as a regular winner of handicap events, even with a handicap of −2½.*

# CHAPTER 10

# WIRING

Nothing prevents an opponent's shot more convincingly than a cast-iron hoop directly in his path. Blocking one ball from another with the wire of a hoop, or with the peg, is called *wiring*. By wiring balls from each other, you can restrict your opponent's options, and force him to take on longer, or more dangerous, shots.

*A problematic Red for Chris Clarke.*

# The Crosswire at Hoop 1

Setting up a wiring takes a few delicate and precise shots, but is often worth the effort. In the classic example of wiring, two balls are *crosswired* at Hoop 1 – that is to say, they are left close to each other, but wired across the hoop.

Red has just taken a break all the way to peg, and Yellow is still for Hoop 1. This is the leave you have laid for your opponent. Blue and Black are just a few feet apart, but separated from each other by the first hoop. Red and Yellow join up in the opposite corner. Whichever of Blue or Black plays, the only available shot is thirty yards. If that shot misses, Yellow can bring all four balls into play immediately, with a ball still a foot away from Yellow's hoop.

## The Set-Up

Setting up a wiring needs some care – if you get it wrong, you risk giving your opponent a three-foot shot. There are only certain positions where you should safely attempt it, and you will need to do some forward planning.

Here is the plan: put the balls roughly in position before the last hoop of your turn, score the hoop, and then fine-tune the layout. With this leave more than any other, you need to make sure that your last roquet of the turn is a rush on Yellow; if there is no prospect of guaranteeing a tight lay-up in the far corner, then you are wasting your time, and you should do something else.

For many players, this is the most intricate thing you will attempt on a croquet lawn, so the description is very detailed. To start off, you need Yellow as a (good) Penult pioneer, Black a bit west of the peg, and Blue (the Rover pioneer) slightly away from Rover, towards Hoop 1.

- Come through Penult and hit Yellow.
- Send Yellow towards Hoop 1, stopping short of Black. Yellow should land a couple of yards from Hoop 1, on the line between Hoop 1 and Hoop 6.
- Rush Black close to Rover. Because Blue is wide of the hoop, you can stop Black towards Hoop 1, getting a good rush on Blue back towards Rover.
- The position you now have is this: Black is by Hoop 1 very close to its final resting place, Yellow is six feet north-east of Hoop 1, and Red is about to approach Rover with Blue.
- Approach Rover carefully, as you need a rush on Blue towards Hoop 1.
- Run the hoop, and rush Blue towards Hoop 1. You have two options: you can either rush Blue to the *opposite* side of the hoop from Black (if Black is north-west of the hoop, rush Blue south-east), or you can rush Blue to the *same* side of the hoop as Black. If you are doing this, you *must* land further from the hoop than Black, by maybe a couple of feet.

If Blue is opposite Black, you need a little take-off from Blue to Black. This is your last shot on Blue, so you need to leave it in its final resting place. At the end of this stroke, you want to have Blue, the hoop, Black and Red (or Blue, the hoop, Red and Black) in a straight line:

- Tap Black to correct its position.
- Take off short of Yellow, correcting Black a bit more if necessary.
- Rush Yellow, and lay up.

If Blue is on the same side as Black, you need to croquet Blue beyond the hoop:

*The standard crosswire at Hoop 1.*

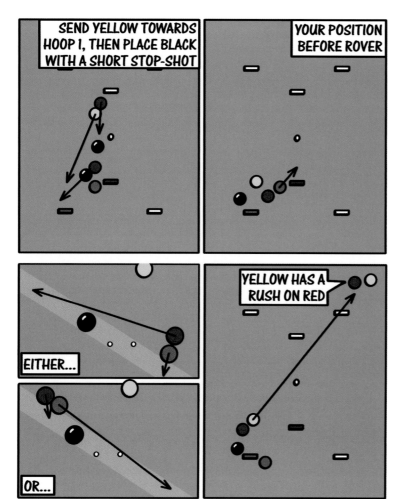

*Setting up the crosswire.*

- Line up your croquet stroke, so Blue just misses the hoop.
- Play a straight stop shot, sending Blue to the far side.
- You now have the same layout. Blue and the hoop are on a straight line with Red and Black. Tap, tap, rush, and you have got your crosswire.

## Aborting the Set-Up

Sometimes you do not know until too late that things have gone wrong. Black rolls on a little too far, or does not roll far enough. Even so, a quarter of a ball visible from three feet is often missed, and you can sometimes get away with leaving a tiny sliver of a target. If you do find that you are a foot off line, and still have not placed Black, it is time to abandon hope. All is not lost – a simple stop shot places Black at Hoop 2, and Red can easily hold for the rush on Yellow. It is not what you planned, but you should not be

disappointed to walk away from your break having laid a perfect squeeze leave.

## The Crosswire in Handicap Play

The Hoop I crosswire is ideal in handicap play when you are playing a strong opponent, and you have plenty of bisques. Because it guarantees you an easy start with Yellow, it is worth using a bisque or two to set it up. Even better, it is the prime example of what to do with a half-bisque.

Because you have bisques available, you do not need such a precise set-up before Rover. What is more, you do not really need the forward rush on Blue after the hoop. Consider the following course of action:

- Approach Rover with Blue and run the hoop.
- Hit Blue, and roll Blue close to Hoop 1, going to Yellow.

*Robert Fulford putting the balls into position.*

- Take off from Yellow to Black, and tidy Black up.
- Finish your turn, placing Red near Blue.
- Now take a half- (or a full) bisque.
- Rush Blue into perfect position.
- Take off to Black.
- Improve Black.
- Rush Yellow, and lay up.

All you are doing is finishing your natural turn with the four balls anywhere in the neighbourhood of Hoop 1. You then take a bisque, and have lots of little shots to tap everything into a precise position. Because your natural turn has finished with all four balls very close together, it is much easier to tidy up in the bisque turn.

Do not be fooled by the charms of the crosswire in every handicap game you play. It is certainly not recommended if your opponent is receiving bisques. It may save you from an immediate hit-in, but it almost guarantees a perfect break for the expenditure of a single bisque.

### CROSSWIRING AND AN UNFORCED ERROR

Players sometimes make so dreadful an error that it becomes the stuff of legend. Two friends of mine, whose embarrassment I will spare by not naming them, were playing in a handicap tournament. Red was using his bisques to play a very well-controlled turn. As it drew to a conclusion, he decided he was playing well enough to lay a crosswire at Hoop 1. He set up the balls perfectly using half a bisque. He decided that one of the balls was an inch off line, so took another full bisque to improve the placement further. He left the lawn beaming proudly at his impressive achievement.

What Red had failed to recognize was that the crowd gathering around the lawn were not fascinated by his technical prowess. Instead, they were marvelling at the fact that he had inadvertently left Yellow and Blue crosswired at Hoop 1, and had given Black a rush on Red.

He lost the game.

## Wiring Angles

Where you place Blue and Black in relation to the hoop makes all the difference between an easy wiring and a hard one, and between one that is tactically sound and one that is not.

Wherever you are, a ball that is level with a hoop is much harder to wire than one that is at an angle. Let us look at each of these cases.

There are four examples shown below:

1 The first example is the least promising for a successful wiring – there is a high chance that a small amount of Black is left visible.
2 The second is not recommended when Red and Yellow lay up at Hoop 3. Blue is likely to be given no shot at all, which could get you in trouble with a referee. (For more on the legal position of that, see page 103.)
3 The third example could leave you looking silly if this is Blue's hoop. A short straight hoop shot, and you have just sacrificed the innings.
4 The fourth example balances all these concerns. Blue and Black are at enough of an angle to make the crosswiring viable to construct, and are square on to the target of Red and Yellow.

You will develop more of a 'wiring instinct' with experience. Some positions make it very hard for you to wire a ball, while others make it very easy. Look at Black in each of these positions, and consider where you could place Blue so it has no shot. Depending on where Black lies, this *wiring area* could vary hugely. If it is level with a hoop, the area is only a foot wide; at a wider angle, as much as three-quarters of the lawn might be hidden from Black.

## Other Wiring Leaves

Most wired leaves are variants on the same theme. Blue might have an open (but very long) shot on Black, but is hidden from Red and Yellow. Blue and Black might be wired by a hoop that is just a foot away, or they might be stuck behind hoops that are at opposite ends of the lawn.

The *wired squeeze* is a low-risk option. This should now be a familiar set-up – Red has gone to the peg, Yellow is for Hoop 1, and Blue and Black are left at Hoops 1 and 2. The refinement here is that Black and Blue are wired from each other by Hoop 2. Black is almost forced to play, and the only shot available is at Red and Yellow.

The *hampered squeeze* presents the same scenario, but in a more sadistic manner. Blue and Black appear to have a straightforward shot at each other, but they have been left so close to the hoop that your opponent cannot possibly get a large enough backswing to hit them the full distance.

In this third example, Black and Blue are wide open – for now. This is a very subtle trap. If Black takes on the shot at Blue and misses, he will land directly behind Hoop 2. Red and Yellow can do what they please on the next turn, in the knowledge that Black has just wired himself by mistake.

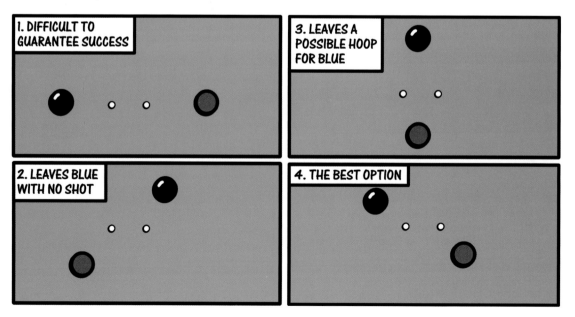

*Aligning the balls is important.*

*There is more room to hide from Black at an angle.*

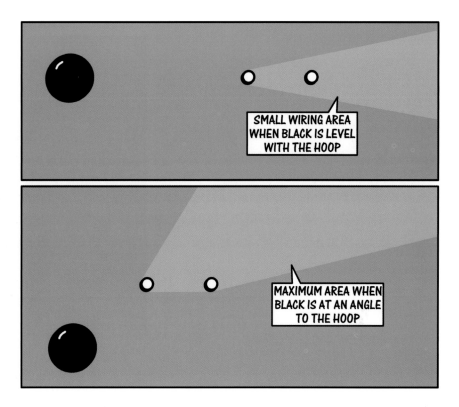

Another leave, and one which is unfairly out of vogue, is the double wiring across Hoops 3 and 6. Red has again played an all-round break, and Yellow is for any one of Hoops 2, 3 or 4-back. Blue is placed northeast of 4-back, and Black is southwest of Penult. There is a huge area available in which to find a wired position; if Blue and Black are not hidden by one hoop, they will almost certainly be hidden by the other.

The set-up for this one should be relatively straightforward. You need to have Blue at 4-back, Black at Penult, and Yellow close by, somewhere between the two. Come through 4-back gently, hit Blue, and just leave it behind. If you find the right spot, there is nothing more to fear – just send Yellow to Rover, and everything will fall into place.

## The Improvised Wiring

Many wiring positions need a great deal of pre-planning but, often, a wired position just appears out of nowhere. Blue might bounce off a hoop into a position where it cannot see Black. Red might mishit a rush on Yellow, only to

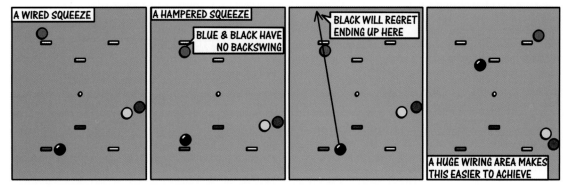

*Using wiring in a leave.*

### HITTING THE 'TEALADY'

The seven extra bonus shots gained from running a hoop are almost essential for anyone wanting to achieve a crosswired leave. One example of a virtuoso display of wiring is now part of croquet folklore.

Joe Hogan, then the reigning World Champion, was partnering Bob Jackson in the New Zealand Open Doubles Championship in 1990, at the United Club in Christchurch. With an odd number of pairs, they decided to play an exhibition game against two lady members of the club, who had been enlisted to provide afternoon tea for players and spectators. Jackson persuaded Hogan to set up a wired leave, giving the opponents the long shot from Hoop 5 towards Corner 3.

Hogan dutifully obliged, but was surprised when their inexperienced opponent shot Blue at Red and hit. She moved the balls around to little avail; Hogan immediately regained control and – with just seven shots – put the balls back into exactly the same position.

This time, the other member of the opposing pair took the shot, and she too hit, to tumultuous cheering from the spectators in the clubhouse. Jackson and Hogan made no further attempt at wiring for the rest of the game.

The two anonymous opponents have entered croquet folklore, and the long shot forced by a tightly crosswired leave now goes by the nickname of the 'Tealady Shot'.

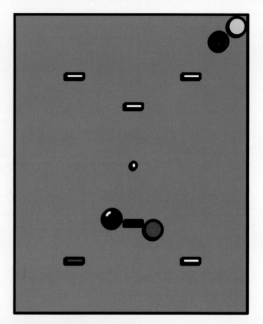

The 'Tealady' leave.

find it is landed in a position that is inaccessible to the opponent. Always get in the habit of checking the position of the balls at the start of your turn, as a lucky wiring will often sway your choice of shot. As a basic principle, the moment when your opponent wires himself is the moment when control of the game passes from him back to you. Now is the time for you to join up with your partner ball.

Very occasionally, you may be rewarded with a rare treat. Blue and Black accidentally wire themselves, allowing you to do whatever you like with no penalty. Nothing is more satisfying than to roll Red and Yellow right into the middle of the lawn, and to leave a rush, knowing that the opponent can do nothing about it.

Be alert. Get in the habit of having a brief look at the start of your turn to see what is in plain sight and what is not. Psychologically, it is always easier to take on that risky shot at a hoop when you know your opponent will not be able to fire at you even when you miss.

### The Pros and Cons of Wiring

Wiring is a very strong tactic, in that it restricts an opponent into a single choice of shot. And if your opponent is not shooting straight, it is often the route to a quick win. But do not get carried away – only force your opponent into a particular course of action if you are happy that that is the shot you want him to play.

If you stop Black from shooting at Blue, he is almost bound to shoot at you. And if you wire him from Red and Yellow, you can bet that he will join up. The choice of shot becomes obvious, and you have robbed your opponent of the need for any further decision-making. Is that a good thing? Well, it depends on the circumstances.

How threatened do you feel by your opponent's ability to hit straight? Is Black likely to win next turn if you leave him a shot at Blue? Maybe he will feel obliged to play safely into a corner – is that what you want? In the psychological battleground of a croquet lawn, it can be worth giving too many shots to choose from rather than too few, and then enjoy watching the opponent dither about what to do.

## The Wiring Lift

### Rule Change

In the early days of croquet, there was no restriction on wiring. A player could play a break to score all twelve hoops, then construct the crosswired leave at Hoop 1, with Red and Yellow tucked tight behind Hoop 3. Neither Blue nor Black has a shot at each other, or at either of the other two balls. Deprived of any shot, an opponent is unable to offer any resistance, so one player retains control throughout the whole, one-sided game.

*Blue is stuck on the wire of Hoop 1. The middle of the lawn is free from attack.*

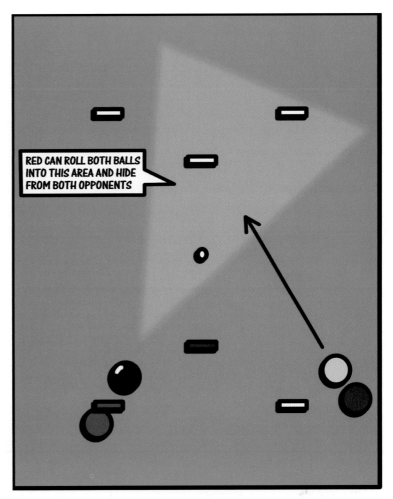

A new rule was added to the lawbook to prevent this situation. It is a complex bit of wording but, put briefly, a player may not leave an opponent ball wired from all three of the other balls.

The penalty for giving an opponent no hittable shot is to concede a *lift* – he is entitled to start his next turn by picking up the wired ball and playing it from anywhere on either *baulk line* (the two start lines are the *A-baulk*, running from the first corner to the middle of the south boundary, and the *B-baulk*, running from the third corner to the middle of the north boundary). That normally gives a much shorter shot. In the case of the crosswire at Hoop 1, it would reduce his hitting distance from thirty yards to a couple of feet. Bear this carefully in mind – each of the opponent's balls has to be given at least one fully visible shot, or you face a potentially disastrous outcome. If you cannot avoid wiring an opponent, there is only one thing you can do: keep away from the baulk lines, and adopt a defensive position.

## THE INTRODUCTION OF THE WIRING LIFT

Association Croquet was quick to see the unfairness of a game in which wiring was allowed without restriction. In 1906, a rule was introduced to get round the problem – the striker could move a ball near a hoop by one foot in any direction. That rule proved unworkable, and the following year, the option of lifting a ball to A-baulk was introduced. Three years later, B-baulk was invented, to allow players to lift a ball to either end of the lawn.

Croquet under American rules was much slower to notice the unfairness of the system. In 1981, an English team of Nigel Aspinall, John Solomon, Bernard Neal and William Ormerod visited the USA. They realized that the USCA Rulebook had no provision for wiring lifts, and spent much of their time jamming the American team's balls into hoops. The heavy defeat inflicted on their hosts precipitated a swift change in the American rules.

*Jonathan Kirby is unable to get an adequate swing.*

## A Wired Ball – The Technical Definition

The latest edition of the *Laws of Association Croquet* provides a full definition of the law on wiring. In summary, you are entitled to a wiring lift with Red, if the following applies:

- it is the start of your turn;
- your opponent placed Red where it is; and
- either Red is stuck in a hoop, or Red has no clear shot at any other ball.

In that case, Red may start the turn from any spot on either baulk line.

Legally, if Red can see 99 per cent of Yellow, it is still wired. The striker has to be able to hit Red cleanly towards either side of Yellow. Put another way, there must be a path three and five-eighths of an inch wide on either side of the Yellow, unimpeded by either a hoop or the peg.

There are two things to note:

1 wirings are not symmetrical – just because Red cannot hit Yellow does not mean that Yellow cannot hit Red;
2 the striker needs to be able to hit the ball as hard or as gently as he likes. If the mallet makes any contact with a nearby hoop on the backswing, the ball is also technically wired. However, the same allowance does not cover the striker's follow-through. If the mallet hits

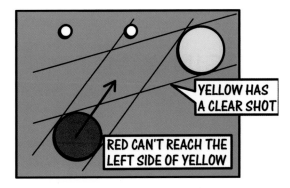

*Red cannot see all of Yellow, but Yellow can see all of Red.*

a hoop immediately after hitting Red, there is no recourse (even though that might result in damage to the mallet, the hoop, and the player's wrists).

Wiring is one of croquet's more refined subtleties. Currently, more and more players have developed an attacking style. Once upon a time, a player would set a defensive trap, in the knowledge that the opponent would decline the dangerous shot. Nowadays, defence is treated with much more disdain. Whether you are playing handicap or on level terms, the use of wiring is the soundest means of repelling enemy fire.

## CHAPTER 11

# PEGGING OUT

You have scored all twelve hoops with each of your balls, and your sole remaining task is to hit each of them against the centre peg. There is always a relief of tension when you reach this stage, in the knowledge that the game is all but won, and you have just one final shot to play. Peg-outs can still go wrong, though. You can still lose, and there are a few points that you need to learn before you can be sure of success.

*Sam Tudor lines up a peg-out.*

# Lining Up the Peg-Out

Almost always, you should try to engineer pegging out a ball with a croquet stroke. As ever, you are playing Red, and you are trying to peg out Yellow with this shot. Yellow will hit on the croquet stroke, and Red will either follow on in the same shot, or you can peg it out with your last continuation shot. Your croquet stroke must have Red and Yellow pointing in a direct line towards the peg.

The peg is a narrow target (1½in, or less than 4cm) and a fractional difference in the lining up of the balls could result in a miss, so you should take as long as you need in preparing for this shot. There are two methods for lining it up.

## The Crescent Method

Whenever you need to judge direction accurately, take a step back and have a good look at the line. You will get a better angle of view if you are lower down, and most players will opt to lie, crouch or kneel on the ground to aid this. With the crescent method, position yourself behind Red and Yellow, and look along the tops of the two balls. Yellow will be mostly obscured, and the only part of the ball showing will be a thin crescent. The peak of this should be in line with the centre of the peg. There are two quick checks you can do to make sure:

- tilt your head very slightly to the left, and the peak of the crescent should now be to the right of the peg; tilting yourself to the right should move the crescent to the left;
- if you are still in doubt, go to the other side of the peg, and look at the line from beyond the target. You will not see much of Red and Yellow, but there should be a symmetrical sliver of each ball on either side of the peg.

## The Edges Method

Instead of looking at the middle of the balls, some players get more accuracy looking along the edges. For this, you have no option but to get down on your hands and knees. Line up the left edges of Red and Yellow; they should be to the left-hand side of the peg. The right edges of the two balls should point to the right of the peg.

# Playing the Shot

It needs only the slightest of pressure on Red to change the alignment of the two balls. So, line them up, check them, adjust and check again. Once you are convinced that the two balls are pointing dead straight at the centre of the peg, you need to play the shot. Here are your three Golden Rules:

1. Do not play a split shot. You must play this stroke absolutely straight at the peg. The further away you are, the more likelihood there is of Yellow curling off its path.
2. Avoid playing a roll shot; there is much more accuracy in a drive or a stop shot. There may be times when a roll is the only way to get Red within distance of the peg, and that is fine, but you should be warned that it will reduce your success rate for Yellow.
3. Do not play the shot gently. Even the best lawn has imperfections and a gentle shot is more likely to find a bump and change direction. If your lining up is good, you do not care where Yellow finishes, so play the shot firmly.

Typically, this shot should be a strong, straight drive.

*The crescent method – check the alignment from both sides of the peg.*

*The edges method – in the first example, Yellow will miss on the right. Align the balls, and repeat the check, looking along the other edge.*

# Preparing for the Peg-Out

You have got a Yellow clip on the peg, and you have just come through Penult with Red.

Ideally, you will have Blue as a pioneer at Rover, so now is your ideal chance to leave Yellow close to the peg, ready for an easy finish. After Rover, you have got seven shots if you need them:

• hit Blue;
• take off to Black;
• rush Black towards Yellow;
• take off to Yellow;
• rush Yellow closer to the peg;
• peg Yellow out;
• peg Red out.

Hopefully, that presents few problems.

## Problematic Set-Ups

Often, you have not had time to organize yourself to that extent. If you have got to approach Rover with Yellow, do not put it right behind the hoop, where you risk blocking your own path to the peg. The rush you need is backwards, so the best place for Yellow is a couple of inches to one side of the hoop, and not far beyond. Unless you have hurtled through the hoop by seven yards, you should have a hittable rush towards the peg.

A harder scenario is where you have limped through the last few hoops with Blue and Black, and have not yet got Yellow into play. In this case, it is time to get creative with a pivot ball.

Score Penult with Black. Blue is down near Rover, so Black no longer serves much use in the break. Send it as close as you can to Yellow. After Rover, revisit the Black, and you have at least a fighting chance of getting your final, important rush on Yellow.

## Dragging the Game Out

Sometimes you will need to call on your discretion. You have tried to get Yellow closer to the peg, and everything has gone wrong. There are examples of players who have achieved a peg-out from 40 yards away near one of the corners. Do not even think about it – it is a ridiculous idea. You will miss, and spend the next twenty minutes waiting for the opportunity to get another shot.

At this point, many players abandon all pretence at sophistication:

• Shove Blue somewhere down near the first corner.
• Put Black somewhere near the second corner.
• Roll Red and Yellow together as close to the peg as possible.
• Yellow misses, so you peg Red out.

Blue and Black have a long shot, and Yellow lays up in the middle of the lawn. The opponent has one last shot. If that misses, Yellow hits the peg and you have won.

That is the theory, and it usually works. By this stage in the game, your opponent is resigned to defeat, and all pressure is off. He will often relax into his last shot, and then hit. You will probably win from here anyway, but you could have a long struggle before you finally get a chance.

A tidier option is to make sure your opponent has the longest possible shot, but to leave both your balls in play. Keep together near a boundary, and try to give yourself a rush pointing towards the peg. A miss from the opponent now gives you your best chance of winning.

*James Death checks a long peg-out.*

## A GRIEVOUS ERROR

It is a good idea to rush Yellow close to the peg, so that Red is pegging it out from a short distance. Even so, it is possible to play the rush with too much enthusiasm, to disastrous effect.

I remember the first time I made this common mistake: Red ran Rover perfectly; I turned round and rushed Yellow back, only to see it roll on and smack full into the peg. I was already walking up the lawn, Red ball in hand, ready to take contact from the Yellow. Then I realized that Yellow was no longer part of the game. My turn had finished, and I had to replace Red back on the ground, next to the Blue.

The accidental premature peg-out of a ball – or *grievous* peg-out – is the one error that is completely irreversible, but almost always avoidable. We have all done it once, but try not to make a habit of it. For the sake of caution, aim your rush a foot to the side of the peg, and a foot short.

### Fighting the Losing Battle

The best games to win are the ones in which you have to claw your way back, catching up against an opponent who reached the peg ages before you. You could have had both

balls still for Hoop 1, and not hit your first roquet of the game until the opponent is just one point from victory. You scrape together two long breaks, and win.

When the opponent is one step away from victory, and it is your last shot, your tactics are simple: you ask yourself the question, 'Will my opponent definitely finish next turn?' If the answer is 'Yes', you should take your shortest shot. If the answer is 'No', you should consider joining up with your partner. If your balls are split, your opponent can play gently to the peg; if you are together, he will be reluctant to lay up mid-lawn. If you do survive for another turn, you have a nail-biting time ahead of you. But the game is not lost. Keep the opponent's single ball away from the peg – keep him towards the corners, wire him from the peg, and give him dangerous single targets at your balls. If you are for Hoop 4, put his ball near Corner 2, and lay up at your hoop with a guarded boundary. His missed peg shot becomes your break opportunity.

## The Three-Ball Game

Croquet often sees an unexpected reversal of fortunes. One player can race ahead, building up a huge lead, but the game is won only once both balls have struck the peg.

*The pegged-out game often presents unexpected puzzles for both players.*

## RIGGALLING

Jargon abounds for the pegging out of balls. A ball that has been pegged out is off the lawn, or off the ground. Whereas a ball whose clip is on Hoop 1 is for Hoop 1, the clip of a ball removed from the game is put back in its box, so a player may be for peg and box.

The action of pegging out an opponent ball is sometimes called *Riggalling*, after the late South African, Leslie Riggall. Originally, the term 'Riggall' applied to the tactic of pegging out one's own ball singly, before the partner had run all its hoops. Leslie had written an article on the subject, the gist of which was that it is a stupid idea. The term has been widened, and is now used for the process of pegging out any single ball ahead of the other three.

One way of tipping the scales in your favour is pegging out the opponent. Once Black has scored all twelve hoops, he becomes vulnerable to being pegged out. Red could be a long way behind, but a good break can allow you to eliminate Black from the game, reducing your opponent's winning chances considerably. Blue no longer has a partner ball. Red and Yellow have permanent control of the innings, and Blue must hit something in order to gain control. The game becomes a chase between the Hunter and the Hunted.

### The Hunter – Playing the Single Ball

Yellow has been pegged out by Blue, and Red has only a few options:

1 run a hoop;
2 shoot at a ball; or
3 threaten.

The first two options need little clarification, but you will need to become creative with your tactics to find the best threatening positions. You can threaten to run your hoop, threaten to hit on the next turn, or just get in the way of where Black wants to be. There are a few simple rules.

**Running a Hoop** If you have an easy chance, it is hardly ever wrong to run your hoop. Think carefully, though, as you may want to look at coming through hard (to reach the next hoop), gently (to guarantee the point), or by a specific distance (to give yourself a double target, or the shortest possible shot at the enemy).

If Blue and Black are joined up, do not bother taking position at your hoop. If you get a good position, Black will only move you out of the way. If you get a bad position, you have just wasted a turn; Black will leave you there, and you lose any advantage.

If Blue and Black are split, take position only if success is 100 per cent guaranteed. Otherwise, it is a wasted shot.

If you manage to take croquet, your best hope is an immediate break. At the very least, you should split the opponents, and get yourself in front of your hoop. An ideal outcome is the *three-ball squeeze leave*. Red can run Hoop 1 hard or softly and have either a pioneer or a rush to his next hoop.

**Shooting** You are unlikely to win the game unless you hit Blue or Black at some point. Choose your moment carefully. You will have more chances earlier in the battle.

The decision to shoot should be based on three elements:

• your chances of hitting;
• your chances of scoring if you do hit; and
• Black's chances of scoring if you miss.

*With Blue pegged out, Chris Clarke has to change his strategy.*

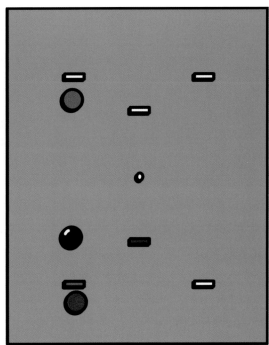

ABOVE: *The three-ball squeeze.*

LEFT: *Phil Cordingley takes the opportunity to run his hoop.*

If Blue and Black are split, it is safe to shoot at Blue. Blue is for peg, so is unable to score. Forcing Blue to play guarantees you more chances later.

**Threatening** Stick to the boundaries. Black's winning break is much easier if you lay up mid-lawn. You are much safer keeping your back to the boundary, and shooting in towards the middle of the lawn.

If you think Black will fail to get position at a hoop, you can lay up near by, and threaten to hit on the next turn. A speculative hoop approach from Black with Blue is dangerous if your ball is on the boundary near by.

If you think Black will get Hoop 1, but struggle with Hoop 2, consider hiding in Corner 2, near his next hoop. Black will be unable to take position.

If you have pegged out Yellow yourself, and Red is for peg, you want to guarantee as many short shots as possible at the peg. Put Red in the middle of a side boundary, and you can shoot backwards and forwards at the peg with a series of thirteen-yard shots. Even the weakest of hitters will win eventually from here. Your opponent will try to move you as soon as he can.

Your tactics in the pegged-out game will depend greatly on what your opponent does. He has two balls left, and will try to set the pace. If you lurk on the boundary, just out of

his convenient reach, you stand every chance of unsettling him. The key to success is to second-guess what his tactics are going to be.

## The Hunted – Defending the Innings

Blue and Black are being hunted. Red needs to gain an initiative by roqueting something, and by stopping Black's progress. Black's strategy is to retain control, and to continue to score without risk of giving Red a winning opportunity. There are two ways of playing this, and often Black will settle for a combination of the two.

The traditional way of playing the game is the *defensive endgame*. Black wants to give Red long, difficult and dangerous shots. Setting up a break is dangerous, as a wrong move will allow Red back into the game. Black decides on the following:

- Do not roquet Red unless absolutely necessary.
- Try to remain in the diagonally opposite corner.
- Always try to lay up with a rush to Black's hoop.

The longer the game continues, the more chances Red will have, so Black will attempt to score as regularly as possible.

ABOVE: *New Zealand's Bob Jackson keeps Blue and Black together.*

LEFT: *Red has a shot, but can he afford to take it on?*

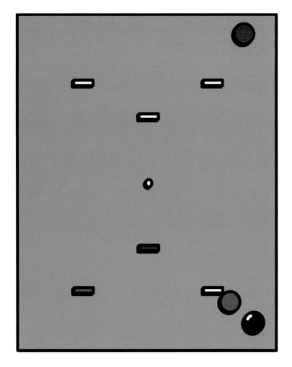

Black will only play a break if it needs no work to set up, but a simple trap may allow this to happen easily. Here, Black is for Hoop 4; a shot from Red at this guarded boundary would be suicidal, and present a rare chance for a break – Black has an easy prospect of at least four hoops. The options are clear-cut – if Red hits, he wins; if Red misses, he loses; if Red hides in a corner or on a boundary, he gets another chance. Most players will opt for the third choice.

Black must steer clear of giving Red a big target, so will stay a long way away. Black should avoid leaving a double, so his best options are as follows:

- Blue and Black pointing straight at Red, giving a perfect single target.
- Either of Blue or Black wired, so Red has no chance of a double.
- A sizeable gap between the two balls.
- A hoop preventing Red from making a double target.

If Black has not moved Red this turn, he can wire Red without fear of a wiring lift. Whatever position Red finds himself

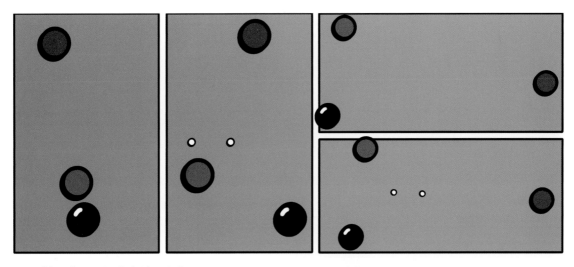

ABOVE: *Ways of presenting Red with a single target.*

RIGHT: *Reg Bamford on target for a long hit-in.*

in is Red's responsibility. Even if Black subsequently manoeuvres himself and his partner into an impossible position, Red has no comeback.

Against an unwary Red, Black can creep round all twelve hoops without allowing Red a single shot. Each turn, Black ignores Red, Red plays, and Black wires Red. Red's best option to defy this demoralizing tactic is to find a spot where Black's ambitions are harder to achieve.

If you are playing Red against an opponent who's intent on playing hide and seek, bear in mind that you can place Red where it is harder for him to find a wired position. Your best option is on the boundary, dead level with any of the first four hoops.

If you are playing Black and Blue, and defence is your plan, there is one extra tip. When Black is for Hoop 1 and Blue is for peg, it is possible to get obsessed with playing Black each turn. If all you are doing is leaving a rush, it is often more convenient to play the peg ball. You are only constrained by choice of colour when you are actually scoring.

However, current thinking is moving away from the defensive endgame, which requires lots of fiddly shots at the expense of making progress. Modern players tend to play in a much more attacking style.

The *aggressive endgame* strategy relies on the principle that Red is unafraid to shoot at Blue, but does not want to join up with Black, for fear of conceding a break opportunity. So, Black can do almost anything he likes: ambitious roll-ups to hoops, leaving Blue in the middle of the lawn, and leaving Red in hitting distance. All is well if Black gets position, but if Black does not get near the hoop, he just retreats to the safest corner.

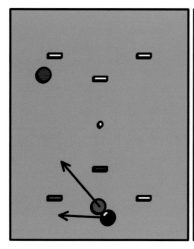
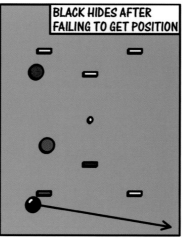

*The aggressive three-ball break. Black has everything to gain, and very little to lose.*

If Red shoots at Blue, a hit earns him nothing. If Red shoots at Black, a miss loses him everything.

Of course, you should not go wild with this. This logic may authorize you to play ambitiously, but it will not make you an expert at shots you would not normally manage. Most players will opt for a combination of aggression and defence.

### Peg and Box

Suppose you have come through Rover with Red. Your plan was to finish this turn, but you have accidentally clipped the Yellow, and are faced with an eight-yard peg-out from behind the hoop. So what do you do? Do you try the long peg-out? A hard drive? A gentle full-roll? Do you leave both balls in play, or peg out Red?

There is a very real chance that you are not going to succeed. In that case, you need to make sure Blue and Black have nothing. Your basic options are either to put Yellow as close as possible and peg out Red, or to roll Red and Yellow to a distant boundary, and leave one a rush on the other.

If your opponent does hit, the first option could force Yellow to spend the next hour thrashing backwards and forwards, vainly trying to hit a long peg-out. The second option leaves you with a better chance of some defensive play. You will have a greater choice of shorter shots and the chance to join wide.

Leaving the opponent with one ball is often your best chance of success. Eliminating your own partner is hardly ever a good idea.

## When to Riggall an Opponent

Blue is on the peg, Red is playing a break – should Red peg out the Blue? While you are out on the lawn, that is the question being asked by all the onlookers, as they sit analysing your game from the comfort of the clubhouse.

It all depends on the clip positions of the other two balls. There are a few considerations.

*Could Black finish, even with just a two-ball break?*

If the answer is 'Yes', then you should not peg Blue out. If Black is for Penult or Rover, it is very rare to see Red go for the peg-out. If Black still needs four or more hoops, he will either need to hit multiple shots, or he will need to find a three-ball break.

*How many hoops does Yellow need?*

If Yellow is ahead of Black, you are in a very strong position: two balls to the opponent's one, and fewer hoops needed for victory. Some players are happy to Riggall Blue if Yellow is still for Hoop 1, even if Black is for 3-back.

*Which of you is the better player?*

Pegging out the opponent will allow you to make hoops at a faster rate. Only experience can tell you whether that will allow Yellow to overtake Black. If you are playing handicap, the peg-out usually suits the stronger player. Bisques are most powerful if used for a four-ball break. Any remaining bisques are devalued when only three balls remain.

*How confident are you?*

Two hours into a game where you have played dreadfully, you finally get the chance to peg out the Blue. If you are playing that badly, you might want to think about *not* pegging out. That gives you all four balls to play with, and the chance of a quick finish with Yellow. Instead of eliminating Blue, and making things hard for Black, you could try repeatedly forcing Blue to play. Here is an example of a *forcing leave*, when Yellow is for Hoop 1, which gives your opponent no alternative except a shot with Blue.

Each shot for Blue/Black is the same length. Blue is close to Yellow's hoop, but Black is useless, stuck on the far boundary away from Yellow's break. Blue/Black has a number of options:

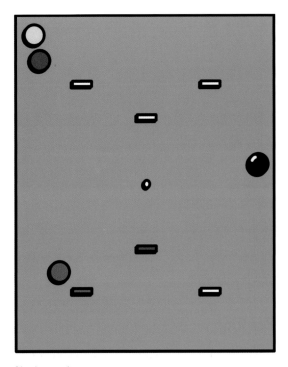

*Blue has to play.*

- Black shoots – suicidal. Black could win if he hits, but should lose if he misses.
- Blue at Red/Yellow – concedes an immediate three-ball break.
- Blue at Black – provided Yellow can make Hoop 1 now, there is a chance of rushing Blue (the forced ball, again) to Hoop 2. Yellow has the chance of a three-ball break, or another forcing leave.
- Blue at the peg – an insane shot, unless Black is much stronger than Yellow, both at hitting and break play. A possible choice if Yellow has a large number of bisques. A miss gives Blue/Black a good defensive wide join.
- Blue to Corner 4 – Blue's most sensible play. Yellow may attempt a two-ball break, in the hope of tidying the balls up later.

Of course, you can change your mind about the peg-out later. You might want to leave all the balls on until Yellow has progressed as far as Hoop 4 (ready for the easy run up the middle). Then you play Red, peg out the Blue, and see how your fortunes lie.

On the other hand, you might rate yourself as a good tactician and your opponent as a lousy shot. In this case, Red can peg out Blue straight away. The way you balance the risks of the two strategies is up to you.

## The Two-Ball Game

### Completing the Hoops First

There is one more option in a pegged-out game. You run Rover, peg out Blue, and then peg out Red. Two balls are eliminated, and you now have a straight battle to the death between Black and Yellow. Neither player has much chance of a break, so the game reduces to a test of whichever player can complete their own hoops first.

Mostly, the two-ball ending is a test of skill rather than tactics. Whoever is better at taking position at hoops and running them will probably win. There are a number of points to bear in mind:

- Running an odd-numbered hoop hard will get you down to the next hoop. Try and get a good distance through on each of these.
- It is often good to be one hoop behind your opponent. It is a bad idea to take position at Hoop 2 when the enemy ball is in front of Hoop 1. Sometimes it pays to let your opponent overtake you by one hoop.
- There are times when it pays to guarantee a hoop, rather than try it speculatively. It may be better to take two turns on a hoop, by tapping Yellow six inches in front before running it hard, than to fail from six feet, and take another two attempts to get through. On the other hand, it may have been a better tactic to gamble on the difficult six-foot shot.
- If you get ahead, do not throw away your lead. The onus is on the trailing player to catch up. If Yellow just keeps scoring, Black will not win unless you make a mistake, or he hits. There is no onus on the leader to

*The two-ball ending is not recommended against a player with Robert Fulford's skill.*

it is raining, and you both want an early finish.

Many players overlook the chance of a late-stage two-ball ending like this:

1 Red pegs out Blue, but not himself;
2 Black misses;
3 Yellow scores a few more hoops;
4 Red now pegs out.

Yellow may have been for Hoop 4 against Black's Hoop 1. At that stage, it is right to leave three balls in play, with the chance of a quick score on the middle four hoops. Later, Yellow may have reached 3-back against Hoop 2. Now the peg-out of Red creates a commanding lead.

If there is a difference in ability between the two players, the two-baller is often the best policy. When Yellow and Black start at the same hoop, the stronger player will usually prevail. In particular, a two-ball finish in a handicap game will render the weaker player's bisques almost useless, whatever the position.

# Peeling

### Introduction

Just as it is possible to peg out another ball, so it is possible to cause another ball to score its hoop. Sending another

roquet the follower. A miss could take you out of position for three turns.

- Beware the position where Yellow and Black are for the same hoop in opposite directions. If Black takes position at Hoop 1, while Yellow is for 1-back, you might not get the chance to go near your hoop until Black is on Hoop 3. Thereafter, you might get tangled up again at Hoops 4 and 3-back, and at Hoops 6 and Penult. If Black can take the initiative, a timid Yellow could see a six-hoop lead disappear.

- Wiring lifts are very common when there are only two balls in play. Whenever you roquet the opponent, there is a very high chance of leaving him no shot. Remember, when you have been wired, you do not need to use the lift to shoot at Black. You could use it to run a hoop, take position, or you could play your shot from where the balls lie.

### When to Create the Two-Ball Finish

This is not a sensible tactic, unless either Yellow is a long way ahead of Black, or Yellow is a much stronger player than Black.

It is sometimes said that a six-hoop lead is the minimum for Yellow's guaranteed success. That may be too rigid; it depends, in fact, on the specific placement of the balls, the temperament of each player, and – to be honest – whether

---

**WALTER PEEL**

Several croquet players have lent their names to strokes or other aspects of the game. None has had a more pervasive influence than W. H. Peel.

Walter Peel was one of croquet's first recorded champions, playing in an open tournament at Moreton-in-the-Marsh in Gloucestershire, in 1868. Tactics were very different then, and hoops were much easier than now, but Peel's proficiency at 'peeling' set him far above his contemporaries. It is said that he once completed a straight run of five consecutive peels during a game, and this certainly proved a winning tactic for him.

Peel's influence was not limited to his playing ability. He conceived the notion of a national governing body, responsible for law-making and the organization of tournaments. In 1896, that came to fruition, with the formation of the All England Croquet Association, of which he was both Secretary and Treasurer. He organized several tournaments in that first season, not least of which was a Wimbledon event, relaunched after years of dominance by lawn tennis.

Alas, Peel did not live to see the game develop further. He died from a short and sudden illness, just twelve days after the first committee meeting of his Association in 1897.

*Stephen Mulliner gets down to line up a peel.*

ball – whether your partner or the adversary's – through its hoop is called *peeling*.

Tactically, peeling a ball through its first few hoops is seldom worth the effort. The area where peeling becomes a profitable strategy is when a ball is being sent through its last hoop (or hoops) and pegged out.

Beginners should be warned away from this tactic. It is a sure way of spoiling a good break, unless you know what you are doing. For a full discussion of this topic, see the chapters on 'Advanced Play', which detail not only the technique, but also the strategy surrounding peeling.

## The Fear of Pegging Out

The fear of being pegged out can often cripple your chances of winning a game. The logic goes like this:

- *If* I play an all-round break to the peg, and
- *If* my opponent hits his next shot, and
- *If* he sets up a break, and goes round without a mistake, and
- *If* he pegs my ball out, then
- I'll probably lose the game.

Many players follow this argument, and arrive at the conclusion that it is best not to play an all-round break. They decide to score eleven hoops and stop short of Rover. Whoever gets the next break, whether it is you or the opponent, would have to peel Red in order to peg it out. That gives some protection from an opponent with a taste for peg-outs.

Sometimes it is sensible. The first rule is this: never leave yourself with peels unless you are confident of being able to do them yourself. If your opponent does not hit, or does not assemble that break, you are just making work for yourself. So, if you are no good at peeling, do not ever think about ending your turn prematurely. Spend your time making that twelfth hoop, and setting up a good leave to freeze out your opponent.

The second rule is this: do not leave a deterrent unless it is an effective one. If you are playing someone much less experienced, the thought of pegging you out might not have occurred to them; against a slightly stronger player, the prospect of a single peel on your Red might be enough to scare them off; against a much stronger player, the single peel is no obstacle at all, and they will peg you out anyway. Some of the time, you will just be making extra work for yourself.

## Towards Technical Perfection

If you play enough croquet, sooner or later you will win games consistently. Your handicap will improve and you will become adept at hitting long shots and putting together breaks from increasingly challenging beginnings.

Put two players together, each of whom is capable of the full range of shots, and the game takes on more and more elaborate tactical manoeuvres. Advanced-level croquet is a game in which long breaks, complex leaves and ambitious peeling turns become commonplace.

---

### PEELING IN DOUBLES

Handicap doubles has one more additional rule. Typically, this a game played between pairs comprising a strong player and a weaker one. Back in the old days, there was nothing to stop the strong player taking all the bisques of the team, performing lots of peels, and winning the game single-handedly. Now, there is a rule that prevents any player at handicap level – and only at handicap level – doing more than four peels on his partner ball.

As a case in point, John Solomon once managed to win a doubles match, without his partner even turning up. Solomon was playing in the British Open Doubles Championship at Hurlingham in 1972; his partner Pat Cotter was late for the game. Solomon played every turn with Red, peeled Yellow through twelve hoops, and kept his opponents split. This tactic won him two games +24 and +21 (conceding an aggregate of just seven hoops in total). His second-round match was less successful, as the same tactic lost him the first game. At that point Cotter arrived. The pair won the two subsequent games, and reached the final of the event.

The moral of the story is that the true expert is unafraid of peeling any other ball. Had this been a handicap game, with Solomon partnering a novice, any opponent would be glad of the four-peel limit. Without it, Solomon would have been invincible.

# CHAPTER 12

# INTRODUCING ADVANCED PLAY

# Advanced Rules

## The Need for a Rule Change

By the 1920s, it was becoming clear that the rules of croquet needed to change. The top flight of players were becoming so proficient at the game that they would regularly score all-round twelve-hoop breaks. The game was becoming very one-sided.

The player who won the toss would play first. More often than not, that would give him the first opportunity of a break. He would play the break round to the peg, and leave the opponent with a thirty-yard shot. If the opponent missed, another break would follow, for a +26 win.

OPPOSITE: *Stephen Mulliner – a difficult man to beat.*

RIGHT: *Reg Bamford considers his options.*

Several years of experimentation came in the 1920s and 30s, in order to improve the game among the top players. That resulted in what are now the Rules for Advanced Play, a variant of the game that has become widespread at tournament level.

## Advanced Rules in Brief

The Rules for Advanced Play attempted to deal with the growing inequalities by reducing the distance of the opponent's shot, to give more of an opportunity of hitting. They also aim to deter a player from racing ahead, and scoring all twelve hoops in one turn early on.

In Advanced Play, hoops 1-back and 4-back become penalty hoops, so that the following applies:

• When a player runs either of 1-back or 4-back, the opponent is entitled to start his turn from either (a) where his ball lies, or (b) from any point on either baulk line. This is called a *lift* shot.

• If a player runs 1-back and 4-back in the same turn *with his first ball*, the opponent is entitled to start his next turn from either (a) where his ball lies, (b) from either baulk, or (c) from in contact with any other ball. Play starts immediately with a croquet stroke, as if the striker had just hit the other ball. This is called a *contact*.

Without the lift shot, a player could be confronted with a shot of over thirty-three yards. The lift first gives more choice of which shot to take, but also reduces the length of the longest shot, typically to between thirteen and eighteen yards.

The contact is usually considered a very severe penalty, resulting in a certain sacrifice of the innings. For this reason,

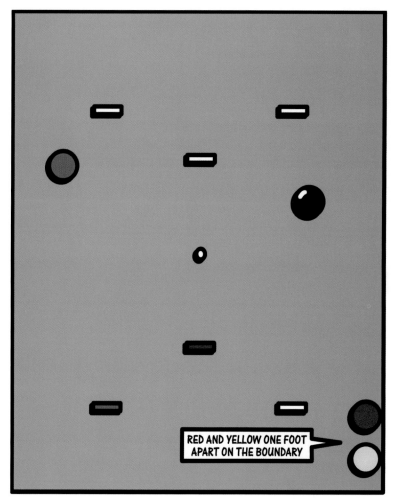

RED AND YELLOW ONE FOOT APART ON THE BOUNDARY

*The old standard leave.*

players very rarely consider running 4-back with their first ball.

You should note the following:

- each side can only ever concede one contact per game (first ball through 1-back and 4-back), and at most four lift shots (either of two balls through either of the two hoops);
- lifts are granted when a ball *runs* 1-back or 4-back for itself, and never when it is peeled by one of the other balls;
- lifts and contacts must be taken immediately at the start of the next turn. They cannot be saved up and played later in the game;
- any player who pegs out any ball (either his own or an opponent's) may no longer claim lifts or contacts under this rule;
- this rule is entirely separate from the wiring lift rule.

Players may still claim lifts for balls in wired positions, exactly as normal.

Under standard rules, it would be possible to win a game in two turns:

- Red scores twelve hoops;
- Blue misses a long shot;
- Yellow scores twelve hoops to win.

Under Advanced Rules, that same result would require three turns:

- Red scores nine hoops;
- Blue misses a lift shot;
- Yellow scores twelve;
- Blue misses another lift shot;
- Red scores three and finishes.

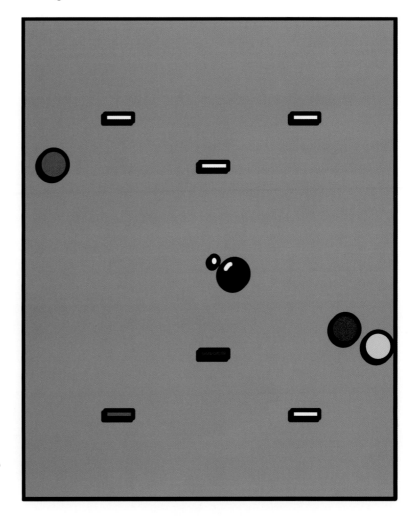

*The diagonal spread.*

# The Importance of the Leave

You are just finishing your first break with Red, and you want to set the balls up in a position that is going to stop your opponent getting an advantage, but also give you a good chance of progressing with Yellow on your next turn. (For more on the technicalities, see page 139.)

The most basic leave in Advanced Play is the *old standard leave*, or *OSL* (see illustration page 120), which has been in use for around half a century. Yellow and Red are together and on the boundary, Blue and Black are split, and any lift shot that the opponent might take from either baulk area is going to be at least thirteen yards. How you place Blue and Black is a matter of personal preference, as long as there is more than thirteen yards between them; you are giving away one relatively short shot, so it is best not to give a choice of similar lengths.

Traditionally, this leave works best when Red is for 4-back, and Yellow is for Hoop 2. Whatever Blue/Black does, Yellow will punish him severely if he misses anything. Even when Yellow is for Hoop 1, Blue/Black needs to hit in if he is going to dent Yellow's prospects.

Back in the 1960s, when this leave was in vogue, players often shied away from the shortest shot – Blue at Yellow from A-baulk. It is only thirteen yards, but it is a possible game-loser. Nowadays, top players are so confident of hitting at this length that the leave is seldom seen at the top level.

An evolved version lengthens the shot by a couple of yards, and finds a clever way of forcing Blue/Black into a restricted set of choices. This is the *diagonal spread* (see illustration page 121), which has become the standard leave for many players. (Indeed, so universal is its use now that it is often simply referred to as 'the spread'.)

After running 1-back, Red will concede a lift to the opponent at the end of the turn. Blue/Black cannot save up that lift until later, so there is no penalty to Red for conceding a wiring lift at the same time. So, Red places Blue in a similar position as for the OSL, but Black is now tucked in close behind the peg. All four balls are in a straight line, so that Blue has no shot at anything, and Black has no backswing towards Red and Yellow. With such a lack of choice, it is almost inevitable that the opponent will lift one of the balls (usually the Blue) to B-baulk, and play the long shot down the boundary towards Red and Yellow (about twenty-five yards). He misses, and Yellow has a straight rush for an instant 3-ball break.

*James Death plays a full-roll.*

# Avoiding the Second Lift: the Triple Peel

You have taken Yellow round nine hoops, and given your opponent a leave. He misses, and you have a turn with Red. Red can score twelve hoops, but you would then have to give your opponent another shot, and another chance of taking control. Ideally, Red would like to finish the game this turn, by scoring twelve hoops for himself, three hoops for Yellow, and pegging out both balls in the same break.

In the advanced game, peeling (see page 116, and Chapter 13, below) becomes a vitally important element. If you can score all the points for Red, and the remainder for Yellow, all in the same turn, you can finish the game off before your opponent has a second chance at a short shot. A break that scores hoops for the striker's ball, while at the same time scoring the last three hoops for another ball and pegging it out, is called a *triple peel*, or 'TP'.

The triple is the crux of the modern top-class game, and its mastery is the pinnacle of achievement for many players. This is a subject that warrants some detailed examination.

## THREE VARIANTS ON THE DIAGONAL SPREAD

It is said that the diagonal spread is a universal leave. Whatever the position of the clips, it is almost never wrong to play. Sometimes it is seen in a slightly different form.

The traditional form has Blue near Hoop 2, and Red/Yellow near Hoop 4. That works fine most of the time, but some circumstances suit reversing the positions. The reversed diagonal has Blue near Hoop 4, and Red/Yellow near Hoop 2 (with Black obviously moving too). The reversed diagonal tends to appear later in a (scrappy) game, when all the balls are clear of the first couple of hoops. The area near Hoop 2 is neutral territory for Yellow, who wants a rush towards the fourth quarter. That is useful if Yellow is for Hoop 3, Hoop 4, Hoop 5, 2-back, 3-back or 4-back.

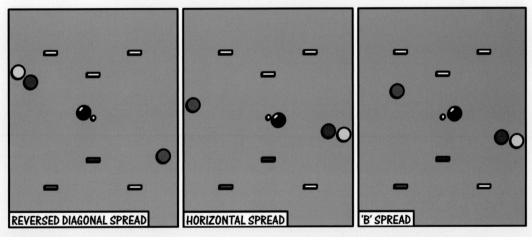

REVERSED DIAGONAL SPREAD | HORIZONTAL SPREAD | 'B' SPREAD

*Spread variants.*

There was a short-lived fashion in the 1990s for the horizontal spread. A standard diagonal spread places Red and Yellow fifteen yards from A-baulk and twenty-five yards from B-baulk. The horizontal spread rotates all four ball positions, so that Yellow and Red are eighteen yards from each baulk. (For those who wish to check, the point on the East boundary, equidistant from each baulk line – or *long point* – is about two feet south of the peg.)

The horizontal spread quickly dropped out of use, once players realized that it lengthened by three yards the shot their opponents did not want to play, whilst reducing their planned shot by about seven yards. Even so, there are circumstances in which it retains some value, specifically against a very good shot, whose hitting chances peak at around fifteen yards. In that case, it provides some defence against the dangerous shot from A-baulk.

The final variant of the spread is what top-class players unkindly call the B-spread. A-class experts have practised the diagonal spread diligently, and can execute it perfectly each game. Less experienced players sometimes produce a B-class version, in which one essential aspect is missing: the ball at the peg is out by a few inches, giving a short shot between Blue and Black, Black has a backswing allowing a shortish shot at Red and Yellow, or Blue is out of position, and has a view of a big double target at your balls. There is nothing better than a good leave, but there is nothing worse than a good leave that has gone slightly wrong.

# CHAPTER 13

# PEELING

When I was a beginner, someone told me that peeling was easy – the hard part is peeling without your break falling apart. Other players told me that a triple peel is nothing more than a three-ball break. With hindsight, those two pieces of advice need elaboration. The best way is to strip it down into simple elements.

## Peeling within the Break

### The Straight Peel

The easiest way of peeling a ball is to wait until you have taken your ball (Red) round, up to the point where Red and

*Placing the balls for a Rover peel.*

Yellow (the ball you are peeling, or the *peelee*) are for the same hoop. Peeling and running a hoop together is called a *straight peel*, and is worth practising for the improving handicap-level player as much as the aspiring advanced-level player.

Yellow should be your pioneer at the hoop, and you should start with it a few feet somewhere in front. When you are ready for the peel, rush Yellow directly in front, and as near as you dare (usually about a foot). It is a common mistake to place Yellow in perfect position – one foot in front of the hoop – before you roquet it. Then, it is impossible for Red to hit Yellow gently enough not to dislodge it from position. Whatever your placement, a straight peel is much easier if it is long and straight, rather than short and slightly angled.

You will need to take a lot of care in placing the Red for the croquet stroke, so this is a moment to take a while lining up. Place Red in contact with Yellow, and look along the edge of the balls. The left edges of Red and Yellow should be aligned so that they are just missing the inner edge of the hoop's left upright. The same should apply for the right side. If you have done that correctly, Yellow will now travel in one direction only – right through the gap, missing both wires of the hoop.

How you play this next shot depends on how far away you are, and how good you are at stop shots. If you are far enough away to send Yellow well clear, whilst stopping in front with Red, then play a stop shot. You are ideally placed to take position while sending Yellow through, and then to run the hoop gently.

If you do not have enough room for a stop shot, you can always play to send both balls through in the same stroke – this is called an *Irish peel*. For this you need a drive shot – Yellow should pass straight through, and Red will follow.

The crucial point with either method is that you should play the croquet stroke dead straight, as if Yellow were not there, and you were just running the hoop with Red. Yellow should sail through the hoop, and Red will either stop in position, or score the point.

## The Back Peel

Straight peeling is the easiest technique to learn. However, in a real game, when you are faced with three peels in a turn, and when something inevitably goes wrong, you are likely to run out of shots. The *back peel* gives you the chance to try peeling earlier in the break.

The back peel occurs when Red and Yellow are for the same hoop in different directions. Suppose Red is for Hoop 3, and Yellow is for 4-back. Red can run his hoop, turn round away from the direction of the break, peel Yellow, and then turn back towards Hoop 4. As well as 4-back after Hoop 3, this method is commonly used at Penult after Hoop 6 and Rover after Hoop 5.

Because Red is switching directions mid-break, a third ball is needed to turn Red back towards the next hoop. The pivot ball needs to be held close by, and is referred to as the *escape ball*.

To set up the back peel at 4-back, you need Blue as the pioneer to Hoop 4, and to have the other three balls at Hoop 3. Before the hoop, Black – the escape ball – should be placed just behind the hoop and to the side. Red rushes Yellow in towards the hoop for the approach. The approach should drop Red in a very good position in front of the hoop, and Yellow in a good position in front of 4-back. For that, you want to play your approach from very close and a bit to the side – if you are directly in front, the hoop will block Yellow's path.

The straight peel.

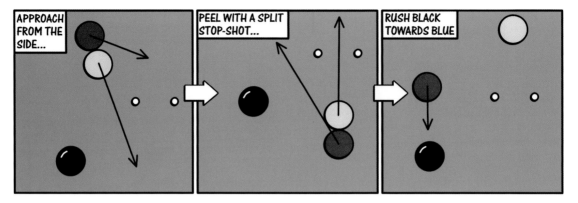

*The back peel.*

Score the hoop, and tap Yellow. Now Red needs to play a split stop shot. Yellow scores the hoop, and Red lands behind the escape ball (Black). Red rushes Black down the lawn, and places it at Hoop 5. The break continues for the next two hoops before Red needs to bring Yellow back into play.

## The Transit Peel

If you learn the techniques of the straight peel and the back peel, you should have enough to complete a break with multiple peels. There is a third type of peel, which presents more opportunity for getting the job done. This is the *transit peel*.

In each of the two previous examples, Red has been peeling through its own hoop, either in the same direction or backwards away from the route of the break. The transit peel allows Red to peel Yellow whilst in transit between two other hoops.

Unless you are very ambitious, expect to carry out this manoeuvre when you are in the right neighbourhood. So, you might want to peel Penult when you are passing from 1-back to 2-back, or from 3-back to 4-back; or peel Rover when you are somewhere in the vicinity of 2-back or 3-back.

There are two ways of doing this, and each one calls for a bit of accuracy and pre-planning. In the following example, you want to peel Yellow through Rover during the journey from 2-back to 3-back:

**Method 1**  You are at 2-back, with Yellow as your pioneer; Blue is at 3-back; Black is level, or just south of, Rover, and on the far side of the hoop. Approach the hoop, ready for a rush on the peelee (Yellow) to Rover. Make the hoop, rush Yellow into perfect position, peel it and get a rush on Black to somewhere beyond Blue. Everything is laid out for you. This is sometimes called a *Wylie peel*, after Keith Wylie, the British master tactician who pioneered the technique.

**Method 2**  You are at 2-back, with Black as your pioneer; Blue is at 3-back, and Yellow is near Rover. Make 2-back with Black, setting up a rush towards Rover. Rather than the difficult rush to peeling position, you want to find a spot where there is a straight stop shot to send Black to 4-back, allowing Red an easy shot to tap Yellow into perfect position. This time, there is no escape ball – you peel Yellow through Rover, going direct to Blue as the pioneer.

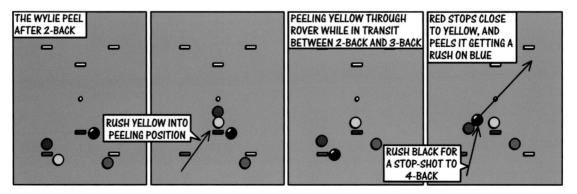

*The transit peel.*

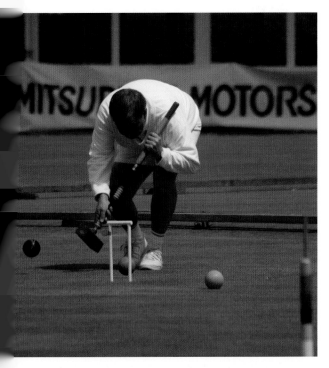

*The mark of an expert: Fulford is unafraid to peel with a split-roll.*

Method 2 is the easier of the two, because Yellow is already in place. All you are doing is playing a standard four-ball break with Yellow as the pivot, but adjusting the position of Blue to allow yourself a peel through Rover. Because there is no escape ball for this method, it is wiser to leave your 3-back pioneer short – maybe halfway between Rover and 3-back. Then you can have the peel with a stop shot, and rush Blue into hoop position.

Do not discount Method 1, though. It is certainly not an easy play, because you have got to be spot-on with your rush. The worst that can happen is that you have got to wait for a straight peeling opportunity at Rover; it is worth considering if that is the way the balls lie.

Be wary of playing this, or any other, transit peel with a roll. A poorly played shot can cause much embarrassment, as the peelee soars clean through the hoop and off the lawn. At this level, finishing your turn prematurely by sending a ball out of play and into baulk will probably lose you the game.

## The Posthumous Peel

One final peeling scenario is the *posthumous peel*. Here, Red and Yellow are for 4-back. Red attempts to peel Yellow and fails. Red runs 4-back, rushes Yellow back into position, and peels it before going to Penult.

There is never any serious threat of pegging out on a turn where you have played a posthumous peel. Once you require more peels than you have hoops to run, you are almost certainly not going to have enough shots to finish the game. Some people like the tactic. It can turn a 4-back and peg position into a Penult and peg position, which puts some pressure on the opponent. That avoids your last lift and gives your opponent one last shot. That is the theory, but is it the best option?

It might be preferable to use your last few shots preparing a good leave for the end of your turn, at the expense of one extra hoop. If you reach this stage, the implication is that you have been playing so badly that you have failed to peel 4-back after Hoop 3, before Hoop 6, after Hoop 6 and before 4-back (at least). That should be enough evidence to convince you that your chances of a peel *and* a good leave are slim.

Try it by all means, if you can confidently peel Yellow before Penult, and then get it safe again after Rover, but it is not necessarily advisable.

## Rush-Peeling

Each of the cases detailed above have assumed that you intend to play your peel as a croquet stroke. You may think it is simpler just to place Yellow in front of its hoop, and rush it straight through with Red. A *rush-peel* is often worthwhile when it is straightforward, but is a definite game-losing tactic if not.

Imagine Yellow is sitting in the middle of the jaws of Penult. Hitting it will inevitably score the hoop. You can play the shot gently, and tap it through by a foot, or you can play it hard, rushing Yellow through the hoop into peeling position at Rover.

Now consider the same thing, where Yellow is three inches dead in front of Penult. Red decides to rush-peel it after 1-back. Red's rush is out by a sixteenth of an inch, and Yellow sticks in the jaws. Red needs a take-off to Blue at 2-back – but there is now no way of playing the shot to get within fifteen yards of Blue. With a lift owing to the opponent, there is a chance that that could be your last shot of the game.

OK, you think you are more accurate than that. Here is what happens if Red's rush is out by a thirty-second of an inch. Yellow gets rush-peeled, but rattles in the jaws, and comes through by just an inch. Red's take-off gets within eight yards of Blue; Red has to shoot hard at Blue to make sure of the roquet; Red approaches 2-back from seven yards behind the hoop; Red sneaks through, but with no rush on Blue (which is on the boundary in A-baulk), no rush on Yellow (which is only just off the wire of Penult), and a nasty roll to 3-back... The moral is that the rush-peel is a shot for a genius or a fool. Play it only if you are 100 per cent confident of a clean peel.

### Jawsing a Peelee

Sometimes you will find a position where you do not have a good peeling prospect, but you can jam the peelee right into the middle of the hoop. There is something to be said for deliberately sticking the peeled ball into the jaws of the hoop, or *jawsing* it. This lets Red set up one of those 100 per cent guaranteed rush-peels, in preparation for a simple point for Yellow immediately after the next hoop.

## Aiming Peels

### Pull

Because croquet balls are not smooth, the friction between them causes a small amount of spin. Normally this is hardly noticeable. The point at which it becomes more apparent is in a peel.

If you play a croquet stroke dead straight, so that Yellow and Red move along the same line, there should be no pull at all. However, if there is an angle of split between the two, the forward ball (Yellow) will curl in slightly towards the direction of the striker's ball (Red). This curl is called *pull*. Players must compensate with their line of aim, because the pull is often enough to cause a peel to miss.

Pull varies depending on playing conditions (there is typically more pull in wet conditions, or in longer grass), on the manufacture of balls (balls with a deeper pattern of milling will probably pull more), and on the type of shot played.

*Ian Lines positioning his Rover peel.*

<br>

**SPLIT PEG-OUTS**

Whenever you play a split shot, the croqueted ball will curl slightly in towards the line of your ball. You will usually only pay much attention to this on an accurate shot where you are trying a peel, but exceptional circumstances can give you a problem elsewhere.

Occasionally, a long split shot can hit a hoop, even when you have carefully lined up the balls to miss. You also need to very wary when pegging out a ball with a split shot – you are in serious danger of missing.

This is largely irrelevant when Red is pegging out Yellow. You line them up, play the shot straight, Yellow hits, and Red follows. When Red is pegging out Black, you might need to watch out. Perhaps you need to roll towards Yellow for a rush. Perhaps you just want to play Red slightly to the side to avoid following the Black out of the game.

Games are lost by players who miss peg-outs, leaving both opponents in play and within easy hitting distance. If you do try to split a ball on to the peg, make sure you allow for pull.

Pull increases with the amount of split between the two balls, but also with how you play it. Stop shots and take-offs have the smallest amount of pull; a big split-roll can sometimes cause a ball to curl by about a foot. It is possible to line Red up towards a point on the right of 4-back, only to see it miss entirely, by several inches on the left.

That might lead you to think that pull is a bad thing, to be avoided at all costs. You might plan to play all your peeling strokes as straight stop shots. Once you become familiar with what is happening, however, there is much less to fear.

The only real way to gauge pull is to practise. Your own technique will give you a different effect from someone else, and experience is the only true way to find out. Nevertheless, there are some basic rules to bear in mind when practising.

## Practising Aiming a Peel

The margin for error on a peel is tiny. If you want to succeed as a peeler, there is only one thing to do, and that is to spend time lining each shot up. There is no substitute for getting down on the ground and having a close look.

If you are peeling in a dead-straight line, the method is straightforward. Look along the edges of the two balls, and check that the left edge of your ball (Red), the left edge of the peelee (Yellow) and the inner edge of the hoop are lined up. Then do the same for the right edges. Play the croquet stroke absolutely straight, and Yellow should sail through the hoop.

If you are peeling at an angle, you should allow for pull. Line the edges of Red and Yellow well inside the inside of the hoop upright. The amount by which you aim off depends on the shot being played, the weather, the grass and your own technique. You will have to work it all out yourself, but there is some advice you can follow.

First, you will notice that a croquet ball is not uniformly milled. There is a point where the grooves form concentric circles, where manufacturers often stamp their logo. This is the *node*. Maybe it makes no difference, has no scientific basis, and is purely superstition, but there is a theory that placing Red so its node is touching Yellow reduces the amount of pull. (Legally, it is acceptable to do this while Red is being placed for the croquet stroke; but it is *not* acceptable to reorientate any other ball, or at any other time in the game.)

The second point is that you should work out a formula for pull versus distance. If you play all your peels as split stop shots, this should provide you with a means of judging consistently. Do not take it as 100 per cent precise, but the following calculation is a good starting point:

*For every foot away from the hoop, Yellow will pull inwards by the width of one upright.*

Therefore, if you are peeling from two feet away, you should line Red and Yellow up to allow a gap of a couple of uprights. Try this in practice, and you should not be a million miles adrift. You will have to adjust it for your own play, but using the width of the hoop as a unit of measurement is a fair guide.

*Reg Bamford checking the angle for his shot after Rover.*

*The node of the ball is the smoothest part, and may impart less pull.*

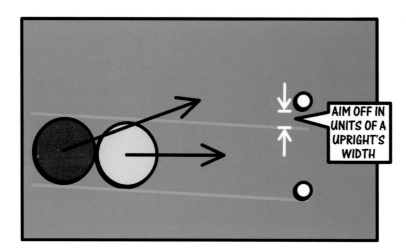

*Calculating the amount of pull.*

For very speculative peels (big rolls from a distance), there is a certain amount of hitting and hoping. Often it pays just to point Yellow to miss the hoop completely by a ball's width; even then, it is exasperating when the stroke pulls by a full foot, or by nothing at all. Unfortunately, in this respect, croquet is not an exact science.

## Putting it All Together

### The Straight Triple

Once you get control of your break, there are several ways of fitting together the triple. The easiest to organize is the *straight triple*, or *STP*.

The straight triple needs no work until you get to 4-back with Red. You are going to do a straight peel on Yellow through 4-back, get a rush to Penult, a straight peel through Penult, get another rush, and a straight peel through Rover. Then rush Yellow to the peg, and the game is over.

It may sound simple, but there is one shot which is *very* difficult, so this requires a bit of luck. You will start off with Blue alongside Penult, Red and Yellow dead in front of 4-back, and Black a foot behind 4-back and to the right. You need the following sequence:

- Red peels Yellow through 4-back.
- Red runs 4-back, and rushes Black to Corner 3.
- Red stops Black back, as far towards Rover as possible, getting a good rush on Yellow.

*A difficult Penult peel for Mark Avery.*

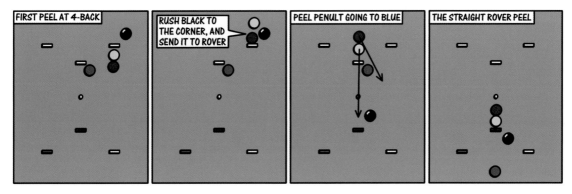

*The straight triple.*

- Here is the hard shot – Red rushes Yellow into perfect peeling position, about a yard in front of Penult.
- Red peels Penult hard, stopping beyond Blue.

## The Straight Rover Peel

That should, hopefully, give you a continuing break, with Yellow now down near Rover. Fast forward to the *straight Rover peel*, where you need the following: Red and Yellow dead in front of the hoop; Black just behind the hoop and to the side; Blue somewhere down near the boundary.

If Red runs Rover, and accidentally roquets Yellow in the same shot, the peg-out becomes close to impossible. Blue and Black are placed as they are to give Red two chances of escape. If Red comes through gently, Black is hittable. If Red is to run Rover hard, Blue is ready. Either way, Red should be able to get the necessary rush on Yellow to the peg.

The downside of the straight triple is that it does not give you any second chances. If anything goes wrong at any stage, the turn is not going to finish the game for you. Lots of things can go wrong at Rover, and Chapter 16 deals with ways of recovering from these. But, if disaster does happen in the straight triple, you have left things far too late to make a dignified exit. It is likely that you will be punished for any error.

## The Standard Triple

The *standard triple* gives you more options, combining back peels and transit peels. If you can organize yourself sooner, you need fall back on straight peeling only as a last resort.

Your timetable for this is as follows:

1 Back-peel Yellow through 4-back after Hoop 3.
2 Organize the balls ready for a back peel through Penult after Hoop 6, then a transit peel through Rover between 2-back and 3-back.

The peeling should be self-explanatory, but the organization side may not be. There is much to bear in mind:

- Avoid using Yellow as your Hoop 2 pioneer, or you will struggle to position it at Hoop 3.
- Place Black as your first escape ball, so it is a foot to the left of 4-back, and a couple of feet south. That gives the best angle of split for the peel, and lets you rush Black towards Blue.

*Chris Williams lining up Rover.*

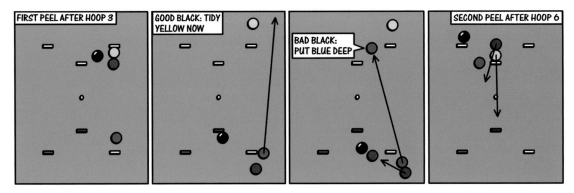

*The standard TP.*

- If Black's a good Hoop 5 pioneer, you can afford to rush Blue up to Corner 3, and send Blue and Yellow both to Penult, before returning to Black.
- If Black's a bad Hoop 5 pioneer, concentrate on keeping the break going. Ignore Yellow, and stop Blue beyond Hoop 6 – putting it a couple of yards towards Yellow will help your next shot.
- After Hoop 5, get a forward rush on Black to somewhere behind 4-back. You can now send Black to 1-back, and get Blue and Yellow into position.
- Put Yellow a foot behind Hoop 6, ready for peeling. Your ideal escape-ball position is to have Blue level with Hoop 6, and two feet to the left.
- After Hoop 6, peel Penult hard, so that Red lands a foot south of Blue, and Yellow goes towards Rover.
- Rush Blue behind Black, and stop it down to 2-back.

From that point, everything should be easy. If Yellow went through Penult cleanly, you have a good chance of a transit peel after 2-back. Otherwise, you have five hoops in which to organize a tightly controlled straight peel at Rover.

## The Delayed Double

Of course, nothing runs smoothly, and you are likely to get peels that fail, or a break that fades in and out of focus. If you do need to peel 4-back later, there are many chances other than after Hoop 3. Your best options are for a transit peel immediately before Hoop 6, or immediately after Hoop 6, or to wait until Red is for 4-back, and have a go at the straight peel.

Assuming that gets you back in control, the timetable for the standard triple no longer applies. Do not worry, as there is still a very good opportunity, by playing the *delayed double*, in which Yellow is peeled through Penult, as another transit peel on the way to 4-back, before you finish with a straight Rover peel:

- Approach 3-back with Black, making sure of a forward rush after the hoop.
- Rush Black to Yellow.
- Leave Black at Penult.
- Peel Yellow through Penult with a hard stop shot.
- Red holds for the rush on Blue to 4-back, Black is the Penult pioneer, and Yellow is down at Rover.

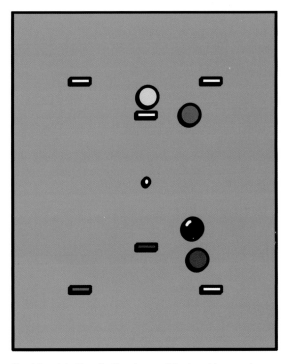

*The delayed double – Red has just run 3-back, and has a rush on Black.*

If the worst comes to the worst and Yellow fails again, you have a perfectly possible attempt at a straight double peel to finish. The details are not hard to work out, as long as you play a hard Irish peel at Penult.

## Practising Peels

There is much to take in on this subject, and the only way of grasping the detail fully is to attempt the shots on the lawn. Practise the techniques for the straight, the back and the transit peel in isolation, and then put them together in a break. Make sure you rehearse the most common likely scenarios:

- back peel of 4-back;
- 4-back in transit before Hoop 6;
- 4-back in transit before 1-back (which works well as a take-off);
- back peel of Penult;
- death roll of Penult going to 2-back (if you fancy the shot);
- transit peel of Penult before 4-back;
- transit peel of Rover before 3-back;
- straight peel of Rover.

There are other opportunities you might want to create for yourself, and ways of putting together the various building blocks within your break. Tony Mrozinski of Surbiton Croquet Club holds something of a record, having once completed all three peels of a triple before running Hoop 4. There is always room for creativity in croquet.

## Advanced Peeling

### The TPO

Assuming you do not have a disaster – miss a short shot or stick in a hoop – there is little to go wrong with a triple on your partner. An aborted triple may not finish the game, but you should be happy if it gives you a twelve-hoop break for Red, and a point or two for Yellow, and you can step off the lawn with an elegant leave.

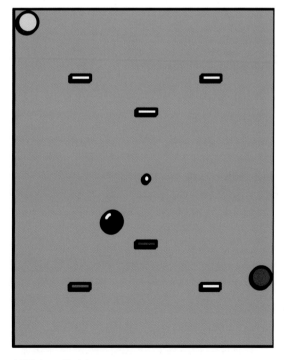

*A TPO leave. Black has a contact.*

A much higher-risk strategy is the *TPO*, or *triple peel on opponent*. Here, your opponent has a ball on 4-back, and you peel him through his last three hoops, pegging him out, and leaving him with only one ball on the lawn. Tactically, it is pointless to do this if the other balls of both you and your opponent have barely started, so the TPO almost always involves giving a contact rather than a lift.

Do not even think of doing a TPO unless you are confident of finishing the turn successfully. There is nothing worse than giving the opponent the three peels he needs, then breaking down at Rover with four balls in the middle of the lawn, and a pending contact for the opponent. Similarly, you should not even think of the TPO unless you can manage a standard – rather than a delayed – triple.

It is paramount that you get a good leave after the peg-out, so you will need an early peel of Blue through Rover. Ideally, you should aim to peel Rover in transit going to 3-back. Then you can concentrate on the leave.

Assuming Blue gets pegged out, you want to leave Black with as meagre a chance as possible. Here is the standard leave with Black for Hoop 1 (Black can play from where it lies, take a lift, or claim the contact): Yellow is placed in Corner 2, from where Black's take-off to Hoop 1 is very difficult. Red is placed level with (or about a ball's width north of) Hoop 4, on the East boundary. This makes a roll approach to Hoop 1 very difficult indeed for Black.

Nothing is guaranteed in croquet. The TPO usually favours the peeling player, but it is still possible to lose from this position. In that case, the score is recorded as *OTP* (opponent's triple peel) rather than TPO (triple peel on opponent).

## Quads, Quins and Sextuples

You know you have the respect of an opponent who deliberately stops at 3-back instead of 4-back. This is a defensive move to stop an attempt at a TPO. More often, a clip on 3-back is a sign that the first break finished unintentionally early. Either way, it then leaves the player needing to do an extra peel on his partner if he later wants to finish in one turn.

The *quadruple peel*, *quad*, or *QP*, is significantly harder than the triple. The 3-back peel can be done as a back peel after Hoop 4, but everything thereafter becomes more and more delayed, with three peels in transit, and, more often than not, at least two peels straight.

Harder still, and very rare, is the *quintuple peel*, *quin*, or *QNP*. Really, this only occurs when there has been a bad mistake with the first break. Frankly, if you ever attain the level when a quin is in your repertoire, you are unlikely to be playing an opponent who will give you the opportunity of demonstrating it.

Much more common than either of these is the *sextuple*, or *SXP*. The standard of play among top players has risen significantly over the last decade, and the sextuple has become

a staple tactic. Rather than playing the triple to avoid the second lift, experts will attempt six peels to avoid *all* lifts.

It is not worth detailing how this works – if you can play one successfully, you do not need the advice. Suffice to say, the sextuple has very few back peels, and is made mostly of transit and straight peels. If you ever see one being performed, you can expect to see the focus move entirely away from conventional break-building – pioneers are replaced with escape balls, and pivots are sent as escape balls to the next hoop to be peeled, rather than the next hoop to be run.

## The Sextuple Leave

By doing away with all lifts and contacts, the sextupler can lay an extremely difficult leave for his opponent. Below are the standard and delayed sextuple leaves, which Yellow has

---

### FRIVOLOUS PEELING TURNS

It is possible to complete yet more complex peeling turns, although the tactical merit diminishes for all but the most flagrant show-off.

Octuple peels have been completed in competition – the first by New Zealand's Bob Jackson in 1987 – even though they present the opponent with a significantly shorter shot than the sextuple. Reg Bamford holds the record for consistency, with four consecutive games at a tournament in Oregon in 2005, in which he completed two sextuples and two octuples.

Paul Hands from Cheltenham holds a unique accolade. He was playing during the late afternoon of a tournament, and realized that he did not have time to complete two all-round breaks and arrive in time for an appointment. His opponent was for 3-back and 4-back, so he completed a quadruple peel on one ball, a triple on the other, and pegged both opposing balls out, to lose -14 OQP OTP. (The trick, for readers who are anxious to try their skill, is to peel Blue and Black alternately.)

The three-ball triple is another rare sight, and is often the act of a desperate player. The opponent has already pegged out a ball and, for some reason, you need to finish this turn with a TP. For much of the time, the three-ball triple is a very complicated version of a two-ball break. There is a lot of straight and accurate rushing, although the turn gets a whole lot harder if any of the peels of the standard triple fail.

Perhaps the most frivolous of all peeling turns, therefore, was the TPO inflicted by Keith Aiton on David Peterson. Peterson scored a nine-hoop two-ball break for Red on the second turn of the game; Aiton hit with Black on the third turn, and went round, peeling and pegging out Red before Yellow had been played into the game; Peterson took the contact with Yellow and won. A great achievement by Aiton, but not a strategy for guaranteed success.

*Sextuple leaves.*

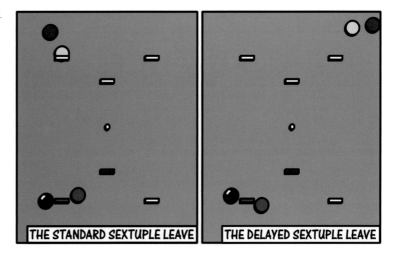

THE STANDARD SEXTUPLE LEAVE | THE DELAYED SEXTUPLE LEAVE

set up for Red (Yellow is for 1-back, and Red is for Hoop 1).

In the *standard leave*, Yellow has finished his turn by jawsing himself in 1-back (his next hoop). Blue shoots at Red and misses. Red brings Blue back into play, and rush-peels Yellow, with the hope of an immediate back peel at 2-back. That gives a chance of a back peel at 3-back, and a healthy prospect of completion.

The *delayed leave* is more common now, giving a harder sextuple attempt, but a much longer shot for Blue. By doing so, Red should be more confident about retaining the innings, but every single peel in the next turn will be difficult.

Robert Fulford has done much to develop the tactics of the expert game, and has further adapted the sextuple leave. The downside of the delayed sextuple leave is that it gives Blue an easy break if the long shot is hit. The Fulford tactic is to peel each of Blue and Black through Hoop 1, then crosswire them and lay up as far away as possible. All of this is done in a short break of six hoops. Even if Blue hits, his manoeuvrability is reduced and there is a difficult chance of a break.

The tactic of peeling the opponent, or *popping*, is not yet mainstream. Achieving it in a game is left as a non-trivial exercise for the interested reader.

## The Coward's Peel

A less satisfactory peeling turn is often seen among inexperienced players of the advanced game. The game has been scrappy, and Red has crawled round to 1-back. Blue and Black, seeing the prospect of a lift, have taken position just outside Corner 3 and just outside Corner 1. When the lift comes, they can pick up a ball for a guaranteed rush. Red will struggle to dig out all four balls, and the innings will change hands immediately.

That is Blue and Black's plan. Red feels unable to thwart it, so lays up at 1-back, waits for his next turn, then peels

Red through with Yellow. The lift is saved, and everything looks good for Red.

It is a terrible tactic for both players. If Yellow takes on the peel, Red ends the turn mid-lawn, with a guaranteed free shot for Blue and/or Black. Even if that misses, Red still has a bad position. However, if Red/Yellow does anything else at all, Blue/Black looks a bit stupid. There are a number of options:

- Run 1-back with Red, rush Yellow to a safe boundary, attempt a roll approach to 2-back from the ball near Corner 1. There is an optional hoop with a wide join available. This scores 1-back, threatens 2-back, leaves Blue/Black with lots of work, and wastes the opponent's lift.
- Run 1-back with Red, rush Yellow towards 2-back, ignore the opponent, and see whether there is a chance of picking the ball up after the hoop. This option is a good confidence booster, bearing in mind your opponent is probably playing worse than you.
- Nominate to play Yellow instead, and lay a rush to Yellow's hoop. You have more opportunity to dig out a good position without the danger of an impending lift shot.

Take your pick. Your opponent has given you control, and it is up to you to choose what tactic to adopt. There is usually something better to do than a single peel, just to avoid a lift.

Once your opponent misses his first lift shot, and you start your second break, you want to get control of the balls as soon as possible. The longer it takes you to tidy up the four balls, the less chance you have of finishing, and the more chance you have of letting the opponent back in.

Peeling turns rarely appear from nowhere. The quality of your leave at the end of the previous turn is the key.

# CHAPTER 14

# FURTHER ADVANCED LEAVES

Once your opponent misses his first lift shot, and you start your second break, you want to get control of the balls as soon as possible. The longer it takes you to tidy up the four balls, the less chance you have of finishing, and the more chance you have of letting the opponent back in.

Peeling turns rarely appear from nowhere. The quality of your leave at the end of the previous turn is the key.

*Stephen Mulliner gives partner David Openshaw an aiming point.*

# The New Standard Leave

The *new standard leave*, or *NSL*, has evolved since the 1970s, but its general design remains intact. It is also called the *two-four leave*, and its current form started to appear about a decade ago. The original version, now relabelled the *MSL* – or *Maugham standard leave*, after its main devotee, David Maugham – has become rarer. As with the diagonal spread, the opponent's balls are placed in wired positions, but the NSL has an extra layer of elegance. Here is the layout:

- NSL: Red has just reached 4-back. Yellow is for Hoop 1, and is left a rush pointing at Blue, which sits a foot or two off the yardline. Black is an inch off the upright of Hoop 4, and has no backswing at Red and Yellow.
- MSL: Yellow is left a rush to Hoop 1. Red and Yellow are in a position on the East boundary so that Hoop 4 blocks a lift shot from A-baulk. Blue and Black are both an inch from the upright of hoops, and are wired from each other by the peg. What is more, both Blue and Black are wired from the end of the nearest baulk.

The shot to take, and it is more or less the only shot possible, is to shoot the long distance (a bit over twenty-five yards) down the East boundary at Yellow and Red. If Black takes that long shot and misses, it lands in Corner 4. Yellow plays the rush, and has an instant three-ball break. But if Blue plays the long shot and misses into the corner, the outcome is often even more severe:

- Yellow taps Red, and leaves it a yard in towards the lawn.
- Yellow takes off to Blue in Corner 4 and roquets it.
- Yellow plays a hard drive/stop shot, sending Blue to Hoop 2, landing level with Black.

David Maugham.

- Yellow rushes Black to Hoop 1, for an instant four-ball break. An immediate pivot swap after the hoop puts Black to the middle, bringing Red up the lawn to become the Hoop 3 pioneer. Yellow is all set for a standard TP on Red.

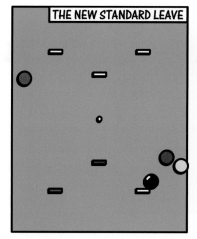

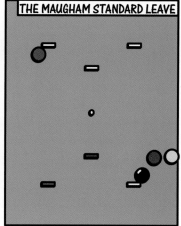

The new standard and Maugham standard leaves.

If you are good at playing big drive shots, this leave is a killer, giving an instant break for one moderately skilful shot. Even if your rush to Hoop 1 goes awry, you have the option of surrendering the break, and returning to Red with a perfect squeeze leave.

Clearly, the NSL, with Blue left out in the open, is much easier to set up than the MSL, in which placement of both Blue and Black is critical. The newer version has one other key benefit – Black's scoring prospects are much reduced if Blue is left close to the boundary and away from Black's next hoop.

## The Vertical Spread

The *vertical spread* is another hoop leave. For obvious reasons, this one is sometimes called the *five-six leave*. It is only really practical very late in the game, when you are giving your last lift. Red is for peg, and Yellow is for either 4-back or Penult. Yellow has a useful rush to 4-back, Blue is wedged on the wire of Hoop 6 and Black is wedged on the wire of Rover. Blue/Black's safe option is to lift Blue, and shoot down the long boundary. The heroic option is to accept probable defeat, play the shorter shot from A-baulk, and hope you hit. Against a strong opponent, it can be better to go down fighting.

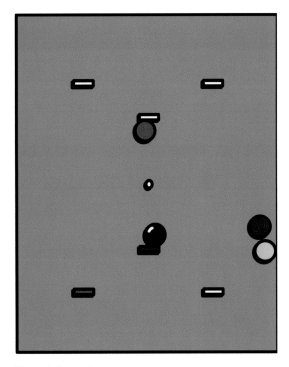

*The vertical spread.*

## Forcing Leaves

Maybe you are playing doubles against two players, where Black is very strong, and Blue is very weak. Alternatively, you may be playing an opponent whose Black ball is for Hoop 1, and whose Blue is for peg.

In each of these cases, you should try to force them to play Blue. Forcing leaves require you to improvise on the standard layouts. You can turn any of the standard leaves into a forcing one by taking a bit more care over which of Black and Blue goes in which position. In the diagonal spread, it is usually the ball near Hoop 2 that is lifted; in the NSL, the ball on the wire of Hoop 4; and in the vertical spread, the ball at Penult.

More generally, you can force a ball by placing it somewhere very useful – right in the jaws of your next hoop, or somewhere mid-lawn with your rush pointing straight at it. At the same time, you leave the other ball somewhere much less productive – slightly behind your break, or buried right in a corner.

---

### WHICH BALL SHOULD I PLAY?

At the start of your turn, there is usually a ball you would prefer to play. It is your opponent's job to leave you in a position where you are forced to play the other one. But, if you do get the choice, which is the better option?

Often, you will decide to take your shortest shot, or move the ball which is most helpful to your opponent. If not, you can base your decision on the clip positions of each ball.

If your forward ball is on 4-back, you will usually prefer to play the backward ball. There is no longer any danger of giving a contact, and you have more time to set up a good break (and a good leave). You can threaten to take a break to peg, and there is even the chance of a cheeky peel of your partner ball through 4-back. That would put you on Penult and peg, with all your opponent's lifts gone.

If your forward ball is on 2-back, it is less clear-cut. A break to peg with the backward ball is still a viable option; a break to peg with the 2-back ball might prove dangerous if you are worried about getting pegged out; alternatively, there is the option of scrabbling through two hoops with the 2-back ball, and going no further than 4-back. That gets you a clip on 4-back, and the chance of a punishing leave without needing to concede a lift. You have a good chance of a peeling break on the next turn.

If you have made less progress than that, it is usually better (tactically and psychologically) to finish what you have started. Play your forward ball and get it round to 4-back. If you have ground to a halt on Hoops 3 and 6, you can regain some momentum by improving your position to Hoops 3 and 4-back. At least then you have a fighting chance of a peeling break with the second ball.

## Scatter Leaves – Giving the Contact

Convention dictates that it is a bad idea to take your first ball all the way to peg. Given a contact, players are likely to get an immediate break, go round, and peg you out. Of course, there are ways of stopping them from doing that, and there are some basic principles if you are giving contact:

- Avoid both baulk lines. The contact is optional, and your opponent can choose a lift – and a rush – instead.
- The only safe place in baulk is *precisely* in Corner 1 or Corner 3.
- The only ball that can be easily placed in a corner is your own, in the final stroke of your turn.
- Never join up. Avoid putting your balls together, or near either of the opponent's balls.
- Keep all the balls as close to the boundaries as possible.

There are a number of types of scatter leave as shown below (experts are quite pedantic about the placement of each ball, so these are far from easy):

- A *standard scatter leave*. Your two balls, Red and Yellow, are in Corners 2 and 4. Blue and Black are six inches off the boundary. A shot from one to the other gives you a big double target.
- Very elegant, but not as good a leave as it looks. Purists insist that the corners should have Blue, Red, Black and Yellow in that order, to match the corner flags. Placing each ball precisely in each corner is very difficult indeed. Do not be surprised if your opponent just joins up and forces you straight back on to the lawn.

- *One for the professionals only.* Yellow is for Hoop 3 and is nearly but not quite through, Red is for peg, Blue and Black are both for Hoop 1. Yellow threatens to run Hoop 3 hard, and finish. It is shockingly hard to achieve.

Be warned. Contact leaves are all very well, provided you are prepared to exploit the immediate advantage they give you when your opponent fails to score. The longer the game drags on, the less that advantage is, and the more chance of your opponent pegging out your peg ball.

## Technicalities of Leaves

As soon as they approach 1-back, panic overcomes many improving players. Previously, with a handful of bisques, this hoop would have presented no threat. Now it symbolizes the point of no return – running 1-back gives a shortened shot to the opponent, who will punish any mistakes. This is the point at which a player's focus shifts away from maintaining the break, and towards building a defensive leave. Red must score the next two hoops, but – just as importantly – must present the opponent with a long and dangerous shot for each of Blue and Black, as well as setting up the best possible opportunity for Yellow to score in the turn after that.

The early pioneer at 2-back becomes much more critical in Advanced Play. Loading 2-back with a good pioneer immediately after Hoop 5 gives Red much more chance of success, as well as giving some extra control in the run-up to 3-back. There is an added benefit to this, too.

With almost any leave, the most important thing is for Red to leave Yellow with a good prospect of a break. Ideally, you

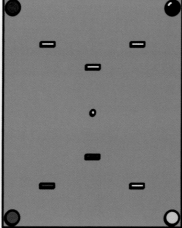
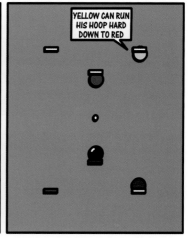

*Some scatter leaves.*

will be walking off the lawn after running 3-back, and Yellow will be set up precisely for an easy one-foot rush. If you want to achieve this reliably, you need to do the following:

- make sure that Red's last roquet of the turn is on Yellow, which should lead you to
- approach 3-back with Blue or Black, which means
- approach 2-back with Yellow; and
- approach hoop 5 with Yellow.

In effect, you should start thinking about your leave five hoops before the end of the turn. That needs less intensive planning than you might think. Nine times out of ten, Yellow will be your pioneer at Hoop 5 anyway. If you do need to swap balls around, Hoop 5 – the midpoint of the easy stretch of four hoops – is the easiest place to do this.

The important point – and it is the only real critical aspect of leave construction – is not to use your partner ball as a pioneer for your last hoop. Sorting this out early takes a load off your mind, but there is plenty of opportunity later to swap pivots, and ensure that the opponent's ball is down near 3-back.

## Laying the OSL

There is so much leeway in placing the balls for this that you can please yourself with its execution. The key point is to have all the balls somewhere in the inner rectangle before making 3-back, and to have Yellow somewhere between 3-back and the peg. Score your last hoop and put Blue and Black into their positions. Ideally, you will rush Yellow somewhere down towards Corner 4, and then leave both balls about a foot apart on the boundary.

If you get no rush on Yellow, it is not the end of the world – point your croquet stroke at the boundary, and play an almost-but-not-quite-straight roll as hard as you like. You can send both balls off in the croquet stroke. Your turn will end prematurely, but you should have the desired position of two balls just apart on the boundary.

Specifically, the ideal points for Yellow and Red are the following:

- Yellow and Red on the East boundary;
- Yellow six inches out of Corner 4 (which makes it slightly harder if Blue/Black hits);

*USA's Jerry Stark preparing a diagonal spread.*

- Red a foot north of Yellow (any closer makes a double from A-baulk, further apart leaves a double from B-baulk).

## Laying the Diagonal Spread

The diagonal spread does not need much early planning, except to make sure you have your partner ball (Yellow) as a good pioneer at 2-back. You need a rush on this ball after the hoop, so you should try to make sure of an easy approach and an easy hoop.

Just before 2-back, you should have a pivot ball (Black) in the middle of the lawn. Place this pivot somewhere on the south-east side, maybe about a yard or two from the peg. Do not be tempted to put it too close, as you are about to dislodge it from its position.

After 2-back, rush Yellow up towards the pivot. Tap Black closer, leaving it a foot or two south-east of the peg. Now take off to Blue, your 3-back pioneer. Now, Black is two feet south-east of the peg; Yellow is a yard away from Black, also somewhere south-east of the peg; and Red is approaching 3-back with Blue.

The next phase goes as follows:

- Make 3-back with a forward rush on Blue, to somewhere a bit short of Black.
- Play a hard stop shot, to send Blue towards Hoop 2, stopping short of Black. Blue should be only a yard or two into the lawn, and Red very close to Black.
- Tap Black into an exactly wired position.
- Use a very gentle take-off to fine-tune Black, and to drop Red behind Yellow.
- Rush Yellow to the boundary, and set up with a perfect rush for Yellow pointing at Blue and Black.

The two most critical shots in the leave are the rush on Yellow after 2-back, and the rush on Blue after 3-back. You need a perfect pioneer at each. If you are struggling with getting a ball down to 3-back, you could always swap pivots after 1-back – put Blue to the peg and send Black to 3-back. As long as you can get your angles right, it is a much shorter shot.

To summarize: after 1-back, put Black a couple of yards from where you eventually want it; after 2-back, nudge it so that it is accurate to the nearest foot; after 3-back, nudge it again so that it is in place to the nearest inch.

## Laying the NSL

Placement for the NSL is easier than for the MSL, as there is little precision required on the ball left at Hoop 2. For the purist, like me, who still clings to the Maugham version, the method is described below.

At 1-back: the leave is all about being able to play lots of little shots accurately. Again, you need to have Yellow as your 2-back pioneer. The key is to have all three of Red, Blue and Black together at 1-back.

Black, your pivot, is placed nearer than usual – a couple of yards south-west of 1-back. Approach the hoop from close up. If you play the shot from the right (nearer the corner), you will avoid getting the upright in your way. Place Blue a little bit behind the hoop, and on your right. As you come through gently, tap Blue. You can take off very finely to Black from this ball, nudging it a tiny amount into a position wired from baulk. Then rush Black towards 2-back, sending it to 3-back, stopping near Yellow.

Of course, if you are playing the NSL, this procedure requires little explanation. Come through 1-back, drop Blue somewhere about a yard off the boundary, and rush Black down the lawn.

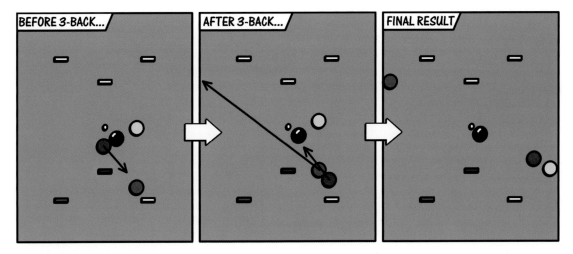

*Laying the spread.*

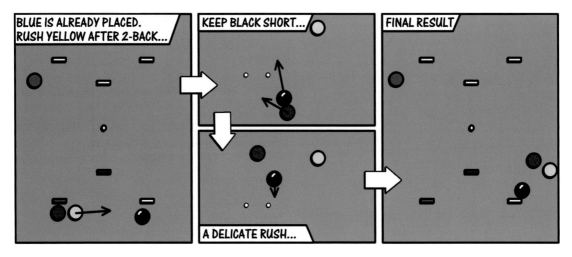

*Laying the NSL.*

At 3-back: Yellow needs to be a couple of yards on the far side of the hoop (north-east), as you approach with Black. To get it there, you ideally want a forward rush after 2-back. The position now is identical to the one at 1-back. You need to approach the hoop from very close and on the right-hand side, so that Black stops only just beyond the hoop, and Red can be guaranteed to come through gently. The only thing to worry about now is leaving Yellow a perfect rush, at the same time leaving no double target of Red and Yellow from either baulk.

Modernists should find everything much easier. There is still the shot to place Black on the wire of Hoop 4, but the placement of Blue should be simple.

### Aborted Leaves

Of course, things can always go wrong. The advantage of the NSL is that it can be salvaged, right up to the last moment. Whatever happens around 3-back, Blue is already in a good position. If it looks like you won't be able to place Black on the wire of the hoop, send it up the lawn, and hit Yellow. Roll both balls off the lawn, and you have created the old standard leave as a replacement.

Placing Black can still produce some worries, particularly when the ground near hoops is uneven. There are a number of options for making the best of a bad job.

*Black stops in the jaws of Hoop 4, where it is not rushable to Hoop 1.* This is a clear forcing leave – Blue will surely take the lift, and make you sort out the mess with Black. Black is useless to both of you, so your position is at least safe. To get yourself out of trouble, leave Yellow a rush on Red, pointing straight at Black. You have a chance of a *promotional cannon*, using Red to dislodge Black, and knock it into a playable position. For more on this (and other Advanced Play), *see* Chapter 16.

*Black misses the wire and lands south of Hoop 4.* Blue has a shot at Black, from just ten yards. Depending on the strength of your opponent, you might try a wide join. Leave Red and Yellow on the boundary, split by ten yards. Blue has some work to do, even if he hits Black. Consider leaving Red in the corner and Yellow beyond Black, rather than the other way round. Yellow's difficult position becomes useful if, and only if, Blue shoots at Black and misses. Yellow is guarding against Blue's shot, which may encourage a nervous opponent to try something different.

The third option is to acknowledge that the innings has been lost, and to play into a defensive position. Black and Yellow are both out of position, so bury Red into an inaccessible position. Try putting it on a distant boundary.

When things go wrong with the leave, take solace in the fact that you have at least scored. You may have lost the innings, but you might be just one hit-in, and one break away from winning.

### Laying the Vertical

In the way of things, the vertical spread is not so difficult to construct, provided you can set Blue and Black as very close pioneers to Penult and Rover. After Penult, you want to place an opponent ball on the wire of Hoop 6. You just need to continue your break through the last two hoops, but with Yellow kept as a very close pivot throughout. Approach Penult with Black from very close, putting Black beyond and to your left. Run the hoop, and tap Black *gently*, full into the wire of Hoop 6. Provided you play this from an angle, Black should stop where it is.

Two things can go wrong. First, you hit Black too hard, it bounces off the wire, and lands in an open position. Blue then has a ten-yard shot at a fully visible Black. Second, you

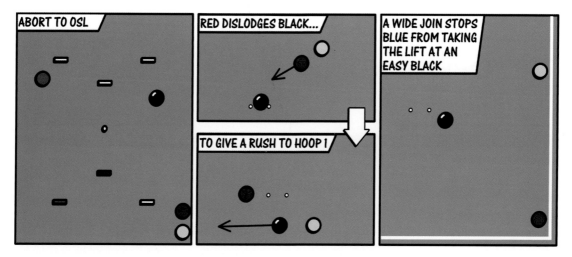

*What can go wrong with an NSL.*

could accidentally peel Black through. As long as you place Black from a slight angle, this should not be a serious risk.

Some people fret about leaving Black a couple of inches short, or not fully on the upright of Hoop 6. This should not be such a disaster. Blue would have to go several yards along the baulk line even to get a half-ball target at Black. You may be presenting a small target rather than no target at all, but it is still a very bad prospect for Blue.

So, you have placed Black at Penult, and you have rushed Yellow down towards Blue at Rover. The technique here is identical. Place Yellow a foot beyond the hoop, and a yard to your left. Approach Rover with a tiny full-roll, leaving Blue very close, and directly alongside. Tap it back into position in front of the hoop. A take-off to Yellow should nudge Blue into an unplayably awkward position. Take your rush on Yellow to the boundary.

Blue and Black should be both wired and hampered from each other and from you. For perfection, Black should be leaning on the left wire of Hoop 6, and Blue should be on the left wire of Rover. If you have achieved that, each ball should be completely hidden from any point on baulk (it hardly matters even if there is a quarter-ball visible – it is a tiny target to aim at).

The odds are that Black will lift, shoot down the boundary at you and miss. You now have a rush to 4-back, and Blue is in the jaws of Rover. As long as you can stagger through the next two hoops, you should finish. Make sure you start your next turn with a perfect rush.

## Summary

By the time you reach the stage in your croquet career when you get to play these more sophisticated leaves, you should be able to figure out most of the steps yourself. The key message is that you need to be in control right until the end of your first break, so you need to have Blue, Black and Yellow in the right order at the right hoops. As early as Hoop 5, you should be thinking about what you are going to do, and by 1-back you should be busy swapping Blue and Black round, in order to place the right ball in the right spot. The stroke play may need precision, but it is a thousand times more difficult if you have failed to plan correctly.

# THE OPENING

The outcome of the game is often determined by what happens in the first four shots. If you play your two balls on to the lawn carelessly, you risk giving your opponent an early initiative. Sometimes that is a gift that you cannot afford to make.

What you do depends on who you are playing against, and the standard of each player. If it is a handicap game, the weaker player probably wants to start using bisques immediately. It suits him to keep all the balls out in the open, where break-building opportunities are easiest. At the same time, the stronger player wants to play defensively, keeping to the boundaries, and waiting for an attacking chance.

Whoever wins the toss at the start of the game gets to choose whether they go first, or whether they have choice of colours. If you are receiving lots of bisques, the sooner you attack the better. Weaker players often opt to go second, with a view to playing a break as soon as all four balls are in play. However, if you are giving bisques and you win the toss, you will probably opt for the same choice – if only to confound your opponent.

In any other game, where there are few bisques or none at all, there is an advantage in going first. You get to influence the choice of opening, and you will probably have the first innings.

# The Standard Opening

There is one opening that is seen at all levels of the game, from handicap to advanced. The theory is that it gives nothing much away for either player. There is a small initial advantage for whoever goes first (Blue), but that is offset by a defensive response.

The sequence of shots goes as follows:

1 Blue is sent off the East boundary beyond Hoop 4, near the neutral fourth corner, and away from the first hoop.
2 Red is sent off the West boundary, a bit past Hoop 1. The length of this shot should be short enough for Black to be tempted, but long enough for it to be missable. This enticing shot is called a *tice*.
3 Black now has a choice. He can decline the tice, and join up with Blue, or he can shoot at the tice, landing near Corner 2 if he misses.

There are four outcomes for Yellow:

*Black has joined up.* Yellow shoots at the tice, and misses into Corner 2. Blue and Black are left to sort out the mess.

*Black has joined up.* Yellow shoots at the tice and hits. Yellow has the advantage, and can try and bring Black and Blue into play.

*Black shot at the tice and missed.* Yellow and Red join up, but progress will need some hard work.

*Black shot at the tice and hit.* Black can remove Red to a safer position, and has a clear advantage. Black's ideal outcome is the *Dream Leave* – a rush at Red threatening immediate control whatever Yellow does.

Essentially, the first person to hit Red has the initiative. Against a strong opponent, Red should leave a long tice, shortening it against a weaker shot. Conventionally, an average shot length is ten yards – a missable distance for most players. In a handicap game, the length could be much less.

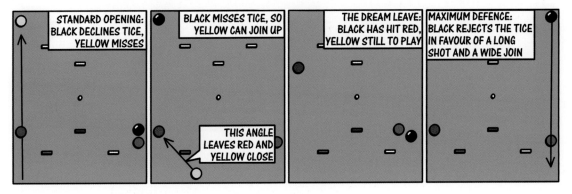

OPPOSITE: *Jonathan Kirby takes aim with his first ball.* ABOVE: *The standard opening.*

## Variations with Blue

Traditionally, Blue is placed on the East boundary level with Hoop 4. This should be far enough up the boundary to avoid giving Yellow a double target when Blue/Black join up. Had Blue been put, say, six inches outside Corner 4, that double target would be almost unavoidable. The further you go away from the corner, the less chance there is of leaving a large target for Red or Yellow.

Alternatively, Blue could be placed further north. There are players who aim their first shot just to the right of Hoop 4. When Blue is replaced, it is then fully wired from the end of A-baulk. Red is unable to shoot at it. There may be some merit to this shot when giving bisques in handicap. Otherwise, the logic in blocking a shot that nobody would take on anyway is not clear. Perhaps it is a layer of subtlety too far.

## Standard Opening (A-Class Variant)

The standard opening has lost some popularity with top players over recent years. Laying the tice forces Black into action – a confrontational warning shot from Red. The distance from A-baulk becomes critical:

* too short, and Black will shoot and hit;
* slightly further, and Black will shoot, but miss;
* further still, and Black will decline the shot, joining up with Blue.

Shooting at Blue from A-baulk leaves Blue/Black vulnerable after a hit-in from Yellow. In this variant, Black shoots at Blue from B-baulk. The chances of a Black hit are lower, but a miss earns an eight-yard wide join.

If Red plays the tice length just right, much of the Blue/Black initiative is dissipated. Red should be wary of placing the tice too far – playing beyond Yellow's reach allows Black to join tightly with impunity.

# The Attacking Bisque Opening

You have won the toss, and you have put the stronger player in first. He will probably start with the standard opening, but you can quickly reshape the layout:

* Blue plays to the West boundary beyond Hoop 4.
* Red plays into the middle of the lawn, between Hoop 5 and the peg. This gives you a ready-made pivot, and declares an intent to use bisques immediately.
* Black plays defensively, possibly into Corner 2.

*A long shot for James Death.*

- Yellow now takes bisques to set up a break. Start by shooting at either Blue or Black, and sending it to a useful position.

If Black has been sensible, you should be able to draw out a four-ball break for two bisques. If Black has greedily tried to hit something at this early stage, you have a good chance of setting up the break for one bisque only.

The advantage is yours, provided your budget allows you the luxury of two bisques for a set-up.

## Shock Openings

### The Bisque-Giver's Options

Handicap openings are often weighted against the stronger player, whose only option is to curl up into a defensive position, and hope that the bisques are put to wasteful use. The bisque-giver has several options. Against a small number of bisques, it is unlikely that there will be much action in the first five minutes. The standard opening is appropriate here.

Against a much weaker opponent, the waiting game is advisable – keep to the corners and be patient. If the weaker player is also very inexperienced, an improvised 'shock' opening is sometimes seen. It is not unknown for the stronger player to leave Blue as a one-inch shot (a *microtice*), just to see what Red's response is. Maybe Red will roll both balls into vulnerable positions, to Black's advantage. Sometimes, a naive Red might opt to ignore Blue altogether.

Novices are advised to think ahead to the fifth turn. What happens on the turn *after* Yellow's? In one avoidable trap, Blue goes to tice position, and Red half-recognizes this position, so plays to the East boundary. This is a familiar layout. Blue and Red are in the positions of the standard opening, but the other way round.

However, it is *much* worse, as Black joins up with Red.

Whatever Yellow does, Black has a one-foot roquet on Red next turn. Yellow's only hope is to hit in, or take an immediate bisque.

If you are the second player, it is generally wrong to play Red to a safe position, whatever the opening; when Black shoots at Red, Yellow is hard-pressed to dislodge it. Try putting Red in any of the spots marked.

### The Solomon Opening

This is the king of the shock openings, invented by Eric Solomon in the early 1980s. Whether in a handicap or an advanced game, it seems to work well, particularly early in the morning, when players are not used to the pace of the lawn.

- Blue goes to the East boundary.
- Red hits Blue, and plays a stop shot up the East boundary.
- Blue lands in tice position, about 10 yards off B-baulk, near Hoop 3.
- Red shoots into Corner 1.

Black now has the choice of taking croquet from Red, in the hope of approaching the hoop, or hitting Blue, in the hope of getting both Red and Blue safe. If Black is a weak opponent, either of those looks pretty good for Yellow. There is a tantalizing prospect of Black limping through two hoops before disastrously breaking down with three balls in B-baulk, and with Yellow still to play his shot.

The opening relies on Red's second turn hit-in. Neither that, nor Black's immediate collapse, are guaranteed. The opening's strength is as much in its entertainment as in its tactical integrity. That, of course, is not necessarily a criticism.

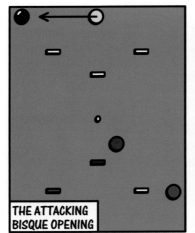

THE ATTACKING BISQUE OPENING

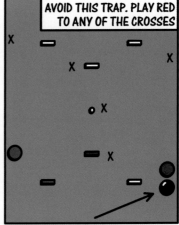

AVOID THIS TRAP. PLAY RED TO ANY OF THE CROSSES

*Openings for handicap play.*

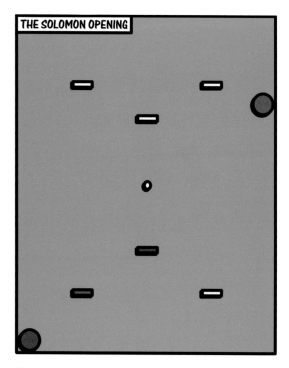

**THE SOLOMON OPENING**

*The Solomon opening.*

# Advanced Openings

### The Duffer Tice

Croquet in the 1920s was dominated by a group of Irish players, principally Duff Matthews. He is credited with the invention of the *Duffer tice opening*, which has become the mainstream opening of the advanced game. The start – Blue goes to the East boundary; Red is placed close to Hoop 6 – forces a more attacking start, and gives Black something to think about. The outcome is uncertain:

*Black shoots gently at Red, and hits.* The outcome is similar to a hit tice in the standard opening, and Black can easily set up the Dream Leave. A good outcome for Black.

*Black shoots gently at Red, and misses.* Yellow is faced with two balls close together between Hoop 6 and the peg, and has the chance of aiming at a double target. Not good for Black.

*Black shoots hard at Red, and hits.* Shooting hard gives a much better chance of hitting, with the possibility of a lucky rush towards Hoop 1. If not, Black has the same chance of the Dream Leave. Either way, a big advantage for Black.

*Black shoots hard at Red, and misses.* Black lands in A-baulk; Yellow automatically receives a rush to Blue, and Red is in the lawn. Instant break for Yellow, and disaster for Black.

*Black takes a long shot at Red from Corner 3.* This very

defensive response is much out of fashion. It gives the (faint) chance of hitting, and setting the Dream Leave. More likely, it just leaves balls scattered around the lawn. Prepare yourself for a slow and very dour game.

*Black ignores Red altogether, and joins up.* If Yellow were to hit Red on the fourth turn, a close join would look grim for Black. Often it is best for Black to play for a wide join, by shooting down the long East boundary towards Blue. It is a good choice if you do not rate Yellow's chance of hitting.

### The Anti-Duffer

The Duffer tice is not a new opening, but it has evolved a great deal over the last ten years, among the current set of risk-taking players. As Black has become more confident of hitting, so Red has lengthened the placement of the tice. Once, people would put Red a yard short of Hoop 6; now it often goes a yard or more beyond. That is something that does not suit Black, so a new leave, the *anti-Duffer*, has recently appeared. Its function is to stop Red from laying the Duffer tice.

Blue plays first, but instead of playing to the East boundary, it is played a yard short. Blue is rushable for whichever player makes the first roquet, so Red is forced into a more defensive position. There is some logic to this for the very best players in the world, but only time will tell whether it becomes a mainstream opening for others within the advanced game.

### The Corner 2 Opening

The *Corner 2 opening* favours a confident Red:

1  Blue goes to the East boundary;
2  Red shoots at Corner 2.

This one should worry Black, as it is a clear declaration of intent. This opening says, 'I have played Red into a very defensive position, because I'm about to attack.'

Red is placed safe, because Yellow is about to shoot at Blue and Black. Black would be well advised not to leave his two balls close enough together to award Yellow a double target.

Technically, it is important that Red is not placed exactly in the corner. It should be shot to a point about six inches south. Skilled rushers can exploit balls that lie tight in corners, and a corner ball often concedes an instant break (for more on this, see Chapter 16).

### Corner 2 Variation

There is a simple way of punishing an over-ambitious Red. Here, Red fancies the shot at Blue on the East boundary:

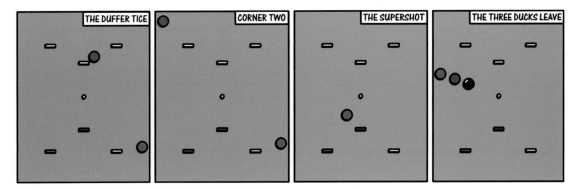

*Advanced-level openings.*

1 Blue goes to the East boundary;
2 Red shoots at Blue and misses;
3 Black goes to Corner 2.

Yellow now needs to hit, or lose the innings.

## The Supershot Opening

Another newly developed opening is the *supershot*. Over the last few years, this has become dominant among some players, although, arguably, it is more dominant than it deserves to be.

*Reg Bamford is at the top rank of supershot players.*

The theory is this. Players at the very top of the game (of whom there are very few) have a very good chance of hitting any ball at any distance. In the opening, there is usually no safe hiding place for their opponent. So, instead of placing Blue safe on the boundary, it is placed right in the middle of the lawn. Irrespective of where Red plays on the second turn, Black threatens to hit, assemble a break, and go to 4-back before Yellow is even in play.

Convention, such as it is, is that Blue is placed somewhere around Hoop 5. Maybe it is slightly – even a couple of yards – further, but it is typically on the side of the lawn nearer Hoop 1. Then, once Black hits Red, Blue is useable as a Hoop 1 pioneer.

To fight against the supershot opening, there are limited options: Red can shoot gently at Blue, which threatens to leave a double target; Red can shoot hard, which is disastrous unless Red hits; or Red can hide, and hope that Black misses. The best place for this is the long point just south of the peg on the East boundary, where Black has an eighteen-yard shot from the end of either baulk.

The shortcoming of the supershot opening is not the tactic itself, but its widespread adoption. If the person playing the opening does not threaten to hit on the third turn, and does not threaten to play an all-round three-ball break, then they are committing their Blue ball to the middle of the lawn for no reason. Imitating the tactics of experts is all very well, but you must be able to follow it up with the technical expertise.

### The Three Ducks

Partly a leave and partly an opening, the *three ducks* opening follows on from the supershot. Fast-forward a few minutes:

*The ideal outcome: an early initiative at Hoop 1.*

- Blue puts out a supershot ball.
- Red plays on to the lawn (wherever).
- Black hits Red, gets a break and goes to 4-back.

Black now lays a leave. Yellow is yet to be brought into play, so the opening has not yet finished. However, Blue threatens to win next turn, with a fifth turn TP. Red and Yellow will each have had one shot in the entire game. Yellow could be about to have his first, and last, shot.

Blue, Red and Black are in a straight line pointing at the peg, with a yard between them. Yellow cannot make a double from either baulk. Missing the (slightly) shorter shot from B-baulk should lose Yellow the game immediately; the longer shot into Corner 2 gives Blue a harder time.

### 26 OR BUST

The supershot opening may not be an everyday tactic for most players, but there are circumstances in which it might be sensible.

You are a weak player in your first big event, and you have been drawn against the World Champion in the first round. Face facts – you are about to lose. All you can do is to play aggressively. Play each turn with the shot you want to play, and do not lose any sleep over what is going to happen if you miss.

Against a very, very good player, playing defensively is usually the wrong tactic. Wide joins and balls hidden in corners are more of an obstacle for the weaker player than for the champion. Shoot at balls as though it is your last shot, and experiment with the supershot opening.

*Chris Clarke at Cheltenham.*

# CHAPTER 16

# ADVANCED TECHNIQUE

The preceding chapters give you as much tactical know-how as you are ever likely to need. But that is not the end of the story. A few essential – and a few rather esoteric – techniques that may prove useful have not been covered. So, pick up your mallet and read on about jump shots, trick shots and multi-ball collisions.

Most problems in the game of croquet can be resolved by tactical planning. Sometimes, however, the best plan in the world will not help you out of difficulty. Below is a com-pendium of advanced shots, ranging from the common to the bizarre, obscure and whimsical. Some of these are use-able on a daily basis; some may remain unused for most, if not all, of your playing career.

This is not, by any means, an exhaustive list, but the adventurous and ambitious player may find some comfort here – if you have encountered an unrecoverable problem, someone somewhere may have found a solution that you could apply.

*Danny Hunnycutt plays a sweep shot.*

# The Jump Shot

The subject of jump shots clearly complicates matters but, as your play improves, the jump shot becomes indispensable. There are three scenarios in which jumping becomes important: failed peels, failed hoop approaches, and hitting an unhittable ball. Generally, the use of a jump means that something has gone wrong. It is a lifesaver.

## When to Jump

**Angled Hoop** Here you are at your hoop. You have just overhit the approach, and the hoop is almost impossible. If you can get your ball airborne, you can make the ball spin, which might carry it through the hoop, and you will be hitting the hoop at a point where it is slightly wider. Hoops are often set in the ground so that the uprights point slightly inwards. There might be a sixteenth of an inch clearance at ground level, but an eighth of an inch nearer the crown.

    **A Blocked Hoop** Consider two possibilities. Red has attempted to peel Yellow through Rover, and Yellow has missed badly. Red's path is blocked, and the only chance of continuing is to jump over the top of the other ball. The second possibility is that Yellow has just crept through – Red can run the hoop, but wants to roquet Blue and Black before Yellow. Again, Red wants to clear the other ball.

    **The Half-Jump** In the third scenario, Yellow has stuck mid-jaws and Red still needs the hoop and the peel. Instead of clearing Yellow completely, Red can play a *half-jump*, or *drag-jump* – a shot which jumps Yellow, but does not quite get enough height. Red lands on top of Yellow, scoring the hoop, and dragging the peelee through at the same time.

    **The Over-Jump** This is a bit of an expert's shot, for lovers of spectacle. You are crosswired, and you do not

*Jumping through a hoop.*

fancy any of your long shots. Rather than a dainty little hop over a ball, you hoist Red two feet in the air – straight over the top of the hoop, smashing right into the Yellow on the far side.

## How to Jump

The technique for all jump shots is the same – hit down to squeeze the ball into the ground, and pull the mallet out of the way quickly enough for the ball to spring upwards. Here is an itemized list of what you need to do:

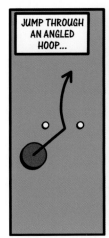
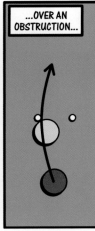

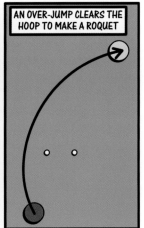

JUMP THROUGH AN ANGLED HOOP...

...OVER AN OBSTRUCTION...

...OR TO AVOID ROQUETING YELLOW.

A HALF-JUMP SKIMS YELLOW

AN OVER-JUMP CLEARS THE HOOP TO MAKE A ROQUET

*Reasons to play a jump shot.*

- Check the shot is possible. If you are too close to the obstacle (hoop or ball), you will not be able to get enough lift into the Red ball. As a general guide, anything closer than six inches threatens to be a fault (Red could bounce back on to the mallet). Six inches is OK for a half-jump, and twelve inches is enough room for a full jump. If you must try to jump over a hoop, you will struggle to get the height if you are much closer than four feet. What is more, you are likely to sail clean over the top of Yellow if it is nearer than six feet on the far side.
- Stalk the shot very carefully. Whatever your reason for playing a jump, there is either a difficult hoop shot, or a difficult roquet. This is not going to be a normal swing, so you need to make sure your shoulders point in the right direction.
- Hold the mallet very firmly. There is a danger of mishitting, and skewing the mallet. You want to exploit the natural whippiness of the shaft, so hold it near the top. You are going to tilt the mallet forwards, so your hands should be in the positions you would adopt for a half-roll. I like to use a standard grip, with the hands together, and about six inches from the top of the mallet, and bracing the back of the mallet with the thumb of my upper hand.

LEFT: *The half-jump – Red has skimmed Yellow, and both balls score the hoop.*

BELOW: *The over-jump.*

- Control the tilt of the mallet with your foot positioning. If your standard stance has Red six inches in front of your toes, you should have your toes level with Red for a half-jump, and Red level with your insteps for a full-jump. For an over-jump, Red should be behind your heels. That will cause you to hit well down on to the ball.
- Focus on hitting Red. For any jump, you will hit somewhere above the horizontal. Just make sure you make a clean contact.
- Punch the Red. With a clean punch, the follow-through becomes less important. You want the ball to spring sharply off the face of the mallet. If you play the stroke half-heartedly, it will not work.
- Get the mallet out of the way. This becomes an issue for big jumps, when you are hitting harder and at a steeper angle. If you do this wrong, the mallet will dig a hole in the turf, which is a breach of etiquette, as well as being illegal. At the point of impact with Red, tense your toes. That lifts you slightly on to tiptoe; the arc of the swing changes, and the mallet should stay clear of the ground. It is easier said than done, of course, and that is why over-jumping is not a mainstream shot.

Until you become proficient, never practise jumping anywhere where you can cause serious damage. Find a practice area off the lawn, and see if you can hop one ball over another.

*The over-jump stance. The ball is behind the heels.*

## Alternative Technique

All is not lost if the standard centre-style jump shot does not suit you. The trick is to do two things that seem illogical: play the shot backwards, and use only one hand.

Hold the mallet half-way down, with one hand only, as if you were using a hammer. Stalk the ball in the opposite direction from normal – stand by your target and walk along the line towards Red. Follow the rules as above, and hit Red with a good crisp punch.

There is some genuine merit to this method, and it is worth practising for anyone who struggles with jump shots. Even with just one hand, some people can play over-jumps like this with nonchalant ease.

# Cannons

## General Principles

A clever player can exploit balls in corners, and quickly turn a negative position into a productive break. The trick is to create a *cannon* – a position where three balls rest on the same spot. If Red has rushed Yellow somewhere where it lies touching Blue, Red's next shot can be played as a croquet on Yellow, with a simultaneous roquet (usually a big rush) on Blue. If you know how to play it, that is a very powerful tool for bringing an awkward Blue ball into play, often delivering an instant break position.

*An alternative jumping method.*

A three-ball group could occur in the middle of the lawn, but it is very unlikely. Usually a cannon will happen when Blue is on the yardline. Here is how a cannon might arise:

- Red rushes Yellow at Blue.
- Yellow is brought on a yard, and is found to be touching Blue.

- Yellow may be placed in any position on the yardline, so long as it is touching Blue. The position of Yellow is now fixed, and it may not be moved again.
- Blue is now removed.
- Blue and Red are placed anywhere in contact with Yellow, as long as Blue and Red are not touching each other.

*A yardline cannon.*

Red is now ready to play the croquet stroke on Yellow.

## Some Common Cannons

Some cannons occur more frequently than others. You can live your whole life never needing to arrange the ball for a mid-lawn cannon, but yardline cannons occur often, especially at the higher levels of the game. Most common of all are corner cannons, which threaten to give an immediate break.

**Corner 1 to Hoop 1** Red has rushed Yellow at Blue, which is in Corner 1. Red needs to get Yellow to Hoop 2, and rush Blue towards Hoop 1. This can be done in one stroke, as a hard drive sending Yellow to Hoop 2. At the same time, Red cuts Blue, rushing it towards Hoop 1. Result: Yellow two yards from Hoop 2; Blue one yard from Hoop 1; Red ready to croquet Blue.

Lining up cannons is a matter for experience. The gap between Red and Blue in this cannon is about one and a quarter inches. Of course, you may not produce a tape measure each time you line the shot up – that would be illegal. You will have to work it out by eye, although there is nothing to stop you trying to measure the gap in widths of fingers or gaps between knuckles.

Line the balls up, and play a hard drive. You might need a few attempts in practice before you have a result you are happy with, so do not expect perfection if your first try happens to be in an important match.

**Corner 2 to Hoop 1 – A Take-Off Cannon** This is a long take-off, nudging Yellow out of the corner towards Hoop 2, while playing a hard cut-rush on Blue to Hoop 1. The trick is to play the shot so that Red goes out of play. In any normal croquet stroke, that would be the end of Red's turn, unless Red makes a roquet or runs a hoop. That is the case here – a take-off from Yellow combined with a cut-rush on Blue. Hit hard, and this should send Blue right towards the first hoop. It goes without saying that you must not miss the cut-rush.

**Corner 4 to Hoop 1 – A Wafer Cannon** There are a couple of ways of playing the cannon from the fourth corner to Hoop 1. Very few people play the old version, which has a perfect result, but is extremely difficult. Instead, most settle for a *wafer cannon*, which gives a perfect Blue and an adequate Yellow. Get to know this technique. If you are starting a break with a cannon, it is probably going to be in this quarter of the lawn. No matter where you are on any of the boundaries, the wafer is often seen as the cannon of preference for getting all the balls into play.

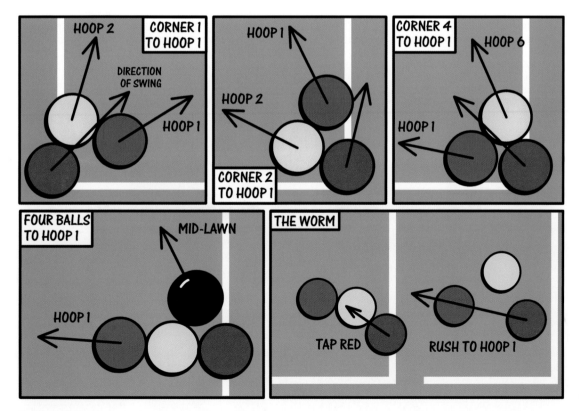

*Five types of cannon.*

Red, Yellow and Blue are placed in a triangle, with Red almost but not quite in contact with Blue. If you point Red-Blue a couple of yards south of Hoop 1, Red-Yellow should point somewhere between Hoops 3 and 6. Play a drive, hitting Red hard somewhere into the middle of Yellow and Blue. Yellow will land somewhere mid-lawn, near Hoop 6; Blue should be rushed towards Hoop 1.

The wafer cannon can be adapted for other situations, depending on where you are. You can change the orientation of the balls, or you can swing the mallet in a different direction to give a very thin contact on either Blue or Yellow. It has become a sort of universal cannon for all sorts of situations. If you plan to collect Black from a distant boundary, try rushing Blue directly at Black rather than your hoop. Play it right and it is the path to an instant four-ball break. You face an interesting prospect if you have a cannon on Blue and Yellow, where Black is in a (reasonably close) corner – a wafer allows you to rush Blue into the corner, and have cannons on two successive strokes.

**Four-Ball Cannon**   If you are so impatient for the four-ball break, the *four-ball cannon* is the top prize. This is such a strong position that any decent opponent should do anything in their power to prevent it from arising. Because it is so rare, many players who see it for the first time do not know what to do. For those who know the secret, it is an instant four-ball break.

Instead of having three balls in contact, you have all four.

The position is most likely to occur very early in the game, and somewhere on the boundary near Hoop 4.

The trick here is to place Red, Yellow and Blue in a dead straight line pointing directly at Hoop 1. Red and Black cannot touch, so put Black touching Yellow, and a millimetre away from Red. Play a hard drive shot from here and the following will happen:

- Red will croquet Yellow towards Hoop 4.
- Red will rush Black.
- Blue (unroqueted) will go directly to Hoop 1.

Take croquet from Black, and you have a ready-made pioneer. You have a wide choice of positions in which to place the Black. Most people favour placing it north of Yellow – Red rushes it towards the peg, from where it can be split to Hoop 2 as you go to Blue. I prefer to put it southside – Red rushes Black off the lawn, to give you a big straightish drive going to Blue. Please yourself and play it how you like: it is one shot and it is giving you two pioneers and a pivot.

There is a variant, which produces a similar result. Here you have a three-ball cannon with Red, Yellow and Blue, but Black is just a few feet away. Align the cannon as a straight line towards Hoop 1, and play a stop shot. Red will barely move, and Black will remain in easy hitting distance. There is a bigger split shot to play here, but you again get everything into play, with an unroqueted pioneer at your hoop.

*Chris Clarke prepares for a Corner 2 cannon.*

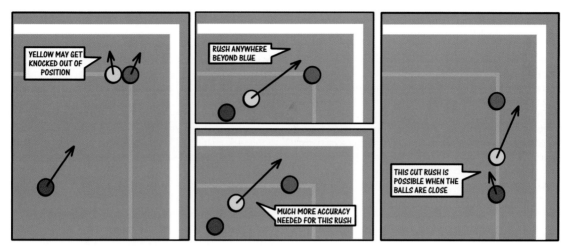

*Creating a cannon opportunity.*

**The Worm** The *worm cannon*, or *banana cannon*, is frowned upon by experts. Red, Blue and Yellow are put in an almost straight line. You then hit Red gently. Yellow squirts out a few inches the side, leaving Red a rush on Blue. Take the rush, and Yellow stays where it is.

Maybe that suits you. Maybe you want to leave Yellow behind, and rush Blue to the far side of the lawn. The complaint of the experts is that it is a lost opportunity – there are usually more ambitious and effective outcomes. Think carefully instead about the wafer, which probably has a much better effect.

**The Superworm** The *superworm cannon*, an Australian invention, is a lively one for the flamboyant exhibitionist and produces an extraordinary effect. Here is how it works. Line Red, Blue and Yellow up in an almost straight line, as if for a worm cannon. The middle ball will be slightly offset. Play the severest pass-roll you can manage, along the exact line of the front (Yellow) and back (Red) balls. Blue, the middle ball, goes forward about eight yards. Red and Yellow will move together, scooting across the lawn two feet apart, but never quite touching, in a sort of travelling dolly-rush position.

This has to be seen to be believed. Practise it, and you will be surprised by the amount of pass required to get the Red far enough. If you do manage to master the shot – it certainly is not easy – it becomes a universal cannon, producing an adequate result from anywhere on the boundary. There are usually better, and more reliable, ways of bringing three balls into play, but none of them is as entertaining.

## The Cannon in Practice

A-class players will often deliberately engineer cannon shots, and can use them to construct an instant break opportunity. If nothing else, the cannon gives a dolly rush to your hoop,

whilst getting the third ball off the boundary. If your opponent is very good at rushes, do not give them that chance.

The easiest way to give yourself a cannon opportunity is when there are two balls – Yellow and Blue – in contact in a corner. Roquet either one, and they will *probably* come back on the yardline in the same positions. Multiple ball contacts are inherently unpredictable, and there remains a chance that the two balls could rock apart. If there is a millimetre gap between them when you come to take croquet, your advantage is lost. Bear in mind, too, that this is a shot you really cannot afford to miss. Your failed ambitions will have gifted the cannon to Blue.

If Blue is tight in a corner, you have an area about four feet across into which to rush Yellow. Play it right, and your croquet stroke on Yellow will be a cannon. This is why A-class players always prefer to put balls to defensive positions six inches outside a corner. The chances of profiting from a ball away from the corner are much less.

Be wary of joining up with the opponent on the yardline, in case you leave three balls very close. There is a chance of Red playing a tiny cut-rush on Blue to somewhere behind Yellow. The closer the balls are, the greater the chance of a cannon.

In summary, the following positions are vulnerable to giving a cannon:

- two balls in contact in a corner;
- a ball tight in a corner, when there is a chance the opponent might get a rush at it; and
- three balls very close together on a yardline.

In addition, four balls together on the yardline could be lethal. Avoid any of these scenarios if you think your opponent knows how to play the shot.

# Hampered Shots

With tight hoops, there is a danger that your ball will not come through far enough. Your next shot is *hampered*, since you are not allowed enough backswing to hit the ball cleanly. All sorts of things can go wrong here, resulting in a *fault*, and an immediate end to your turn.

You can improvise ways of playing a hamper, depending on where the balls lie. Lack of a backswing might make you kneel down, holding the mallet near the base of the shaft, with your arms reaching through the hoop. That might give you some control, and you can play a short, sharp punch. Otherwise, there are a few nifty trick shots that might prove useful.

## The Horizontal Sweep

This has become the default way of playing hampered shots for most players. Keep your hands apart, with your lower hand near the mallet head. Crouch down, hold the mallet horizontally, and rest the base of it against the wire of the hoop. Now push forward with the lower hand, sliding the mallet head along the hoop.

Apart from the danger of a push shot, which is illegal, there are three avoidable faults to think about: do not rest the mallet shaft or your hands on the ground; do not rest your arms on your legs; and do not let your hand touch the head of the mallet while you are playing.

*A referee watches as Mark Avery plays a sweep shot.*

The advantage of the shot is that the hoop steadies the mallet, and the shot needs no backswing. As you swing, bring your lower arm in towards your body. The mallet will swing inwards, and shots that appear unhittable become possible.

## Ricochet

I was shown this novelty shot one day, and had cause to use it the very next day. It only works on a fast lawn with firm hoops, but it saved me a game that I would otherwise have lost.

You have just come through a hoop by a tiny amount. There is a ball a foot away, but there is no way you can swing at it. Bounce Red off the wire of the hoop, and try to ricochet on to the other ball. You cannot afford to go hard, or you will risk a fault when the Red comes off the wire.

## The Hammer Shot

The *hammer shot* is a ghastly stroke, which is very much out of favour. Stand with your back to the target, and hit down on to Red. The theory is that, by facing backwards and hitting towards yourself, you can see what is happening on the backswing. However, it is almost always a push shot. You need to hit sharply so that Red bounces. If it does not, it is bound to be illegal.

*The hammer shot.*

## THE FOOT SHOT, AND OTHER ILLEGALITIES

The foot shot is a very recent innovation, which has resulted in a quick amendment to the Laws (it was outlawed during 2008). It involved using the foot as a guide for the shot, by sliding the mallet head along the instep of the striker's shoe. The striker needs virtually no backswing, and, in theory, it allows all shots to be played dead straight. It was considered to be an undesirable development, so has been quickly dropped.

Cheating is almost unheard of in croquet, and it is a matter of personal pride to declare any mistake to your opponent. But that does not stop inventive players from getting what legal advantage they can. That has given rise to a long battle between the game's lawmakers and its more imaginative would-be lawbreakers. Previous outlawed shots include kicking the mallet (useful for hitting the ball very, very hard, but with absolutely no backswing); the cue shot (striking the ball through the hoop with the tip of the shaft); and holding the head of the mallet with the hands. This last style of play is left as an exercise for the reader, just to see how much undeserved control it provides.

Just do not bother. The hammer shot is never the best option, and is frequently the worst.

# Before the Hoop

When you are in front of a hoop, but very close and at an angle, there is a serious danger of playing a fault. The commonest fault is a *crush* (mallet, ball and hoop form a sandwich, with all three momentarily in contact – effectively becoming a push stroke).

## The Swipe

There are two ways of avoiding a crush shot: hit more gently, or swing the mallet in a different direction. In the swipe shot, the mallet points in the direction of the shot at the exact point of impact, but moves in a different direction throughout the rest of the swing.

You are at your hoop, but you are tight up against the upright. You have just about got the angle to hit Red into the jaws, but you cannot hit it hard enough to get it through.

*The swipe shot.*

Stalk the ball along the line that would hit Red into the jaws, but adopt the stance and grip for a full-roll. Instead of swinging forwards, swing across your body, driving with the lower hand.

This can be played with a fair amount of force, provided you have the angle right. By the time Red is in contact with the far upright, the mallet head is travelling somewhere towards your shoulder. If you play it right, Red will run the hoop by several feet, arcing round with lots of side-spin.

The downside is that the shot only works from one side. You are swinging sideways with your lower hand moving across your body. The left-hander can run impossible hoops hard when Red sits near the left wire, but will be at a loss when it is tight on the right side.

## Vertical Shots

Rather than swinging forwards, and threatening a crush, or sideways, by playing a swipe, there is a family of shots in which the mallet is swung vertically downwards. The mallet never moves closer to the hoop, and the crush is avoided.

One such stroke is the *freefall shot*, with the mallet held above the ball, tilted forwards and then dropped on to the ball. The back edge of the ball receives a glancing blow from the mallet, the ball rolls forwards, and the mallet falls backwards. The striker then catches the mallet. That is the theory – it is a shot that has no follow-through, so it is impossible to play a crush shot. The shot is useless, however, completely ineffective, and likely to damage the grass. Unsurprisingly, it is illegal, since it is tantamount to throwing the mallet at the ball. Nevertheless, it does address the possibility of mallet and ball moving in opposite directions, in order to avoid crushing.

The *guillotine shot* is slightly better, but extremely difficult to achieve. The principle is the same – the angled mallet falls quickly and vertically down on to the ball. The only difference is that you do not let go. Because you cannot see what you are doing, there is a real danger of not stopping the mallet soon enough, and smashing it down into the surface of the lawn. Damage to the grass should be avoided at all costs.

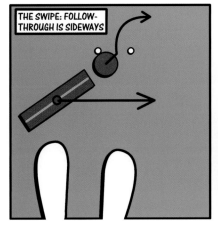

*Avoiding follow-through.*

## THE MAD AXEMAN

The bizarre and alarming Mad Axeman shot is really only for completists who insist on collecting such things. It is almost certainly illegal in any number of ways, and will probably result in a lifetime ban for the perpetrator from any club at which it is played. It first surfaced in a Test Match in the 1980s, and referees were so astonished that no one really knew what to do, so it was declared legal. A few weeks later, two members of the International Laws Committee convened a hasty meeting to discuss a ruling. In demonstrating the shot, the Chairman picked up a nearby mallet, which shattered as he played the stroke. Only then did he discover that he had destroyed a prized possession beglonging to his Vice-Chairman.

Red wishes to run his hoop hard, but his ball sits in contact with one of the wires. The player stands level with the hoop, facing away from the direction he wishes the ball to go. The mallet is raised above the head, and brought down as hard as possible, so that the lower part of the shaft hits the crown of the hoop. The ground around the hoop ripples with the shock, and the mallet flexes with the contact. If the mallet head is still attached to the shaft, it then hits Red. At this point, the hoop, bent well away from the vertical, is nowhere near Red, which rockets through. Now, the hoop twangs back into an upright position. If the mallet has survived this long, there is a good chance that the recoil from the hoop will finally end its productive life.

That is the theory. This shot will damage equipment (probably), the lawn (certainly), and your wrists (quite possibly). Do not even think about playing it.

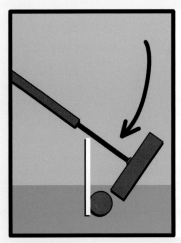

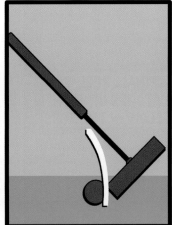

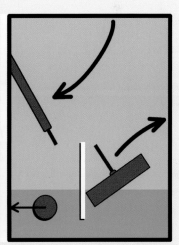

*The Mad Axeman.*

The current innovation in this field is the *Pirie poke*, invented in the Australian town of Port Pirie by Vern Potter and John Riches. It involves hitting the ball in a forward direction – towards a hoop – while the mallet moves backwards, away from the hoop.

The shot is very similar to the guillotine, except that the striker kneels down with a horizontal mallet. For visibility, your eyeline should be right over the mallet head, which is flicked on to the ball by a twist of the wrists. The ball receives a glancing blow as the mallet travels down and backwards, away from the hoop, and towards the striker's body.

This shot is so new that it has yet to find much popularity. There are four big worries: first, there is a serious danger of an airshot that fails to hit Red; second, there is a chance of lawn damage; third, if the contact is not right, you risk playing a push shot; and fourth, it is a shot that just does not seem to be very reliable.

When it works, it is possible to cause Red to jump several inches vertically, before rolling through the hoop. It is a pleasing little trick shot, and one that may have some merit, although it is certainly not a novice's technique. Because there is no conventional backswing at all, there may be some use in difficult hampered positions behind hoops. It remains to be seen whether the poke achieves any of the success of the sweep.

## The Aspinall Peel

Nigel Aspinall, one of the dominant figures in English croquet in the 1970s and 80s, devised this neat solution for peeling hoops from impossible angles.

The *Aspinall peel* is played as a croquet stroke from an acute angle. The peelee lands in the jaws of the hoop and stops. A split second later, the striker's ball catches up with it and rehits it. The hoop is scored.

The shot is only possible from an angle where the peeled ball (Yellow) will land in position. The croquet stroke should be lined up so that Yellow will hit the opposite upright of the hoop dead centre. Various schools of thought suggest playing it as a stop shot or a big roll. As with all trick shots, practise first. See what is most effective.

## The Bounce Approach

You have rushed Yellow into the jaws of your hoop. You have now got the easiest approach you will ever play. You can place Red in contact with Yellow, and play a tiny tap of the ball. Red has had an approach shot from a quarter of an inch away. Guaranteed approach, guaranteed hoop and guaranteed straight rush forwards.

Suppose your rush on Yellow had dropped a tiny distance behind the hoop. You place Red in contact with Yellow, but

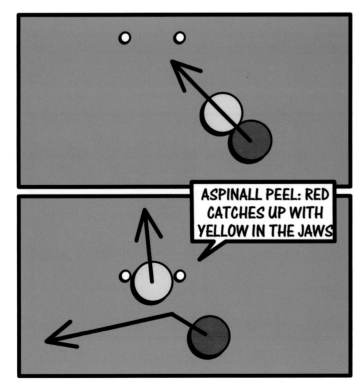

*The Aspinall peel.*

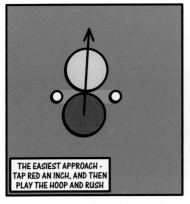 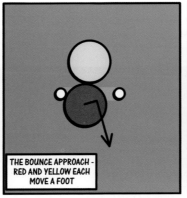 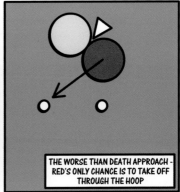

THE EASIEST APPROACH - TAP RED AN INCH, AND THEN PLAY THE HOOP AND RUSH

THE BOUNCE APPROACH - RED AND YELLOW EACH MOVE A FOOT

THE WORSE THAN DEATH APPROACH - RED'S ONLY CHANCE IS TO TAKE OFF THROUGH THE HOOP

*Approaching the hoop from impossibly close positions.*

Red is sticking out a very small amount through the hoop. You have picked up Red, and placed it part way through the hoop. That means you will not be able to score unless you hit Red back on to the playing side first.

This is a neat trick. Place Red in contact with Yellow, wedging Red tight against one upright. A sliver of Red will be visible behind the hoop. Play a gentle shot so that Red hits the opposite upright of the hoop. Yellow will move forward six inches, and Red will bounce off the wire, and back out of the hoop, by about the same amount. That is your perfect hoop approach.

### The 'Worse Than Death' Approach

There is a position immediately behind a hoop called the *'worse than death'* point. This is the spot about six inches clear of the hoop on the wrong side. From here, you are so close to the wires that you cannot take off to any position in front. The nearest you can hope for is an angled running position from about a yard away on the playing side.

There is a solution, which relies on being in the *exact* spot where there is nothing else to do, and having the same playing conditions as those where you have practised it. (Remember, balls of other manufacture may provide a different effect.) Even so, it is an elegant shot to get you out of an unforeseeable disaster.

Line up the balls for a take-off, placing your Red ball between Yellow and the hoop. Align Red so that the 'V' where the balls meet points directly at the centre of the far wire. Now strike Red, swinging the mallet directly at the same point, and watch it run the hoop backwards, landing one foot right in front.

The shot is just a take-off that runs the hoop from the wrong side. Anywhere else on the lawn, this would not work, and, at any other time, it would be utterly stupid to try to take-off through a hoop. Here it could be your only way forward.

## Promotion

### Rushing a Jawsed Ball

It serves you right if you have got into this position. Yellow is in the jaws of 4-back, you are taking croquet from Blue, and you need a rush to Hoop 1. Yellow will only move in one direction – you can peel it and rush it north up the lawn, or knock it out and rush it south down the lawn.

If you are close, and only if you are close, you can *promote* Yellow. Blue hits Yellow, Yellow pops out, and you have the chance of hitting it towards your hoop. This is hard, and will probably not work unless you play very gently from close up. You need a little split shot. Blue will pull sideways, and may miss Yellow completely. There is a chance that Blue hits Yellow far too hard, or not hard enough. Also, you should be prepared for Blue promoting Yellow out of the hoop, but landing in the jaws itself. That may give you the rush to Hoop 1, but you might find yourself having to play another promotion to get Blue into play. Sometimes luck is with you, and sometimes it is not.

### Promotion in the STP

There is a point at which the technical wizardry of promotion makes sense, and is arguably worth every bit of effort – when you are attempting a straight triple.

Suppose you have just tried to peel 4-back. Yellow has stuck, and you have had to jump over it to run the hoop. You hit Black (your escape ball), and nick it back in front of 4-back. Now you can promote Yellow through the hoop, for a posthumous peel, and rush it towards Penult. You may have to play the last hoop without Black, but you are back on schedule, you have peeled a lift hoop, and you have a chance of finishing.

That is not the only point in the STP where promotion comes in handy. Your big headache in the peeling turn is just after the 4-back peel when you have to get Yellow to peeling position in front of Penult. Traditionally, the sequence is played by rushing Black away to Corner 3, stopping it back towards Rover, and getting a rush on Yellow to the next hoop. There is a modern alternative, like this:

*A final flourish. Reg Bamford is playing Black, and is about to croquet Red into Blue, promoting it through Rover. At the same time, Black goes beyond the hoop, getting a winning rush to the peg on Blue.*

- peel Yellow through 4-back;
- run 4-back with Red;
- tap Black;
- point Black at Yellow, and split-roll over to Blue. Black promotes Yellow to Penult.

You now have a good chance of a close peel at Penult. Yellow becomes the Rover pioneer, and you just need to sort out Blue and Black.

That is very impressive if you can get the promotion just right, but it is a bit of a lottery over that distance. To save your embarrassment, try not to clip Yellow on the wrong side with Black. Sending Black off the lawn will end your turn – a ball in baulk and three balls around Penult is not a good outcome.

### The Combination Peg-Out

Here is a final test of skill. Yellow is for peg, and you are about to run Rover with Red. You come through, skim the wire, and an unlucky rebound sends Red full-face into the Yellow. With an unwanted roquet, you now have a nine-yard peg-out, and you are not confident of hitting. The *combination peg-out* is a way of finishing the game when you have run out of roquets on Yellow:

- Play a stop shot dead-weight; Yellow lands as close to the peg as possible, and Red lands close to Blue.
- Rush Blue at Black.
- Rush Black a foot away from Yellow.
- Croquet Black into Yellow, which is promoted on to the peg, and out of the game.
- Peg out Red with your last shot.

At least two of those shots are very, very difficult. If you need to ask which two, you probably want to steer clear of making an attempt.

## Go and Experiment

There is a limit to the practical advice that a book can give you, and every game you play will present its own challenges. However you confront those challenges, feel free to heed the advice or ignore it. There is no right way to play the game, except to enjoy it.

# CHAPTER 17

# THE FUTURE

It is 150 years since Walter Jones Whitmore won croquet's first championship, and published the game's first treatise on tactics. Strategy has evolved immensely since then, and Whitmore would be both proud of and awestruck by the depth of thought in the modern game. Which direction will croquet take over the next few years?

## Development Worldwide

Croquet fulfils a role that many other sports cannot – it appeals to young and old, and equally to men and women.

With a growing population of retired people, croquet is well placed to meet the needs of a increasingly large section of society. If the game continues to see a resurgence in interest, there are likely to be more clubs and more tournaments, and a rise in competitive play at all levels.

This trend is already apparent in the UK, where it is possible to play a different tournament at a different venue every weekend of the season. The wide circle of A-class players competing at championship level has certainly contributed to the dominant position of Britain on the world croquet stage.

*Reg Bamford, three times World Champion, lifts the Wimbledon Cup.*

The World Croquet Federation continues to develop the game globally. At present, the English-speaking world dominates Association Croquet, while Egypt is pre-eminent in Golf Croquet. Many of the top Association players – Reg Bamford and Robert Fulford among them – have crossed the divide between the two games. As yet, no Egyptian, despite their awesomely accurate firepower, has ventured far in the other direction.

The game continues to develop throughout Europe. After years of development, mature players are emerging from Sweden, Italy and Spain. Denmark, with an organized base of thousands of registered players, promises much, although the Danes, with their one-handed playing technique, have yet to be persuaded to embrace the international community. Perhaps, in ten years' time, they will take their place among the great croquet-playing nations.

## The 14-Point Game

As playing standards have risen, some players have begun to claim that the game is too easy. Certainly, at the top level, many players are confident of picking up a four-ball break from very little, playing round to 4-back, and laying a diagonal spread. When the opponent misses, the TP finish is now seen very widely at championship level.

An experimental version of the game has been trialled recently, using the same rules relating to lifts and contacts, but halving the number of hoops. There is one circuit of the hoops (six hoops twice + two peg points = 14, instead of the standard 26), and there are lifts and/or contacts after Hoops 3 and 4 rather than 1-back and 4-back. That forces players to spend less time on break-building, and more time on leaves.

As yet, this format has made little progress in capturing the enthusiasm of many at the top of the game. At present, it seems a step too far towards difficulty. Many players are reluctant to surrender a version of the game that gives them frequent wins, in favour of one in which they would be less successful. Time will tell whether it takes a hold, and whether there are enough expert devotees to allow it to develop.

## The Super Advanced Game

Another experimental form – the *super advanced* game – was trialled in England in 2009. The rules are similar to those of the advanced game, but a third lift hoop, Hoop 4, is introduced. Lifts are conceded earlier in the game, and the contact is granted after 1-back, rather than 4-back. The penalty for running Hoops 4, 1-back and 4-back in the same

turn is now very punitive – the opponent may start their turn from *any* position on the lawn. This 'lift to position' gives any opponent an immediate rush, rendering most leaves useless.

The trials seemed successful and popular with players. Further events are expected, but it is too early to say whether the form has any long-term future.

## The Rise of the Supershot

Since 2001, when Reg Bamford won the WCF World Championship in London, the top-level game has seen much more of a focus on hitting long shots very straight. With confident long-hitting, players can allow their break control to slacken, in the knowledge that a four-yard rush in the middle of the turn can revive their scoring possibilities.

Of course, the fact that Bamford *can* play a loose break does not mean that he *does* – his are some of the most tightly controlled croquet strokes of any player in the game. Equally, David Maugham can unite the disciplines of an inch-perfect break with the ability to blast through a five-yard angled hoop.

The point is that straight hitting has opened the opportunity for more and more ambitious tactics. Defence – traps, cornering, wide joins – now play a much smaller part at championship level. Choice of openings and leaves depends on an assessment of the probability of an opponent's hitting. Tactics for this hinge on the evaluation of a player's *critical distance* – the distance at which their hitting chances are 50 per cent.

Supershot tactics remain in their infancy, and have been covered only briefly here. Often a game can be decided on the arithmetic of weighing up two probabilities. Perhaps this advent heralds the loss of a more delicate and subtle game. For those who aspire to lifting the Wimbledon Cup, it may be an issue to confront. For the majority, it is something of an irrelevance. Whether your intention is for mastery of the sextuple peel, or for playing for the sheer enjoyment, croquet remains a game to satisfy your ambitions.

This book has aimed to pull apart the tactics and technique, and to examine each element in some detail. It is up to you to fit those elements back together. It cannot hope to give the answers to all problems you might face on a croquet lawn – indeed, attempting to do so might well spoil your fun.

It is the ambition, and the curse, of every coach to look forward to losing to each of his students. Maybe we will meet some day on a croquet lawn. Hopefully, you will be able to put into practice some of what you have read here. I hope you win.

# GLOSSARY

**26** The target winning score – twelve hoops with each ball, plus two points for hitting the peg. In British notation, scores are given as a difference, for example, +17, rather than the absolute scores, for example, 26-9. To '26' an opponent is to beat them by the maximum margin, +26 or 26-0.

**14-point** A shortened game where each ball completes half a circuit (six hoops) only.

**1-back, 1b** The seventh hoop.

**2-4 leave** The Maugham standard leave.

**2-back, 2b** The eighth hoop.

**3-back, 3b** The ninth hoop.

**4-back, 4b** The tenth hoop.

**A-baulk** The baulk line on the South boundary.

**A-Class player** A technically accomplished player who plays Advanced Rules.

**Advanced Rules, Advanced Play** Additional rules with penalties for running certain hoops, to prevent one-sided games between A-class players.

**All-round break** Twelve hoops scored in a single turn.

**Alternate colours** Balls of different colours, allowing two independent games to be played on the same lawn. Usually, Green, Pink, Brown and White replace Blue, Red, Black and Yellow.

**Anti-Duffer** An Advanced Play opening, to discourage an opponent from playing a Duffer tice.

**Approach shot** A croquet stroke to place the striker's ball in position to run the next hoop.

**Aspinall peel** A peel from an acute angle, in which the peelee is jawsed in a croquet stroke, and then hit again by the striker's ball.

**Association Rules** The official international rules of croquet.

**'Aunt Emma'** A player who appears more concerned with hindering their opponent rather than trying to progress themselves. Generally considered to be a dull way to play the game.

**B-spread** An inadequate attempt at a diagonal spread leave.

**Back peel** A peel immediately after the striker has run the hoop from the other side, for example, through 4-back after Hoop 3.

**Backward ball** The ball of a side which has made fewer hoops than the other.

**Baillieu double** A large target where all of the other balls are almost in line, but often with one ball further away than the others.

**Ball in hand** A ball which must be picked up and placed – either the striker's ball before a croquet stroke, or any ball which has left the lawn.

**Baulk lines** The starting lines, covering the left half of each of the South and North boundaries.

**B-baulk** The baulk line on the North boundary.

**Bisque** An extra turn in handicap play.

**Blob** To fail a hoop, with the ball landing in the jaws of the hoop.

**Boundary** The edge of the playing area.

**Box** The clip position of a ball after it has been pegged out.

**Break** An uninterrupted series of strokes in which a player's ball runs a number of hoops in order.

**Break down** To make an unsuccessful shot, which causes a break to end.

**Cannon** A croquet stroke in which three or four balls are touching, and may be moved at the same time.

**Casting** Taking practice swings above the ball.

**Centre stance** The traditional stance in which the mallet is swung between the legs.

**Clang** To fail a hoop, with the ball bouncing off one of the uprights. Often played with considerable force.

**Clip** A marker coloured to match each ball, indicating which is the next hoop.

**Clippage, clip positions** The position of the four clips. Hence, the status of the game.

**Clips of death** An awkward clip position, particularly under Advanced Rules, where one ball is for 1-back and one is for 4-back.

**Condone** To let an opponent's fault go unclaimed; the fault becomes a legal play, with no penalty on the striker.

**Contact** A penalty under Advanced Rules, allowing the opponent to start their turn with an immediate croquet stroke.

**Contact leave** An Advanced Play leave made after conceded a contact, designed to make progress difficult for the opponent.

**Continuation stroke** The extra stroke played after a croquet stroke or running a hoop.

**Controlled hoop** A hoop run so that the striker's ball comes through to a specific spot.

**Corner** The intersections of the four boundaries; to play a ball defensively into a corner.

**Corner ball** A ball positioned precisely in one of the corners.

**Corner 2 opening** An Advanced Play opening, where the second ball is placed just outside Corner 2.

**Court** Formal name for a croquet lawn.

**Critical distance** The distance from which a player expects to have a 50 per cent chance of hitting.

**Croquet stroke** The stroke following a roquet in which the striker's ball is placed touching the roqueted ball, and hit so that both balls are moved.

**Croqueted ball** The ball that is moved but not struck in a croquet stroke.

**Crosspeg** To position two balls so that the peg lies directly between them.

**Crosswire** To position two balls so that a hoop lies directly between them.

**Crown** The top of a hoop.

**Crunch up** To beat someone decisively and quickly, generally +26 in two all-round breaks.

**Crush** A fault in which the ball is squeezed between the mallet and the hoop.

**Cut-rush** A rush in which the object ball is sent off at an angle.

**Death roll** A transit peel with no escape ball, played as a full-roll – usually peeling Penult while going directly to a pioneer at 2-back or 3-back.

**Deem** To decline to play a stroke to which a player is entitled (so ending the turn).

**Deep** (A pioneer) placed well beyond the hoop.

**Delayed** (A peeling break) where the peels are made later than the easiest schedule.

**Diagonal spread leave, D-spread, DSL** An Advanced Play leave in which all four balls are placed in a straight line diagonally across the lawn, so that the opponent's balls are wired by the peg.

**Distance ratio** The ratio of distance travelled by each of the balls in a croquet stroke.

**Dolly rush** An easy rush – a straight rush with the two balls less than a foot or so apart.

**Double banking** Playing two independent games simultaneously on one lawn.

**Double tap** A fault where the ball is struck more than once with the mallet.

**Double target** A target of more than one ball so that a player may shoot at the middle of the group of balls.

**Dream leave** A leave (usually in Advanced Play) played on the third turn of the game, where two balls are left with a rush at the third. The fourth ball has to hit or face the prospect of a break from the opponent.

**Drive** A basic croquet stroke in which the croqueted ball moves between three and five times as far as the striker's ball.

**Duffer tice** An Advanced Play opening, in which the second ball is placed mid-lawn, near Hoop 6.

**East** The side of the lawn on which Hoops 3 and 4 are placed.

**Enemy ball** A ball of the opposing side.

**Escape ball** A ball positioned ready to be roqueted after peeling another ball.

**Fault** An error made in hitting a ball, resulting in the immediate end of the turn.

**First colours** Blue, Red, Black and Yellow.

**For (a hoop)** Requiring the next hoop in order.

**Forcing** Restricting the tactical choice of the opponent.

**Forestall** To intervene during the opponent's turn before a fault is likely to be played.

**Forward ball** The ball of a side which has scored more hoops than the other.

**Forward rush** A rush after a hoop, pointing in the direction of the break.

**Four-ball break** A break using all three of the other balls.

**Free shot** A shot at a ball(s) which gives little or no advantage to the opponent if missed.

**Full bisque** A form of handicap play in which both players have a number of bisques.

**Full-roll** A roll in which the striker's ball moves the same distance as the croqueted ball.

**Furniture** The hoops and the peg.

**Golf Croquet** A version of the game in which each hoop is scored only by the first player to run that hoop, and there are no continuation strokes.

**Grievous** An accidental, and undesirable, peg-out – usually by rushing a ball on to the peg.

**Guarded** Positioned near a boundary, to exploit a miss from the opponent.

**Half-jump** A jump shot that (deliberately) does not quite clear a ball.

**Half-bisque** A restricted extra turn in handicap play, in which no score may be made for any ball.

**Half-roll** A croquet stroke in which the striker's ball moves about half the distance of the croqueted ball.

**Hammer stroke** A stroke hitting down on the ball, and played facing away from the direction of travel.

**Hampered** Prevented from a normal swing by a hoop, other ball, or the peg.

**Handicap** A number assigned to a player to indicate his ability.

**Handicap play** A version of the game in which the weaker player receives a number of extra turns equal to the difference in the two players' handicaps.

**Heel** The mallet face that does not strike the ball.

**High-bisquer** A player with a numerically high handicap.

**Hit in** To make a long roquet at the start of the turn.

**Hogan roll** A massive full-roll from a corner to the furthest hoop.

**Inner rectangle** The area enclosed between the first four hoops.

**Innings** Control of the game, by being joined up when the opponents are separated.

**Inplayer** The player with the innings.

**Irish grip** A grip with both palms facing forwards.

**Irish peel** A straight peel in which both the striker's ball and the peelee score the hoop in the same stroke.

**Jaw**  To place a ball in the jaws.

**Jaws**  The area within the uprights of a hoop.

**Join up**  To position the striker's ball close to the partner ball.

**Jump shot**  A shot that causes the striker's ball to leave the ground.

**Lay a break**  To position the balls ready for a subsequent break.

**Lay up**  To prepare a leave.

**Leave**  Deliberate placement of the balls at the end of a turn.

**Level play**  Play without bisques.

**Lift**  To remove a ball from its position on the lawn, and play it from one of the baulk lines, either because of a wiring, or under Advanced Rules.

**Long-bisquer**  A high-bisquer.

**Long point**  The point furthest from either baulk – roughly in the middle of the East or West boundaries (about nineteen yards from either baulk line).

**Low-bisquer**  A player with a numerically low handicap.

**Maugham standard leave (MSL)**  An Advanced Play leave, where the opponent's balls are left very close behind Hoops 2 and 4.

**New standard leave (NSL)**  An Advanced Play leave, where the opponent's balls are placed near to Hoop 2 and close behind Hoop 4.

**Non-playing side**  The area beyond a hoop, from which the hoop may not be scored.

**North**  The side of the lawn on which Hoops 2 and 3 are placed.

**Object ball**  A ball that is being croqueted.

**Octuple peel (OCP)**  A break in which another ball is peeled through its last eight hoops and pegged out.

**Old standard leave, OSL**  A simple Advanced Play leave, rarely used at the top level.

**Open**  Not wired.

**Opening**  The first four turns of the game, in which each of the four balls is brought into play.

**OTP (opponent's triple peel)**  Describing a game in which the opponent completed a TPO, but went on to lose the game.

**Outplayer**  The player who does not have the innings.

**Partner ball**  The ball of a side that is not the striker's ball.

**Pass roll**  A roll in which the striker's ball travels further than the object ball.

**Pawnbroker**  A target that is three balls wide.

**Peel**  To send another ball through its hoop.

**Peelee**  A ball that is peeled.

**Peg out**  To remove a Rover ball from the game by causing it to hit the peg.

**Pegged-out game**  A game in which one or two balls have been pegged out.

**Penult**  The eleventh (penultimate) hoop.

**Pick up**  To create a break, usually from an uncompromising position.

**Pioneer**  A ball placed at the next hoop, to make the approach to that hoop easier.

**Pivot**  A ball, usually placed near the middle of the lawn, used to simplify croquet strokes in a break.

**Playing side**  The area in front of the hoop, from which a hoop may be scored.

**Plummer**  A measure of lawn speed – the number of seconds taken for a ball to travel thirty-five yards (stopping on the North boundary when struck from the South boundary).

**Policeman**  A ball placed within hitting range of an opponent, in the hope of exploiting any mistake.

**POP**  A peel on the opponent, intended to reduce their manoeuvrability.

**Posthumous peel**  A peel through a hoop that the striker's ball has already scored earlier in the break.

**Primary colours**  Same as first colours.

**Promote**  To cause a croqueted ball to collide with another, to improve its position.

**Pull**  The inward curl on a croqueted ball caused by side-spin.

**Push**  A fault in which the mallet is kept in contact with the ball after impact.

**Quadruple peel (QP)**  A break in which another ball is peeled through its last four hoops and pegged out.

**Quintuple peel (QNP)**  A break in which another ball is peeled through its last five hoops and pegged out.

**Reverse take-off**  A hoop approach from the non-playing side, played as a take-off.

**Riggall**  To peg out a single ball, usually the opponent's.

**Roll**  A croquet stroke in which the striker's ball travels further than in a drive.

**Roquet**  A shot in which the striker's ball hits another ball, earning two extra strokes.

**Rover**  The twelfth (and last) hoop; a ball that has run Rover.

**Run**  To send the striker's ball through its hoop.

**Rush**  A roquet which sends the object ball to a specified position.

**Rushline**  An imaginary line along the direction of a rush.

**Rush-peel**  A peel scored with a rush stroke.

**Scatter shot**  A continuation shot, which hits a previously croqueted ball, to try to leave a defensive position.

**Score**  To send a ball through its hoop.

**Scratch player**  A player whose handicap is zero.

**Second colours, secondary colours**  Alternate colours.

**Sextuple peel (SXP)**  A break in which the striker peels another ball (usually partner) through its last six hoops, and pegs it out. Used under Advanced Rules to avoid all lifts.

**Short-bisquer**  A low-bisquer.

**Short Croquet**  A 14-point handicap game played on a half-sized lawn, popular with less experienced players.

**Side stance**  A method of hitting a ball in which the mallet is swung alongside the body.

**Solomon grip**  A grip in which the knuckles of both hands point forwards.

**South** The side of the lawn on which Hoops 1 and 4 are placed.

**Split shot** A croquet stroke in which the striker's ball travels in a different direction from the object ball.

**Squeeze** A leave in which both opponent balls are advantageously placed. Whichever ball is moved gives a promising outcome for the striker.

**Stake** American term for the peg.

**Stalk** To aim a shot by standing back and walking towards the striker's ball from a distance.

**Standard grip** A grip in which the lower hand holds the mallet with the palm forward, and the upper hand with the knuckles facing forwards.

**Standard opening** The traditional tice opening.

**Standard triple (peel)** A triple peel where the three peels are completed at the first, and theoretically easiest, opportunity.

**Stop shot** A croquet stroke in which the striker's ball travels less far than in a drive.

**Straight peel** A peel in which the striker's ball and the peelee are for the same hoop.

**Straight triple (peel)** A triple peel well behind the standard schedule, in which all three peels are played straight.

**Striker** The player whose turn it is.

**Striker's ball** The ball being played by the striker throughout the current turn.

**Supershot opening** A high-level Advanced Play opening, in which the first ball is placed mid-lawn.

**Sweep** A means of playing a hampered shot with a horizontal mallet.

**Take-off** A croquet stroke where the object ball barely moves.

**'Tealady'** A leave giving a crosswire and a long shot; also used to describe the subsequent attempt to hit the long shot.

**Three-ball break** A break using the striker's ball and just two others.

**Three ducks** An Advanced Play leave, played after a break has been completed before the fourth ball has been brought into the game.

**Tice** A ball placed close enough to tempt the opponent into shooting.

**Tice opening** A common opening, in which a tice is placed on the West boundary.

**TPO** A winning triple peel on the opponent, gaining the advantage of a pegged-out game.

**Transit peel** A peel played when the striker's ball is in transit between two other hoops.

**Trap** Laying up near the boundary, to deter an opponent's shot.

**Triple peel (TP)** A break in which the striker peels another ball through its last three hoops and pegs it out. Most common in Advanced Play.

**Triple target** Three balls almost in a straight line, to give a wide target for the striker.

**Two-ball break** A break using just the striker's and one other ball.

**Two-ball game** A game in which two balls have been pegged out.

**USCA Rules** The rules published by the United States Croquet Association.

**Vertical spread (VSL)** An Advanced Play leave, where the opponent's balls are hidden behind Hoops 5 and 6.

**Wafer Cannon** A cannon where a third ball is arranged, almost but not quite touching the striker's ball.

**West** The side of the lawn on which Hoops 1 and 2 are placed.

**Wicket** American term for a hoop.

**Wide join** A defensive position on the boundary, where two balls are close enough to hit but far enough apart to make the opponent's progress difficult.

**Windscreen-wiping** Successive missed roquets requiring the use of several bisques.

**Wire** The upright of a hoop; to position a ball so its shot is blocked by a hoop.

**Wired** Blocked from hitting another ball by a hoop or the peg.

**Wiring lift** A lift granted when a player is left with no open shot at any ball.

**Wylie peel** A transit peel in which the peelee is used as a pioneer at another hoop, then rushed into peeling position and immediately peeled.

**Yardline** The unmarked line one yard in from the boundary, usually measured by a mallet's length.

**Yardline area** The space between the yardline and the boundary.

# USEFUL CONTACTS

## World Croquet Federation
The WCF co-ordinates and develops croquet throughout the world, and should be the first point of contact for any countries not listed below.
Website: www.wcfcroquet.org

## EUROPE

*England/Wales*
The Croquet Association is the governing body for croquet in England, Wales, Northern Ireland, the Channel Isles and the Isle of Man, with around 175 member clubs.

### The Croquet Association
Cheltenham Croquet Club, Old Bath Road, Cheltenham Glos GL53 7DF
Telephone: 01242 242318
Website: www.croquet.org.uk
Email: caoffice@croquet.org.uk

*Scotland*
The Scottish Croquet Association has eight member clubs, details of which are available online. The National Croquet Centre is located at Meadows Croquet Club in Edinburgh.
Website: www.scottishcroquet.org.uk

*Ireland*
The Croquet Association of Ireland has eight member clubs. The annual Championship of Ireland is held at Carrickmines Club, south of Dublin.
Website: www.croquetireland.com
Email: secretary@croquetireland.com

*Italy*
Italy has seen a surge in popularity in croquet, and the Federazione Italiana Sport Croquet has eleven member clubs.
Website: www.croquetitalia.it

*Rest of Europe*
Croquet's spread across the rest of Europe has been gradual, and up-to-date details of member organizations may be accessed online via the WCF website.

## NORTH AMERICA

*USA*
The USCA oversees the game played in both its American format, and under the international rules of Association Croquet. Its offices are located at Florida's National Croquet Center.

### United States Croquet Association
700 Florida Mango Road, West Palm Beach, Florida 33406
Telephone: (561) 478-0760
Website: www.croquetamerica.com
Email: USCA@msn.com

*Canada*
Croquet Canada has twenty-two member clubs, mostly in Ontario. They play both USCA and Association Rules.

### Croquet Canada
Bedford Park Postal Outlet, PO Box 94069, Toronto, Ontario M4N 3R1
Website: www.croquet.ca

## AUSTRALASIA

*Australia*
Croquet in Australia is largely organized at state level. The Australian Croquet Association website gives links to each of its member organizations. Croquet NSW is the largest of these, with sixty-eight clubs.
ACA Website: www.croquet-australia.com.au
Email: secretary@croquet-australia.com.au
CNSW Website: www.croquet-nsw.com

*New Zealand*
Croquet New Zealand has twenty member associations, each of which has several member clubs.

### Croquet NZ
PO Box 11259, Manners Street, Wellington 6142

Level 5, Davis Langdon House, 49 Boulcott Street, Wellington 6011
Telephone: (04) 916 0258; fax: (04) 916 0259
Website: www.croquet.org.nz
Email: croquet@croquet.org.nz

# INDEX